The Amateur
Archaeologist's
Handbook

Excavation of an area that was formerly the site of a nineteenth-century barn. The building in the upper right late seventeenth-century is the Major John Bradford house, Kingston, Massachusetts (formerly part of Plymouth). (Plimoth Plantation Photo)

The Amateur Archaeologist's Handbook
Second Edition

MAURICE ROBBINS

with Mary B. Irving

Thomas Y. Crowell Company

New York: Established 1834

Acknowledgments appear on pages v, vii, and viii.

Manufactured in the United States of America

ISBN 0-690-05569-2

1 2 3 4 5 6 7 8 9 10

Library of Congress Cataloging in Publication Data

Robbins, Maurice.
    The amateur archaeologist's handbook.

    Bibliography:
    1. Indians of North America—Antiquities.
    2. North America—Antiquities. 3. Excavation
    (Archaeology)—North America. 4. Archaeology—
    Methodology. I. Irving, Mary B., joint author.
    II. Title.
E77.9.R6 1973   913′.031′028   73–245
ISBN 0–690–05569–2

Preface to the Second Edition

Since the original edition of *The Amateur Archaeologist's Handbook*, which is now the standard reference on techniques and methods for many amateur societies as well as a college-level text, has enjoyed such encouraging comments from both amateurs and professionals, this second edition has been prepared to help amateur archaeologists keep abreast of the latest developments in the field.

Included in the second edition are the new and exciting discoveries regarding the original migrations to America, the latest information concerning radiocarbon dating, a revision of the data on early cultures in America, and a discussion of a new process called flotation, which is yielding amazing information on subsistence patterns. Also included is a new chapter, "Historical Archaeology," for those who prefer history to prehistory.

Our thanks must go to Plimoth Plantations and Dr. James Deetz, assistant director of Plimoth Plantations, for the photographs that accompany the new chapter.

Preface to the First Edition

This handbook is a practical guide to archaeological methods for the general reader. It is intended to encourage the reader to acquire a good background in archaeology and to gain practical experience in the practical aspects of field work.

Although interest in archaeology, both as a science and a hobby, has grown steadily during recent years, the beginner often is frustrated in locating a single volume that supplies the type of assistance he needs. Many of the books available deal only with Old World areas and methods. Others are either too technical or too limited in subject matter or locale.

This book bridges the gap for the American amateur who wishes to take up the hobby of archaeology in a serious, orderly, and professional manner. Its scope is limited to the North American continent. Just enough of the prehistoric background and cultures is sketched to provide a frame of reference for, and to give meaning to, the archaeological materials that will be uncovered by methodical excavation. Many of the problems concerning cultural areas, chronology, and terminology that continue to baffle archaeologists have been omitted or have been treated quite cavalierly in the process of presenting the simplest and briefest accounts for the general reader. The amateur who wishes to extend his knowledge and fill in the missing details of the outline is urged to read widely in the literature suggested in the bibliography.

The principal focus of the book is on the *how's*, *why's*, *when's*, and *where's* of archaeology. Anyone wishing to acquire more extensive knowledge in this field should contact active workers in the particular area of interest in order to learn the special techniques applicable at the local level. In archaeology there is no substitute for personal observation and participation.

The methods and techniques described in the following pages are the result of more than a quarter of a century of personal experience. In developing them I have been aided by many amateurs who have been associated with me at a number of archaeological sites in New England.

Special acknowledgment is due the members of the Cohannet Chapter of the Massachusetts Archaeological Society, with whom I have worked at several important sites. Many of the special techniques are the results of experiments by this group of sincere amateur archaeologists.

I also owe much to my wife, who has spent many weary hours correcting the manuscript, suggesting changes, and smoothing out my mode of expression. To my editor, Miss Mary B. Irving, goes my heartfelt thanks for her valuable technical assistance and skilled editorial judgment.

The material in the appendices is the result of considerable correspondence; I am indebted to the many individuals who took the time to respond to my questions. Some of the concepts concerning early man in America are drawn from the published papers of Dr. Ronald J. Mason and Dr. H. M. Wormington, who kindly allowed the author to make use of their texts and illustrations. Several of the drawings that accompany the text in chapter 4 appeared first in the Newsletter of the Arkansas Archeological Society and are reproduced by permission of its editor, Charles R. McGimsey III. The geological maps are copies of those published by the U.S. Department of the Interior, and I wish to acknowledge their permission to use the material. Chapter 8 includes a description of a unique device called the Cohannet Line, the brainchild of Mr. Rei Heino; I am grateful to him for permitting the use of his technique in this book. The several record sheets recommended in chapter 8 are reproduced with the permission of the publishers, Chandler Publishing Company (604 Mission St., San Francisco, Calif.).

I am deeply indebted to Dr. R. G. Glover of the National Museum of Canada for the use of the preservation techniques presented in chapter 9. Chapter 6 is based upon a paper prepared by Mr. Arthur C. Lord, Jr., and published originally in the Bulletin of the Massachusetts Archaeological Society, Vol. 23, 1. Thanks are due him for permitting the use of his material. Data with reference to carbon 14 dating and methods of sample collection are used by permission of the Geochron Laboratories of Cambridge, Massachusetts.

In my text concerning photography and its application to archaeology, I have leaned heavily upon the knowledge and experience of my good friend Mr. Robert Ashley. Without the illustrations taken from the Bulletin of the Massachusetts Archaeological Society and drawn by its editor, Dr. William S. Fowler, it would have been difficult to provide such excellent drawings. I am greatly indebted to both for their kind permission to reproduce them herein. I am also in the debt of Mr. Jean-Jacques Rivard, another of my very sincere colleagues, for illustrations, in particular for the fine examples of the skeletal parts of the human body.

In conclusion, my thanks to the many contributors whose names do not appear here, but whose assistance is, nevertheless, deeply appreciated.

MAURICE ROBBINS

Contents

Illustrations

1 : Before You Start to Dig

Out of the random threads of man's prehistory—delicately chipped stone tools, a handful of potsherds from an ancient burial, a carved stone head from the meso-American jungle—archaeologists are painstakingly reweaving the tapestry of antiquity. Some artifacts have been buried in the earth for untold centuries. Many are found by accident, while others are discovered only after careful planning and years of patient excavation. Significant finds are sometimes unearthed by amateurs, who are often unaware of the importance of their discovery While new territories are being excavated almost continuously, the task is still far from complete, for in many areas the threads of prehistory are frayed or missing, and the pattern is blurred. Both professional and amateur archaeologists must continue to search diligently for the material needed to complete the fabric.

Perhaps your interest in archaeology, like mine, was aroused by tales of ancient cities and vanished civilizations. Perhaps your search of plowed fields has resulted in a modest collection of stone artifacts. But something is missing. A mere collection of stone tools without records is meaningless. An understanding of the people who made the tools and what part they played in the life of aboriginal America not only greatly enhances the thrill of discovery but allows the discoverer to make a contribution to archaeological knowledge. To accomplish this, one must know the theories and techniques of archaeology. Where does one start to dig? How does one learn the arts of the archaeologist? This book is intended to tell you not only where to start to dig, but how and why, as well as what to do after you have started.

Before beginning, however, it might be useful to consider briefly what we mean by archaeology. According to Webster, the word comes from two Greek words—the first, *archaios,* meaning "of the past," and the second, *logos,* meaning "discourse." Archaeology is the

1

story of the past. It is concerned with things—objects, or artifacts, of stone, bone, and clay—as well as with the people who made and used them. Often the conditions under which the artifacts are found —as in conjunction with a burial or in evidence of fire, for instance— are more important than the artifacts themselves. The way in which material remains are associated with other features reflects ancient man's mode of living in much the same way that a contemporary mail-order catalog reflects ours. From a careful study of these telltale clues the archaeologist is able to interpret them for us and so add to our knowledge of the past. We learn not only what people of the past wore and ate, what tools and weapons they used, and what kinds of dwellings they built, but something about their religion and their social organization as well.

Much of our knowledge of the past comes from the lowly kitchen midden, or garbage heap. Here we find the utensils and artifacts used for cooking and eating, the bones of animals whose flesh furnished food, the evidence of fire and pottery. But these things are not found simply lying around on the surface of the ground waiting to be picked up. Often they occur in layers, indicating successive occupations at a given site. The first occupants doubtless chose the site because of its sheltered location and proximity to water for transportation and sustenance. The next occupants covered over the debris left behind and established their settlements on top. And so it went. This continual process of burial helped to preserve the remains of human habitation for the archaeologist, who must recover them with spade, trowel, and hoe.

Archaeology encompasses a wide scope of time, area, and subject. It is concerned, for instance, with reconstructing the story of humanity before the time of recorded history. This age of prehistory may have occurred many thousands of years ago or a mere few hundred years ago, depending upon the particular people and places, or sites, with which we happen to be dealing.

But the work of archaeology does not stop with the beginning of written history. Often written records are only recovered in the course of archaeological excavations. Much of our more recent past is gradually coming to light as a result of the new interest in historic site archaeology—the restoration of colonial settlements, ironworks, fortifications, and so on. The archaeologist has even turned scuba diver and spelunker as he seeks clues to man's past under the seas and under the surface of the earth. New techniques are adding new dimensions to the search.

Until about one hundred years ago archaeological discoveries were accidents. Now the study of man's past has become a science, aided in turn by many other sciences. Like physics, chemistry, or any other science, archaeology has its skills, procedures, methods, and disciplines. These must be learned and the reasons for them understood.

I have compared archaeology to a tapestry. We can also think of it as a book, unique in the fact that it contains the entire story of the past. Each site is a page, the only one of its kind in the world. The stone, bone, or clay artifacts found there are the illustrations. As you excavate, you destroy a page from this record of the past; only the illustrations remain. Much priceless information has been lost to posterity through the activities of people ignorant of archaeological discipline who wish merely to amass loot. The relic hunter, with his pack rat mania for collecting, is an example, or the commercial collector and the dealer, who aid and abet the wholesale destruction of sites for personal gain. The true archaeologist, on the other hand, welcomes the discipline because it has given him the skill to interpret and reconstruct a page of history. Amateur or professional, he accepts his moral obligation to record and preserve his findings so that others may trace the story they have to tell.

A sincere interest, love of the outdoors, and willingness to work and to learn the necessary skills are the only qualifications required of the beginner in archaeology. Here, indeed, is a hobby for the whole family—from their individual tasks all members can derive knowledge, satisfaction, and many hours of enjoyment.

In the following chapters you will learn something about the earliest Americans—who they were, where they came from, where they went, how they lived, what tools and implements they made. You will learn how to locate and excavate an archaeological site, how to preserve, restore, and date your finds, and how to write your final site report.

As you gain experience, you will want to learn more about archaeology and may even decide to concentrate on some particular aspect of it. At the end of this book are suggestions for further reading, as well as information about study courses, sites and museums to visit, and opportunities for taking part in a "dig." The local, regional, and national societies listed are excellent sources of information on archaeological activity in specific areas.

2 : Who Lived Where

Evidence is rapidly accumulating that seafarers from the Mediterranean area found their way across the Atlantic to America many years before Columbus made his famous landfall in 1492. It is certain that explorers from Greenland visited the northeastern coast of North America and even established temporary settlements a half century before the voyage of Columbus. Traits that seem to be of African origin have been found in eastern South America, and early traits of western South America point to an Oriental source. Europeans who crossed the stormy Atlantic during the fifteenth century found both American continents already occupied by a people whom they called Indians, thus perpetuating the original error of Columbus who, believing that he had found a new way to Asia, had given them the name *Indios*.

Just how long men have occupied the New World is still a matter of dispute. Some evidence suggests that his residence goes back 40,000 years, but the oldest universally accepted date for his presence in the Americas is 13,000 B.C. But even if the older date is accepted, it seems clear from the far greater antiquity of finds in other continents, particularly Africa, that modern man did not originate in the New World. The physical characteristics of the Indians strongly suggest that the basic stock was Asian. Regardless of other strains that also seem to be present, it is highly probable that a majority of the first inhabitants came to America by way of a land connection in the Bering Strait. There, even today, only about 50 miles of open water separates Asia from America.

How and when was this land connection formed? Beginning more than a million years ago, there were four major glacial periods, or Ice Ages. Large amounts of water were withdrawn from the oceans and deposited upon the land as snow. Thus, continental ice caps were created that at times covered the northerly latitudes with an unbroken mantle. Because of the intense cold in the glaciated areas, more snow fell during the winter than melted in the summer. As a

4

result, the level of water in the oceans was lowered by several hundred feet, thus allowing a land connection between Asia and America to appear. The Pleistocene epoch, however, was not one long, unbroken winter. The four major ice advances of the Pleistocene were separated by periods of comparative warmth, called interglacials. For example, the Wisconsin Ice—the most recent glacial period— was preceded by the Sangamon interglacial; perhaps we are now living in an interglacial to be followed by yet another glacial advance. And even during the major glacial periods, the ice retreated temporarily in what are known as interstadials.

The Bering Strait connection between Asia and Alaska has often been referred to as a "bridge." This was more than a bridge, however, for the area exposed constituted a veritable continent in itself. The huge unglaciated area extended from the sixtieth to the eightieth parallel, and included hundreds of square miles of inhabitable land. In this ice-free area, man, and the mammals upon which he depended for food, could live and move about in comparative comfort.

The Wisconsin glacier was composed of ice lobes that advanced from three major centers. The two eastern lobes, the Laurentian and the Keewatin, quickly coalesced and moved westward to meet the Cordilleran lobe, which originated in the Pacific coastal and the Rocky Mountain ranges. These masses of ice formed a continent-wide barrier, sealing off the rest of the continent from the Bering area.

During interstadials—at least four occurred in the Wisconsin period—the ice drew back and opened a corridor leading southward into the American heartland. However, at the same time, the rising water barred any return to the Asian homeland. Thus, a sort of one-way valve action existed that at various times allowed a southward movement, but forbade a return westward to Asia. Several times during the Wisconsin the alternate routes opened and closed. Men and mammals must have moved in spurts, eastward from Asia and then southward into America. The generation that made the original move was long dead and forgotten before their descendants were able to continue southward. Some species of mammals became extinct during this long period and other species took their place. As the subsistence pattern changed, the material culture of man adapted to it. The changes in culture took place over so long a period and were so gradual that it is now difficult to understand them and to relate them to the movements of people. The great question facing archaeologists is which cultural traits were imported from Asia and which were invented in the New World. About 15,000 years ago the Wisconsin reached its maximum and began to retreat. The land connection between the continents slowly sank beneath the ocean again. Although some migration of peoples continued across the narrow water barrier, the mass movements were at an end.

The original peopling of the Americas was more of an infiltration than a migration in the generally accepted sense of the word. That is to say, it was not a mass movement of people who had discovered that a great unoccupied continent lay across the strait to the east. Primitive man did not think in terms of continents or wander for the sheer love of adventure. He moved after food, which he had to seek on the hoof. The animals were the real trail blazers; man simply followed. Small bands of hunters, ranging far from their usual haunts, were probably the first arrivals. Perhaps they were driven by a scarcity of food or water and were forced to seek new hunting territory where game was more plentiful and competition less intense. Finding what they sought, they remained, and others followed, some perhaps by different routes.

CULTURAL CHRONOLOGY

Every human group has a distinctive pattern of culture. *Culture* is a term used by anthropologists to describe the way in which members of a group live and think, the way they do things, the tools and other products they make. Many different Indian cultures developed in the two Americas. Understandably, there is no acceptable terminology applicable to all of the New World; instead, anthropologists have developed a preferred pattern for each area. At the risk of over-

NO. AMERICAN PLEISTOCENE	
GLACIAL	INTERGLACIAL
NEBRASKAN	
	AFTONIAN
KANSAN	
	YARMOUTH
ILLINOIAN	
	SANGAMON
WISCONSIN	
	PRESENT

The four major glacial advances of the Pleistocene in North America began about 1,000,000 years ago and ended about 10,000 years ago. The first migrants may have crossed to the New World during the last stage of the Sangamon interglacial period.

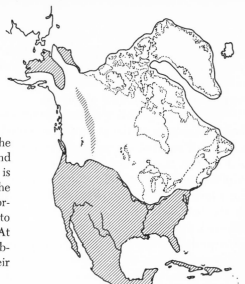

Pleistocene America. At the time represented, the land connection with Asia is flooded by rising waters. The suggestion of an opening corridor leading from Alaska to the south is indicated. At this time the shorelines probably extended beyond their present boundaries.

simplification, I have chosen to use a very generalized terminology to describe the several major stages of prehistoric culture.

Until a few years ago the culture of the *Paleo-Indian* was thought to be that of the first people to enter America. However, continued research showed this to be a highly developed pattern, of which there were only meager traces along the migration routes. Excavations in the supposed Asian homeland did not produce the typical artifacts or their prototypes. Most anthropologists now believe that the Paleo-Indian culture was purely American, developed after the migration from the Old World. Consequently, an earlier and less sophisticated culture must have preceded it.

Recently certain evidences of this simpler culture have been found in both the southeastern and western areas of North America. Called the *Pebble Tool culture,* its name is derived from the rather crude implements made from naturally shaped pebbles only slightly altered to fit them for use as tools. There are no projectile points with these larger tools, at least none have been associated with them to date. The pattern is poorly defined and has never been found in stratigraphic context, and the culture has not been reliably dated. However, some scientists have accepted this culture as authentic. Future study may validate it and better define its distribution.

At the moment the earliest well-known and definitely dated American culture is still the Paleo-Indian. It has been dated as early as 11,000 years B.C. at several southwestern sites and at about 10,000

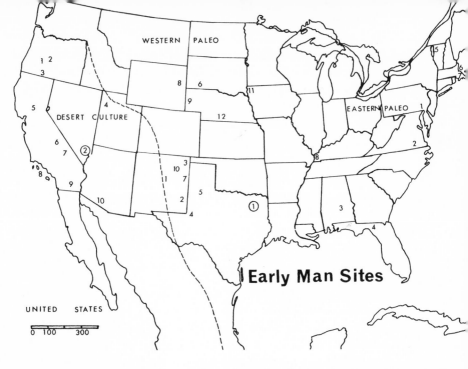

Early Man Sites

UNITED STATES

0 100   300

Evidences of early man have been found at a number of sites in the United States.

Very Early Sites (circled): 1. Lewisville, Tex. 2. Tule Springs, Nev.

Desert Culture: 1. Fort Rock Cave, Ore. 2. Odell Lake, Ore. 3. Klamath Lake Area, Ore. 4. Danger Cave, Utah. 5. Borax Lake, Calif. 6. Stahl Lake, Calif. 7. Lake Mohave, Calif. 8. Santa Rosa Island, Calif. 9. Pinto Basin, Calif. 10. Ventana Cave, Ariz.

Eastern Paleo: 1. Shoop, Pa. 2. Williamson, Va. 3. Quad, Ala. 4. Silver Springs, Fla. 5. Reagen, Vt. 6. Bull Brook, Mass. 7. Wapanucket #8, Mass. 8. Parish, Ky.

Western Paleo: 1. Sandia Cave, N.M. 2. Clovis, N.M. 3. Folsom, N.M. 4. Midland, Tex. 5. Plainview, Tex. 6. Angostura, S.D. 7. Milnesand, N.M. 8. Agate Basin, Wyo. 9. Scottsbluff, Nebr. 10. Meserve, N.M. 11. Simonson, Ia. 12. Allen, Nebr.

years B.C. in the East. The Debert Site in Nova Scotia, for example, has produced several radiocarbon dates between 8,000 and 9,000 years B.C. *Desert culture* refers to a stage partially contemporary with the Paleo-Indian in the Great Basin and the Southwest. *Archaic* refers to the cultures (from about 6000 B.C.) prior to the introduction of agriculture. To designate the beginning (about A.D. 1000) of settled village life based on agriculture, the term *Woodland* is applied to eastern cultures; this stage in the Southwest is represented by the later *Mogollon, Hohokam,* and *Anasazi* cultures. In *historic* times (from about A.D. 1500) American aborigines came in contact with Europeans, and their cultures changed rapidly. Occasional contacts between the Eskimo and the Norse occurred several centuries earlier.

Paleo-Indians

Among the first Americans were the Paleo-Indians, nomadic herd hunters whose cultures were adapted to the pursuit of the great Ice Age mammoths and mastodons. They are best represented at present in the Great Basin and the Southwest, but Paleo chipped stone points, knives, and other artifacts have been found in practically all areas of North America as well as at scattered sites in Mexico and South America.

The Paleo-Indian cultures are divided by some archaeologists into an eastern and a western tradition, with the boundary between the two roughly at the Mississippi River. The western Paleo peoples found abundant big game on the vast grasslands of the Plains, as proved by the great variety of implements found at their "kill" sites in association with extinct forms of bison, musk ox, camel, horse, giant sloth, mammoth, and other Ice Age animals.

Among the oldest known artifacts are the long lanceolate, or lance-shaped, spear points left by Paleo hunters who lived in Sandia Cave, in New Mexico, about 13,000 years ago. More commonly found are the various types of fluted points, where a large longitudinal flake has been removed from the central part of the point. The fluted Clovis point, first discovered near Clovis, New Mexico, dates back about 11,000 or 12,000 years. Somewhat later is the type tool from these sites, the fluted Folsom point, first found in 1926 near the town of Folsom, New Mexico.

The people who drifted into the region west of the Rockies encountered a variety of environmental conditions that caused profound changes in their way of life. They continued to hunt what game they could find but came to rely more on gathering wild plant foods. They left behind grinding stones, choppers, and scrapers and a more limited number of projectile points. Those who wandered farther south subsisted primarily on plant foods.

Then, about 15,000 years ago, the ice sheets to the north began their final retreat. The cool, moist climate of the Plains and Great Basin areas gradually became hot and dry. Between 8,000 and 10,000 years ago the giant Ice Age animals disappeared. With the extinction of the giant herds, men largely deserted the Plains for a considerable period of time. In the eastern forest regions they turned to hunting smaller game and to gathering plants and shellfish.

Desert Culture

The disappearance of Pleistocene animal life had little effect upon the Desert culture. If one source of food became scarce, the people shifted to another source, changing with, and conforming to, the environment. The area in which they lived stretched from Oregon in the north to Mexico in the south and from the Pacific Ocean eastward to the Rocky Mountains. Here wild plant foods were plentiful. In time the hunters became gatherers of herbs, roots, nuts, and berries. The first recognizable traces of this early seed-gathering Desert culture date back to about 11,000 years ago.

The Desert culture people lived in scattered settlements, often in caves. At their camp sites have been found digging sticks, mortars and pestles, chopping tools, and other specialized implements developed for the gathering, harvesting, and processing of plant foods. Flat milling stones with manos, or handstones, for grinding seeds were in use as far back as 8000 B.C., 2,000 years before their known use in the Old World. From the dry caves of the region have come well-preserved basketry containers, trays, and seed beaters.

About 3,000 to 4,000 years ago the late Desert culture seed gatherers were planting primitive Indian corn, or maize (*Zea Mays*), a hybridized form of wild grain, as evidenced by remains discovered in Bat Cave, in New Mexico. But the unfavorable climate of the region limited its cultivation.

In the southern part of the United States, especially in Arizona and western Texas, the latter phases of the Desert culture lasted with only minor changes for several thousand years. They formed the basis of the early farming cultures that succeeded them in parts of the Southwest. Indeed, there are indications that this culture provided the prototype of the Archaic cultures that spread over the entire country at a somewhat later date.

Archaic

Various types of Archaic cultures are found in every state of the Union and in all the provinces of Canada. They are best known in the northeastern and southeastern United States.

While hunting was still important to the Archaic people, they supplemented their meat diet with fish and shellfish. They had no agriculture and no domesticated animal, except perhaps the dog. Camp sites were small. They were occupied by a comparatively few people and were used for short periods of time. This is understandable, for the purely natural resources of a given area are limited and quickly exhausted by intensive hunting and food gathering. Caves and rock shelters often served as protection from the elements and provide a great deal of useful information. The refuse pits, or kitchen middens, that mark the sites where the Archaic people lived are also informative. Here you will find the burned and broken bones of the animals that were used as food. Scattered about the camp sites are characteristic stone tools and implements of the period.

The Archaic people's way of life underwent gradual changes throughout the entire time range of the period. Toward the end of the period, about 1000 B.C., fired clay pottery came into use. This was followed by the beginnings of maize agriculture, which had spread northward from Mexico and Middle America over a long period of time. The transition from Archaic to Woodland was now complete.

Woodland

The introduction of agriculture produces a radical change in the life and habits of a people. Instead of depending upon the chance products of nature, they can rely on a fairly stable food supply. Nomadic days end. After the harvest the comparatively bulky stores of food must be protected, and there is no transportation to move them any distance from the fields.

With agriculture the rather simple society of Archaic times gave way to the much more advanced society of Woodland times. Villages increased in size and were more permanent. Hunting, although still important, became a secondary source of food supply. With their leisure increased, the Indians were able to develop the nonmaterial aspects of their culture (language, social customs, religious concepts), and these became more sophisticated. The increasing complexity of society quite naturally resulted in a more complicated political organization. The culture was on its way to civilization. As a consequence, tool types and other archaeological finds recovered from a Woodland site are more numerous and varied than those recovered from an Archaic site.

In many villages the people built great burial mounds, some round and others that appear from the air to have the shape of animals, snakes, or birds. Burial-mound building flourished particularly in the Upper Mississippi and Ohio River valleys among Adena and Hopewell cultists, but its influence reached into Kentucky, Virginia, and Pennsylvania and has been noted as far north as the Great Lakes, New York State, and New England. In these mounds the dead were cremated or buried with extensive offerings accompanied by elaborate funerary rites. The mound-builders had long disappeared in this area by the time the white men reached it. They found the region populated by numerous tribes and bands, some of which had united into leagues or confederacies, such as the league of the Iroquois.

Some time later a mound-building culture, influenced by contacts with Middle America, flourished in the lower Mississippi River valley. These people built stockaded towns around flat-topped earthen pyramids, on which wooden temples were constructed. This southern Temple Mound, or Mississippian, culture lasted for many centuries, reaching its peak after A.D. 1300. Remnants of it survived until the coming of the Spaniards, the first white men to explore the region.

Mogollon, Hohokam, and Anasazi

Agriculture and pottery-making apparently reached southern Arizona and the Rio Grande region by the beginning of the modern era, perhaps introduced by immigrating people or by contact with others possessing these arts. Here arose two sedentary agricultural societies, the Mogollon and Hohokam.

Mogollon, which takes its name from the mountainous Mogollon Rim country of New Mexico and Arizona and is the oldest southwestern tradition in agriculture and in the making of fired clay pottery, developed out of a Desert culture base. Partially contemporary with it was the Hohokam culture, which arose in the Gila Valley of Arizona during the first century A.D. To cultivate their crops of maize and cotton, the desert-dwelling Hohokam (from the Pima Indian term for "those who have gone," or "the ancient people") about A.D. 700 began to dig large irrigation canals, some eventually covering distances as long as 22 miles. Their culture flourished almost until historic times.

In the highlands to the north of the Hohokam lived the Basket Maker–Pueblo, or Anasazi (from the Navajo Indian term for "the ancient ones"). From the Archaic cultures of the early Basket Makers evolved villages of "apartment-dwelling" farmers, whose multistoried communal type of dwelling has been given the name of *pueblo,* from the Spanish word for village.

The development of agriculture was accompanied by characteristic advances in the social, religious, and political fields. The highly organized religion was based upon weather and climate, the important environmental aspects of an agricultural economy. Ancient ancestral underground houses became ceremonial rooms, or *kivas.*

During the late 1200's, drought and invasion by nomadic Indians from the north caused the Anasazi to leave the area. Village after village was abandoned as they drifted southward along the Rio Grande into New Mexico and northern Arizona, where the modern Pueblo Indians of the Southwest live today.

CULTURE AREAS

There are as many different schemes for dividing the North American continent into geographical divisions, or culture areas, as there are archaeological experts. The culture area is a convenient way of describing the different ways of life followed by many peoples over an entire continent or an even larger part of the earth. Most details of a culture do not fit exactly within the framework of an area but tend to overlap at its boundaries. The use of geographical terms for these areas helps to keep in mind where they are located. A simple map divides the continent into these culture areas, which will be described briefly: Arctic Coast, Northern, Northwest Coast, Intermediate and Mountain, Southwest, and the four subareas of the vast Eastern expanse—Plains, Middle West, Southeast, and Northeast.

A simplified pattern divides the North American continent into these following culture areas: A. Arctic Circle; I. Intermediate and Mountain; MW. Middle West; N. Northern; NE. Northeast; NW. Northwest; P. Plains; SE. Southeast; SW. Southwest.

NO. AMERICAN CULTURE AREAS

Arctic Coast

Except for some areas of Alaska, this Arctic coastal region that includes northern Canada is cold, forbidding, and inaccessible. It can be occupied only by a people extremely well adjusted to the environment. The original inhabitants, like those of today, were fishermen and hunters, primarily of sea mammals. Tools and implements fashioned by an ancient "core and blade" industry (see section on Paleo-Indian Artifacts in chapter 4) have been found at several Alaskan sites. The blades struck from these cores, called micro-blades, are in some instances quite similar to those from Mongolia.

Gravers, or burins, similar to those found at sites in the neighboring part of Siberia are associated with the Denbigh flint complex from excavations on Alaska's Bering Sea coast. They may date from about 4000 B.C.

Eskimo origins are not definitely known, but evidence from village middens at various western Arctic sites points to a relatively recent immigration from Siberia. The earliest Arctic-dwellers probably crossed into Alaska long after the Sandia and Folsom herd hunters. From about the first century A.D. to 400 the early Kachemak, Okvik, and Iputiak hunters of caribou and sea animals were following an Eskimo way of life. Their stone-floored houses, built partially underground, had walls of driftwood timbers. Walrus oil, burned in shallow pottery lamps, provided heat and light. Spoons and ladles were made of wood, bone, and ivory, the two latter materials often being skillfully carved into animals and abstract designs. Seal and walrus were hunted with the toggle-headed harpoon, a throwing shaft with stone spear point fitted into a detachable foreshaft. For transportation the distinctive Eskimo sled, kayak, and umiak, or woman's boat, were employed.

Artifacts found at Cape Dorset near Hudson Bay revealed the existence of an eastern culture similar to that of the ancient western Eskimo. Scattered villages of the Dorset Eskimo have also been found as far east as Greenland and as far south as Newfoundland. Although their tools, implements, and craftsmanship were cruder and more primitive than those of their western cousins, the Dorsets may represent an early development from the Denbigh people. It was in Greenland between A.D. 1200 and 1400 that the Eskimo came in contact with the first European settlers, the Norsemen.

Northern

Included in this area is the entire northern portion of the continent, with the exception of the Arctic coastal area. Essentially, this is an area of lakes and streams, forest, and the level treeless plains known as tundra. Because its subarctic climate is not suitable for agriculture, the people followed a largely hunting-fishing-gathering subsistence pattern. Evidence of occupation by Paleo-Indian, Archaic, and Woodland people has been found throughout the area.

Northwest Coast

Few Paleo-Indian specimens have been found along the coastal sections of British Columbia, Washington, and Oregon. They may lie along the coastal plain that is now submerged beneath the waters of the Pacific, but at present there is little evidence of sites earlier than Archaic. The later cultures of the Northwest Coast were adapted to a fishing economy and relied heavily upon salt-water and fresh-water resources.

Aside from the procuring of food, woodworking and the accumulation of wealth for the ceremonial potlatch were the chief economic activities. A strong and vigorous art characterized their work in wood. Their highly organized social system was almost feudal in its hierarchy of nobles, commoners, and slaves, with titled families showing their "coats of arms" on totem poles. The workings of the social system took place through the institution of the potlatch, a ceremonial gift-giving held to celebrate any socially important event. Its object was to uphold the prestige of a family through its head by mobilizing all of the family wealth and resources.

Textiles are prominent in the final stages of this culture, which is one of the most distinctive in North America. It was probably less influenced by Middle American sources than any other North American culture, although there are indications of considerable Asian influences.

Intermediate and Mountain

This area of the Great Basin, homeland of the Desert culture, includes parts of California, Nevada, Utah, Oregon, Washington, Wyoming, Alberta, British Columbia, and all of Idaho. Within its bounds is the important Danger Cave site, near Wendover, Utah, dating back about 11,000 years.

The cultures were primarily Archaic but differed from one another in their subsistence patterns. In the north they were oriented toward fishing; in the south they tended toward food gathering and primitive agriculture. But in general, archaeological differences between the two regions are slight.

Pottery traits of Asian rather than Middle American origin appear in northern Utah. Anasazi traits (the Hovenweep pueblo vilages, for example) are found in the southern portion of the area.

Southwest

This area has been the scene of much archaeological activity. Its prehistory probably is as well understood as that of any area north of Mexico. Although the Desert culture was prominent in earliest times, Paleo-Indian tools and implements (such as the lance-shaped Sandia and fluted Clovis and Folsom points) have frequently been recovered, as these two ancient cultures were partially contemporary.

t remarkable of the Adena or Hopewell effigy mounds is
ong Serpent Mound, in Adams County, Ohio. Resembling
y coiled snake, it holds a 30-foot "egg" between its jaws.
Department, State of Ohio)

ed evidences of hundreds of farming towns lining the
Great Plains, principally along the Nebraska and Re-
s and other tributaries of the Missouri. These Plains
ated corn, squash, and tobacco, and lived in round or
n lodges. Some of their villages lasted almost into

e 1500's, however, the Plains bison began to increase
nd to spread over a wide area. Abandoning the hard,
arming, the plains Indians took up bison hunting. These
y ancient Americans ever to abandon farming after
d it.

archaeology in this area is important because it in-
iod of rapid change. The horse, a common animal in
during the Ice Age, became extinct when it ended.
ion of the horse about 1700 from Spanish settlements in
t greatly increased the hunting efficiency of the Plains
ell as their ability to defend or enlarge their territory.
Woodland people were forced out of their homeland by
l pressure of colonial settlements along the Atlantic
ere compelled to forsake their traditional way of life
t of the Plains bison hunters.

In post-Paleo times at least three cultural centers arose in the
area—the Mogollon, Hohokam, and Anasazi. The Mogollon people
lived in the mountainous country of southern New Mexico, chiefly
along the Mimbres River valley. A primitive type of maize, dated
about 300 B.C., came from Tularosa Cave I, in Mogollon territory;
from Tularosa Cave II in the same area came the earliest known
pottery, dated about one hundred years later.

The Mogollon culture reached its peak during the Mimbres
period, between A.D. 1050 and 1200. This period was characterized
by beautiful black-on-white pottery decorated with naturalistic figures. Burials were often accompanied by handsome pottery bowls
of this type, which were ceremonially "killed" by having a hole
knocked in the bottoms. The spirit believed to be in the pottery
was thus released to accompany the spirit of the deceased to a
better world.

The Hohokam were lowland desert-dwellers who inhabited
central and southern Arizona, to the west of the Mogollon. They were
skilled shell and stone carvers and made a distinctive buff-colored
pottery with red painted decoration. Their homes were single-room
lodges of adobe (brush and mud). The greatest Hohokam town,
called Snaketown by its excavators, lay near the site of present-day
Phoenix. Here were found vestiges of the overflow ditches and
irrigation canals that explain the ability of the Hohokam to grow
maize and cotton. Ball courts uncovered at Snaketown and other
large Hohokam villages bear marked similarities to those built and
used for ceremonial games by the early Mexicans and Maya to the
south. Because the Hohokam cremated their dead, little is known of
their physical appearance.

During the late 1200's intruders from the north began to drift
into Hohokam territory, settling near the Salt River. These "Salado"
people, so-called after the Spanish word for salt, brought with them
such Anasazi traits as multistoried communal houses and burial of
the dead. Casa Grande, in Arizona, is the only surviving example of
the "great houses" built by the Salado people. Although differing
from each other in almost every respect, the Hohokam and Salado
peoples lived peacefully side by side.

The Anasazi (Basket Maker and Pueblo) lived in the "four
corners" region where the states of Utah, Colorado, Arizona, and
New Mexico meet. Before the year A.D. 400 the early Basket Makers
had an essentially Archaic culture. They lived in underground dwell-

Above, this striking petroglyph of a mountain lion was found in Arizona's Petrified Forest. (U.S. Dept. of the Interior, National Park Service)

Left, the famous Cliff Palace was one of the first major ruins discovered at Mesa Verde, in Colorado. It dates from the Great Pueblo period (about A.D. 1200 to 1300). (U.S. Dept. of the Interior, National Park Service)

ings, or pit houses, used a primitive spear and thrower as their chief weapon, and were skillful weavers of baskets. In addition to basketry, they wove sandals and other articles of clothing, utilizing plant fibers and strips of rabbit fur.

Significant changes took place as farming became more important in the Anasazi economy. Underground dwellings were roofed over with poles and adobe to provide better protection from the weather. From the pit houses gradually developed more permanent, multiple-room dwellings of coursed masonry (stone set in adobe mortar), which were built on the open mesa, or tableland. Often rising as high as four stories, these houses were joined together to form compact villages. Cotton cloth was woven, the bow and arrow came into use, and fired clay pottery of fine design and decoration replaced the earlier basketry.

After about 1200 the Anasazi moved from the mesas to caves. There they built pueblos, or cliff dwellings, perhaps as a defense against intruders who had moved into the area. Important pueblo centers rose at Chaco Canyon in northwestern New Mexico, at Mesa Verde in southwestern Colorado, and in the Kayenta region of northeastern Arizona. Pueblo Bonito ("beautiful village"), one of the most famous of the Chaco Canyon apartment houses, contained in its heyday 800 rooms and 32 kivas, or ceremonial chambers. It

housed over 1,200 inhabita
apartment building anywhe

Other arts also reached
Pueblo period (Pueblo III
1000 to 1400. The striking
of Chaco, Kayenta, and Me
utilitarian ware. Pottery of
manship—jugs, water jars,
people.

Then, in 1276, drought
of a century little rain fell,
economic decline was follo
vasion of the territory by
Navajo. The Anasazi moved
led to an intermixing of the
some of the old Anasazi trait
cultures, still survive in the
others.

Plains

From southern Alberta
stretches the great grassy st
herds of grazing animals for
of the last great ice sheet, m
horned bison, and other Ple
portion of the range. But th
Ice Age. Their final disappea
severely that man, too, vanishe

When climatic conditions
once more on the western Pla
time the modern bison (buff
returned, following his prey a
artifacts had undergone consid
with hand-thrown weapons ti
sessed the bow, and arrows tip
of the eastern Archaic culture.

Later, Woodland people e
with them cordmarked (decora
pottery and agriculture. Arch

One of the mo
the 1,350-foot-
a huge, partial
(Development

have discover
rivers of the
publican rive
farmers cultiv
square earthe
historic times.

During th
in numbers a
dull work of
were the on
having learne

Historica
dicates a per
the Americas
The introduc
the Southwe
Indians as w
When other
the westwar
coast, they
and adopt th

Above, the Leo Petroglyph, in Jackson County, Ohio, is typical of the picture writings made on rock by early Indians in this area. (Development Department, State of Ohio)

Right, this decorative eagle claw of mica was one of the ceremonial objects found in Hopewell burial mounds of the Mound City Group in Ohio. (Ohio State Museum)

Middle West

This subarea includes the Upper Mississippi and Ohio valleys, the states of Missouri and Kentucky, and part of southern Ontario. Paleo-Indians were the earliest inhabitants, as evidenced by Clovis-like fluted points found at the Parish site in Kentucky. They were followed by Archaic food gatherers and hunters, who supplemented their diet with fish and shellfish. River banks in Kentucky are heaped with the shells of fresh-water clams left by these Archaic people.

About 1000 B.C. the art of mound-building and its associated elaborate cult of the dead appeared in the area with the early Woodland cultures, accompanied by agriculture and the making of pottery. Many of these earthen mounds were used for burials.

Some of these burial mounds are round or conical in form, such as the 78-foot mound at Miamisburg, Ohio, built by the Adena people. Geometric forms appear in the Ohio Valley, through Indiana, Illinois, and into Iowa. The Seip Mound and Hopewell earthworks, near Chillicothe, Ohio, are of this type. Effigy mounds in the shape of birds and animals are concentrated in southern Wisconsin and adjacent areas in Illinois, Minnesota, and Iowa. Fortified hills are found in every state east of the Mississippi but are especially numerous in

Ohio, Kentucky, and Tennessee. Fort Ancient, near the Seip and Hopewell mounds, is such a fortification.

Some of the earliest Mound Builders, the Hopewell cultists among them, built the most elaborate mounds and had the most highly organized and colorful religious rituals. Using only digging sticks or primitive hoes, the builders scraped up the earth and carried it in baskets, load by load, to complete the mound. Breastplates and head-dresses of copper from the Great Lakes, knives of obsidian from the Rocky Mountains, drinking cups of shell from the Gulf of Mexico, and mirrors of mica from the southern Appalachians, carved stone statuettes, ornamental pipes, and other lavish grave goods accompanied the burials, which were probably reserved for persons of high rank.

Builders of the later flat-topped temple mounds penetrated this area as far as southern Wisconsin, perhaps conquering many of the earlier Burial Mound peoples. Cahokia Mound, at East St. Louis, Illinois, dates from this period. Covering an area of 16 acres at its base and rising to a height of over 100 feet, it is the largest of all mounds and originally dominated a group of more than 100 similar mounds arranged nearby.

Southeast

This large subarea encompasses the coastal states south of Maryland and Pennsylvania and shares a common western boundary with the Middle West subarea. Paleo-Indians roamed over the entire area north of Florida and left considerable evidence of their presence. Then, some time after the retreat of the last great ice sheet, they followed the grazing Pleistocene herds northward. Just how early this movement occurred and how long Paleo man lingered in the south is not known.

Considerable archaeological evidence has been unearthed concerning the period immediately following the Paleo-Indian. A number of projectile point forms of an early Archaic type have been found in association with Paleo types, as well as tubular stone pipes and mortars, pestles, and grinding stones for use with nuts, seeds, and berries. Great piles of clam and mussel shells heaped along the Atlantic and Gulf coasts and lining the banks of the Mississippi, Tennessee, Savannah, and St. Johns (Florida) rivers mark the temporary camp sites of Archaic inhabitants of some 4,000 years ago.

The restored circular earth-covered temple, or earth lodge, at Ocmulgee National Monument, Georgia, appears much as it did 1,000 years ago. (U.S. Dept. of the Interior, National Park Service)

Clay pottery appeared at an early date in the Southeast. Woodland clay vessels tempered, or mixed, with grass or moss fibers, dating back to 1600 B.C. have been found in Florida and southern Georgia.

In later Woodland times innovations appeared that seem to have marked, but still unexplained, Middle American influences. One of these new ingredients was agriculture. Another was the art of mound-building, closely associated with the highly organized, ritualistic religion developed by the sedentary farming communities of the period.

This mound-building culture flourished somewhat later than in the north and centered along the lower Mississippi River basin. The mounds were flat-topped and usually surmounted by a wooden structure, usually a temple. Builders of the Great Temple Mound at Ocmulgee, Georgia, hauled about 1,000,000 basketloads of earth to construct the 40-foot-high earthwork. At Etowah, Georgia, they built a gigantic temple mound rising 66 feet and covering 3 acres at its base.

Burials were made, not in the mounds themselves, but in cemeteries around them. From the cemeteries and ceremonial caches nearby have come pottery, stone bowls, copper plaques, and shell disks carved with elaborate linear designs of birds and various motifs, such as swastikas, human skulls, hearts, and severed arms. These latter designs indicate the existence of a kind of "death cult," possibly of Mexican origin, that was practiced by the builders of the temple mound at Moundville, Alabama, as well as at Etowah, Ocmulgee, and other centers.

The Temple Mound culture lasted for several centuries, reaching its peak sometime after 1300. Mound-building faded away as quickly as it had begun, its art and ceremonies unknown to most of the Indians of historic times with whom the Europeans came in contact.

Table A. The Chronological Progression of Cultures
*(The progression of cultures in various areas is presented
in the simplest and most generalized form possible. The
intention is to give only an approximate concept of chronological relationships in the areas selected.)*

	Northeast	Southeast	Middle West
A.D. 1700			Historic
A.D. 1500	Historic	Historic	
A.D. 500	Late Woodland	Late Mississippian	Western Farmers (E. area)
A.D. 1	Middle Woodland	Early Mississippian	Woodland in High Plains (non-agricultural)
1000 B.C.	Early Woodland	Early Woodland	
2100 B.C.			
2500 B.C.	Late Archaic	Late Archaic	
4000 B.C.			
6000 B.C.	Early Archaic	Early Archaic	Archaic
6700 B.C.			
7000 B.C.			
8000 B.C.			
9000 B.C.	Paleo-Indian	Paleo-Indian	Paleo-Indian
10,000 B.C.			
11,000 B.C.			
12,000 B.C.			
13,000 B.C.		Pebble Tool	

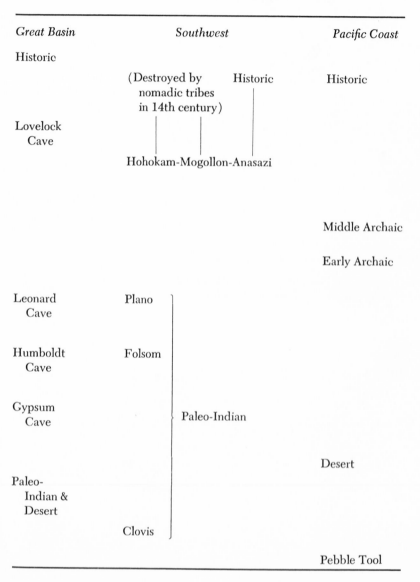

Great Basin	Southwest	Pacific Coast
Historic		
	(Destroyed by nomadic tribes in 14th century) Historic	Historic
Lovelock Cave		
	Hohokam-Mogollon-Anasazi	
		Middle Archaic
		Early Archaic
Leonard Cave	Plano	
Humboldt Cave	Folsom	
Gypsum Cave	Paleo-Indian	
		Desert
Paleo-Indian & Desert		
	Clovis	
		Pebble Tool

The circular Archaic lodge was probably quite a general type of dwelling east of the Mississippi. This model is part of a diorama in the Bronson Museum, Attleboro, Massachusetts.

Northeast

This subarea encompasses southwestern Ontario, the St. Lawrence Valley in the United States and Canada, New England, New York State, Pennsylvania, New Jersey, Virginia, and Maryland. The first inhabitants were Paleo-Indian hunters who left behind a variety of Clovis-like points, gravers, scrapers, and miscellaneous small tools. These have been recovered from a number of sites, including Reagen in Vermont, Bull Brook and Wapanucket #8 in Massachusetts, Shoop in Pennsylvania, and Williamson in Virginia. They indicate that rather than utilize inferior local materials, the Paleo hunters often traveled considerable distances to obtain the best stone for the implements on which depended their food supply.

Shells of mussels, clams, and oysters consumed by the Archaic peoples have been found heaped along the region's rivers and coasts and buried in the refuse heaps of ancient villages in New York's Finger Lakes region. The Boylston Street fish weir, discovered deep in silt under the Back Bay section of Boston, was part of a system of weirs for trapping fish that was installed in the Charles River tidewater over 4,000 years ago.

Pottery came into use in late Archaic or early Woodland times. It was generally gray in color, tempered with shell, sand, or grit, and with a coarse, fabric- or cordmarked surface decoration. Much Siberian pottery has a similar tradition of cordmarked decoration.

At former Archaic camp sites sedentary farming communities grew up. Woodland tools and implements have come from a number of sites in New York, Rhode Island, Maine, and Massachusetts. From descendants of these Indians the first European settlers in this area learned to cultivate corn, beans, pumpkins, squash, and tobacco.

The first Americans crossed into the New World during or toward the end of the last Ice Age glaciation. They came over a long period of time, perhaps following different routes. It seems probable that each wandering band was a self-contained unit, with its own language, tools, and traditions. Over the course of years they moved into different regions of North America and adjusted themselves to the environment they found there. The longer they lived in a particular region, the more varied and complex their culture became.

Natural disasters and human enemies triggered the decline of the early civilizations. The coming of the white man sealed their doom. Although these ancient peoples have vanished forever, it is possible for the archaeologist to reconstruct their way of life, often in startling detail. Each site plays its part in filling in the puzzle.

Table B. The Migration Valve

Period	Onset Date	Passage to Asia	Southern Corridor
Sangamon (interglacial)	120,000 B.P.°	Closed	Open
WISCONSIN I	70,000 B.P.	Open	Closed
Port Talbot (interstadial)	55,000 B.P.	Closed	Open
WISCONSIN II	45,000 B.P.	Open	Closed
Peorian (interstadial)	35,000 B.P.	Closed	Open
WISCONSIN III	25,000 B.P.	Open	Closed
Cary-Mankato (interstadial)	14,500 B.P.	Closed	Open briefly
MANKATO (substage)	14,000 B.P.	Open	Closed
Two Creeks (interstadial)	12,000 B.P.	Open	Possibly open
VALDERS (substage)	11,000 B.P.	Possibly open	Possibly open
ANATHERMAL	10,000 B.P.	Closed	Open permanently

° The initials B.P. refer to carbon 14 dating and mean "Before the Present."

3 : How to Know Where to Dig

There are so many different kinds of sites that it is impossible to supply a blanket answer to the question: "How do you know exactly where to locate an archaeological site?" The answer depends upon such basic considerations as whether the site is prehistoric or historic, underwater or above ground. It depends, too, on the geographic area and on the cultural level of its inhabitants. Prehistoric Indian sites may comprise, for example, one or more of the following:

Caches	Mines and quarries
Camps	Mounds
Caves and rock shelters	Petroglyphs and pictographs
Cemeteries	Shell heaps or middens
Fortifications and ceremonial areas	Temporary villages
	Villages
Huts or houses	Workshops

To narrow down the field a bit, let's assume that you are interested in the possible existence of a prehistoric Indian site in your area. Next, let's consider the necessary steps to take in locating it. This involves preparing a survey of the area compiled from research, notes, and maps. The survey tells you what natural features to look for and where to look for them. Possible sites are plotted on your maps, and you are ready to go out into the field to check your observations on the spot.

THE AREA SURVEY

You must start by making a thorough study of the Indian cultures that were present in your area, by familiarizing yourself with its geography and topography, and by using a considerable amount of good, plain common sense. This research is an excellent occupation for those days or seasons when the weather is unsuitable for field work.

Basic Research

The first step is to read the local history with a critical eye. Glean from it the location of all Indian sites referred to, the trails used by Indians and settlers, and any forts that are mentioned. Next, read all of the scientific reports and papers in which the Indian cultures that existed in the area are discussed. In a notebook or card file list all the pertinent facts under appropriate headings.

Natural Features

Make a list, based upon your research, of the various natural features sought by the Indians of the area. Don't overlook those that common sense tells you they would have required. You will probably notice, for example, that the location of permanent year-round villages was determined by certain subsistence requirements. These involved proximity to certain natural features as well as the stage of cultural development reached.

Drinking water. Fresh water was a common need in all cultures and in all periods. The Indian could not store up this commodity in any quantity, so he had to locate his camp or village near a good supply. For an overnight stop or small family camp, a spring might be sufficient. A village of some size required a much larger permanent supply of fresh drinking water.

Keep in mind this fact: water tables have dropped or risen over the years. In ancient times water may not have existed in its present location. On the other hand, a good water supply in aboriginal times may have disappeared by now, and the only indication of its former presence may be found in the topography of the region. For example, the large lakes that existed in the American Southwest in interglacial times are now deserts. The only indications of their former presence are the ancient terraces that mark the position of their shorelines. Many of the Anasazi apartment houses and cliff dwellings are found in areas that now are waterless. You must search for water, past as well as present.

Although drinking water was a prime requisite of an Indian site,

MAN MADE

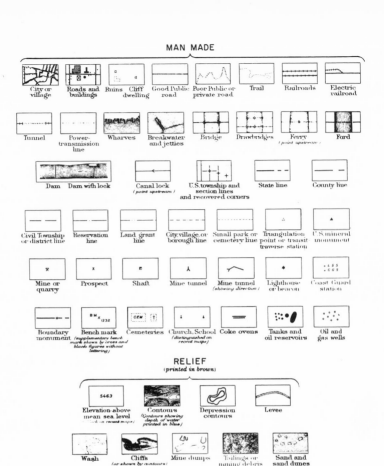

City or village · Roads and buildings · Ruins · Cliff dwelling · Good Public road · Poor Public or private road · Trail · Railroads · Electric railroad

Tunnel · Power-transmission line · Wharves · Breakwater and jetties · Bridge · Drawbridges · Ferry (point upstream) · Ford

Dam · Dam with lock · Canal lock (point upstream) · U.S. township and section lines and recovered corners · State line · County line

Civil Township or district line · Reservation line · Land grant line · City, village, or borough line · Small park or cemetery line · Triangulation point or transit traverse station · U.S. mineral monument

Mine or quarry · Prospect · Shaft · Mine tunnel · Mine tunnel (showing direction) · Lighthouse or beacon · Coast Guard station

Boundary monument (supplementary bench mark shown by cross and black figures without lettering) · Bench mark · Cemeteries · Church, School (distinguished on record maps) · Coke ovens · Tanks and oil reservoirs · Oil and gas wells

RELIEF
(printed in brown)

Elevation above mean sea level (shown on record maps) · Contours (Contours showing depth of water printed in blue) · Depression contours · Levee

Wash · Cliffs (or shown by contours) · Mine dumps · Tailings or mining debris · Sand and sand dunes

WATER
(printed in blue)

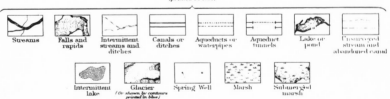

Streams · Falls and rapids · Intermittent streams and ditches · Canals or ditches · Aqueducts or waterpipes · Aqueduct tunnels · Lake or pond · Unsurveyed stream and abandoned canal

Intermittent lake · Glacier (Or shown by contours printed in blue) · Spring Well · Marsh · Submerged marsh

WOODS
(when shown, printed in green)

These symbols represent the three groups of features shown on Geological Survey topographic maps. Water is shown in blue, relief in brown, and culture (man-made works) in black. (U.S. Geological Survey)

too much of it constituted a menace. No sensible Indian selected for a village site an area that could be flooded in time of high water. In the mountain desert regions, where flash floods are an ever-present threat, the Indian avoided narrow valleys. Look for relatively high, well-drained spots near good drinking water. In forested areas the preferred sites were usually located at the point where a stream entered or left a pond or lake, provided, of course, that high land was present.

Navigable streams. There were other advantages in being near water. Streams, rivers, and lakes were natural highways of the aboriginal world. As surely as highways lead to modern towns and cities, streams led to ancient villages. The forest trails were winding and narrow, made many detours to avoid wet spots, and climbed endless hills. Water travel was much quicker and easier.

Swamps and fishing spots. Water was also a source of food. Animals, too, must drink, and some species grazed in the lush river bottoms. Wild fowl and small game were plentiful in marshlands, fish swam in the streams and lakes, and shellfish could be found along the shores.

Wood and workable stone. The need for fresh water was only one of the natural features necessary in the daily life of the Indian. A supply of dead or down wood for the campfires was essential. So, too, was workable stone for the manufacture of implements and tools. If good supplies were not present in the vicinity, the Indians often sought them at considerable distances.

Protection. The Indian also had to consider protection from the elements, particularly in the case of a winter village. A ridge or hill in the proper direction warded off the bitter winds and diverted some of the snow. Temperatures were somewhat higher near swampland. In summer the onshore breeze from the ocean or lake helped to dissipate mosquitoes and to give some relief from the heat.

During certain periods natural features that would aid in the defense of the village against surprise attack were desirable. Often selected were islands in lakes or swamps, areas that had to be approached across water or swampland or that could be reached only by climbing steep ridges or cliffs.

Cultural influences. The culture of a given group exercised considerable effect upon its choice of a village site. The Archaic hunting-fishing-gathering people, for instance, looked for good hunting and fishing grounds, for burned-over areas where berry bushes might be found, and for protection from the winter weather as well. In coastal areas the sea furnished a welcome change of diet. People who were oriented toward the sea needed sheltered harbors, shellfish flats, and fresh water. In other areas the gatherers of wild rice and acorns were attracted to sites most suitable to their specialized economies.

Agricultural people had a whole new list of requirements for their village sites. The achievement of a relatively stable economy had immobilized them to some extent, and they no longer roamed widely in search of game. The villages were larger and more permanent in nature. Although still important, hunting had become secondary to farming. Lands that could be cleared easily for planting crops loomed large on the list of requirements. After the crops were gathered, there was the problem of storage and, because these food supplies were valuable, there was the problem of defense as well.

In looking for sites, you must forget your twentieth-century ideas and put on the moccasins of the Indian. Think as he thought, in terms of the necessities of life. As you become adept at this sort of thinking, you will learn to recognize the most likely sites, both in the field and on the map.

Maps

For this purpose you will need good topographical maps (those indicating surface forms, or relief) of the area. The familiar motorist's road map will not be satisfactory; usually it is quite inaccurate concerning the natural features of the terrain that were of great importance to the original inhabitants. The best topographical maps of the United States are those published and sold by the U.S. Geological Survey. This series of maps covers nearly all of the continental United States. The unit of the series is the quadrangle, which is an area bounded by parallels of latitude and meridians of longitude.

Several sizes and scales are available: quadrangles covering 7½ minutes of longitude at a scale of either 1:24,000 (1 inch = 2,000 feet) or 1:31,600 (1 inch = 2,600 feet), quadrangles covering 15 minutes at a scale of 1:62,500 (1 inch = 5,280 feet or 1 mile), and quadrangles covering 30 minutes at a scale of 1:125,000 (1 inch = about 10,500 feet). I prefer the 7½-minute series at a scale of 1:24,000 because the large scale is more appropriate for an archaeological survey, the scale of 1 inch = 2,000 feet making for easier plotting of sites. For some of the western states quadrangles are available cover-

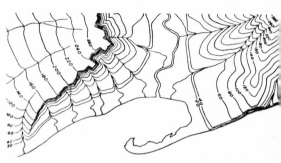

Contour lines show the shape, elevation above sea level, and grade of the hills, mountains, and valleys. Twenty-foot intervals of elevation are represented on this sketch map. (U.S. Geological Survey)

ing 1 degree of latitude and longitude at a scale of 1:250,000 (1 inch = about 4 miles).

Each quadrangle is identified by the name of a city or town or of some prominent landmark within it. The names of the adjoining quadrangles appear on the margins. Natural features of relief—hills, mountains, and valleys—are indicated in brown; water features are shown in blue; roads, railroads, cities, and towns appear in black. In some, even individual houses appear as black rectangles. The intervals between the brown contour lines vary with the scale of the map and the relief shown. On some maps additional colors are used; for example, some quadrangles can be obtained with a green overprint showing forest cover. A descriptive folder and an index map of any state is available free of charge from the Geological Survey. On these index maps the individual quadrangles are outlined in black to indicate the area covered.

The price of the standard quadrangle is 30¢ each, but a discount of 20 per cent is allowed on orders amounting to $10 or more, and 40 per cent on orders amounting to $60 or more. Payment is required with the order. Maps of states west of the Mississippi (including all of Louisiana and Minnesota) should be ordered from the U.S. Geological Survey, Federal Center, Denver, Colorado 80225. Maps for areas east of the Mississippi River should be ordered from the U.S. Geological Survey, Department of the Interior, Washington, D.C. 20405. Specify the minutes and scale desired; if forest cover overprint is desired, mention this in your order. Information and maps for most parts of Canada (scale 1 inch = 8 miles) may be obtained from the Map Distribution Office, Department of Mines and Technical Surveys, Ottawa, Ontario, Canada.

As your collection of survey maps grows, you will begin to make many interesting and worthwhile observations. You will begin to notice, for example, a relationship between topographical features and the location of sites. Springs or sources of good drinking water, good fishing spots, swamps where game was plentiful, sources of workable stone, and good planting grounds will coincide with ancient village sites. Navigable streams and lakes particularly will be rich in archaeological sites. All of these observations, in fact, provide grist for the mill of archaeology. Eventually you will be able to forecast the probable location of hitherto unknown sites simply by studying the map. These new and undisturbed sites are the ones you will want to excavate later.

Plotting Possible Sites

A small portion of the Assawompset Quadrangle of Massachusetts is shown as an example of the Geological Survey type of map and the way in which it is used for archaeological survey purposes. Notice first the number 54 in the water area at the upper right. This number represents the height of mean water above sea level (at New Bedford, Mass.). The brown contour lines are at 10-foot intervals, with a heavier brown line at the 100-foot contour above sea level. Thus, the first brown line that parallels the lake shore is at 60 feet, the next at 70, the next at 80, and so on. Note that there are several points at which the 150-foot contour is reached. By noting the levels shown in the water bodies, the direction of flow in streams and rivers, and the level shown at the various permanent location sites, or bench marks (B.M.), you soon learn to see the surface in three dimensions.

This particular section of the quadrangle was selected as an illustration because it represents excellent Indian country where many possible sites can be plotted. Lying within the valley of a major river, it contains considerable low, swampy land as well as gentle and relatively sharp relief. The elevations were probably islands in glacial Lake Assawompset, and the swampy areas began to form after the lake drained. Probably in Paleo-Indian times these swamp areas were small lakes or ponds. Note that there are several

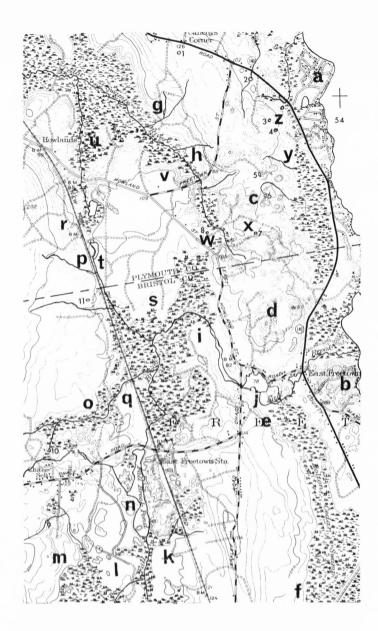

This section of the Assawompset Quadrangle of Massachusetts shows the topographical and natural features to look for in an archaeological survey.

springs (1–11) and a number of small, spring-fed ponds interconnected by streams. Keeping these details in mind, let us scan this map looking for possible Indian sites.

a] Here is an attractive area for a summer village. High enough above the water to avoid flooding, protected by an encircling swamp and stream, it could be easily defended against an enemy. A small, spring-fed pond offers a good supply of drinking water. The one drawback is that there are many houses in the area, and there would be considerable disturbance of the aboriginal sites. Excavation of a site, if located, would be done under adverse conditions. However, it would be well to check gardens and other disturbed surfaces here for your record.

b] Here is an unlikely spot. The relief is quite abrupt; in other words, there are few level areas where a site could be situated. Perhaps you might find some evidence of occupation in the area bordering the swamp west of County Road.

c] At this point we also have abrupt relief; the area is quite hilly. However, the presence of two springs (6, 7) might have made it attractive to Indians for a small winter camp.

d] There are some excellent prospects in this area. Note the broad areas between the 60- and 70-foot contour lines, which are spaced quite widely, indicating fairly level ground. I would look carefully on both sides of the stream west of Howland Street and north of the road as it turns to join with County Road. Along Fall Brook at the north end of Bolton Cedar Swamp the area looks most attractive.

e-f] In the area between Braley Road and Bolton Cedar Swamp there is considerable flat land at a good elevation. Although no springs are shown on the map, there may be indications of dried-up springs. It would pay to examine this area carefully as it does not seem to be heavily built up at the present time.

g] Here the rise from the swamp is very abrupt (note closeness of the contour lines). You should look at the area between the branches of the small brook that empties into Cedar Swamp River.

h] Both sides of Freetown Street look like good prospects.

i] If you were looking for a good, defensible location, here it is: a long, narrow peninsula fairly high above the water table, a good stream on the east, and a swamp on the west. There is high land, water to drink, a swamp full of game, and a narrow entrance between stream and swamp to defend—what more could an Indian ask?

j] A likely spot, just south of the small pond at an 80-foot elevation. A good summer location.

k] Good, high, level land here. Don't overlook it in your survey.

l] Another likely spot, between arms of the swamp, with a small
stream.

m] Here is a gentle southeastern exposure. It would be pleasant
in the summer, with land for planting and water for drinking.

n] Be sure to look closely at this spot above the pond. Don't
miss the little island in Fall Brook Pond.

o-p] Spend plenty of time here. This looks like excellent Indian
country. Note the spring at 11.

q] Here in the area between two streams is another easily defended spot.

r] Maybe, but the rise is rather abrupt.

s] Excellent, don't miss this area.

t] The small pond and the level land make this spot a possibility.

u] Here is the spot for a fort or small camp hidden away in the
swamp.

v] A rather abrupt bluff above a swamp and a river; has pos-
sibilities.

w] I wouldn't pass up this spot because of the spring at 8.

x-y-z] Again, you see springs (3 to 5) that would have provided
good sites for small hunting camps. Note the protection by hills to
the east; also the swamp between the sites and the lake. Good in
winter.

Aerial Photographs

In some areas aerial photographs are available. Find out whether
an aerial survey has been made in your area; if so, obtain prints.
These will be extremely helpful to you. Ancient features, such as
old water-courses, old terraces around present-day lakes, mounds,
fortifications, even individual lodge or house sites, can often be
seen from the air even when they aren't visible from the ground.

THE FIELD CHECK

Now that you have thoroughly examined a section of your survey
map and have marked the spots that seem to be likely areas of

Indian occupation, you are ready to test the accuracy of your forecasts by a field expedition.

Equipment

Here is a suggested list of equipment you may need, to which you will doubtless add items as you grow in experience:

Knapsack or bag of some sort to carry small tools.

A small shovel; the folding variety known as a trench shovel or trenching tool is handy.

Several sizes (2 to 6 inches) of masons' pointing trowels. These can be obtained at any hardware store and should cost between 25¢ and $1, depending upon quality. The cheaper trowel has a blade welded to the shank and will break quickly at the weld after a few hours' use. The drop-forged variety, in which the blade and shank are in one piece, is much more satisfactory.

A short-handled hoe is a most satisfactory tool for ordinary excavation. It is much easier on the wrist than the trowel, and with it one can maintain a level surface with ease. You will want a hoe with a comparatively small blade, about 6 inches wide by 2 inches high. The so-called rose hoe has a blade about this size; a larger blade can be ground down. A larger and heavier blade than this will tire your wrist and will also tend to remove a deeper cut than desired. The hoe, which should cost between $2 and $3 at your garden supply or hardware store, will have a long handle. This should be cut off about 15 inches from the blade.

A small camp axe and jackknife.

A small paintbrush for cleaning artifacts.

A pair of cotton gloves (necessary in poison ivy or sumac).

Paper or cloth bags for artifacts, with tags for identification.

Compass, which should be kept in your digging bag to assist in recording artifacts and features.

Tape measure, preferably the steel variety, in inches or centimeters depending upon the system you elect to use. In a container in your kit keep a small rag saturated with oil or kerosene to clean the tape after use and to prevent rust. Tape measures cost $1.50 to $2.50 at the hardware store.

Pencils, notebook, sketch pad (see chapter 8).

Camera and extra film.

First aid equipment, snake kit in some areas, matches, flashlight.

A small supply of celluloid-acetone solution (chapter 9) or other preservative material is handy to have along. Although you will not be undertaking extensive preservation in the field, it may be necessary on occasion to strengthen a fragile artifact or fragment of clay pottery before removal.

Good stout clothing and comfortable shoes. Waterproof shoes are needed if you expect to examine low land; a pair of rubbers or rubber boots are good to have in the car. In snake country be sure your boots are high enough to protect both the foot and lower leg.

Precautions

Don't trespass without permission, particularly on fenced or cultivated lands. *Don't* leave the bars down so that cattle can wander. In other words, treat the property with due care and don't wear out your welcome. The courtesy of asking permission to walk over someone's property is due owner or tenant and may save you considerable embarrassment. Many "No Trespass" signs have been erected because of thoughtless invasion of privacy and lack of respect for property rights. Most people will respond favorably if you explain your mission and treat their property with care and consideration. In fact, you may acquire some valuable information if you talk with the owner for a few minutes. Often he has picked up artifacts that he will show you, or perhaps he will tell you of others who have found signs of Indian occupancy on his land. Do not invade federal or state lands without special permission (see Appendix V).

Field Note-taking and Collecting

Work slowly, covering each section of the map or a part of it thoroughly. Compare the landscape with the features and contour lines shown on your map so that you become familiar with the relationship between the actual topography and geography and the manner in which the cartographer has shown it on the map. Before long the map will suggest to you a photographic representation of the actual terrain.

Keep a running commentary in your notebook. (For example:

"This field has not yet been plowed, check back in a week or so; at such a point the brook has overflowed and flooded to the 70-foot contour line; a new road is being built from X street eastward.") The flooded area you noted may appear to be dry later in the season, but your note will explain why it was not occupied; the field that was not plowed may be checked later for signs of occupation. Take plenty of photographs as you explore, but identify them so that they can later be related to your survey map. (For complete details on survey records, see chapter 8.)

Now that you have selected a promising area, you must look for the telltale signs of ancient habitation. They are often easy to spot, because they will be marked by debris accumulated about the camp or village. Scattered from the fireplaces will be burned and broken bits of stone—small, angular bits of stone from the manufacture of stone tools—which are called rejectage, or just plain "chips." Blackened areas may mark a lodge site or a refuse pit. These are the signs for which you are looking.

If the site, or a portion of it, has been plowed or if the surface is otherwise disturbed, you have a good opportunity to find these telltale signs. Otherwise, look for down trees, water gulleys, animal burrows, or other disturbances. If there is no disturbance at all and you have permission to dig, do a bit of testing in the spots where natural features indicate likely habitation.

If you find signs of Indian occupation, look closely for whole or broken artifacts that can tell you the nature of the occupation. Try to determine the extent of the occupation and then note the areas of concentration (see chapter 8). Label your finds. Bring home some of the chips so that you can determine later the kinds of stone used at this site. A heap of broken shells (particularly if it is intermixed with charcoal) along the seashore or on the shores of inland lakes and streams is an excellent sign of Indian occupation. Of course, some shell heaps may be recent, but don't pass any of them by without a close look. In the areas where mounds were built (see chapter 2), low mounds are always suspect; caves or rock shelters are worth a careful inspection. A word of caution concerning caves: these are also attractive to snakes and other dangerous vermin, so watch for them as well as for Indian signs.

If it is evident that someone has beaten you to it and is actively working the site, don't disturb his excavations. Find out who he is; if you have found artifacts, offer them to him. Your cooperation will be appreciated, and you will have made an archaeological friend.

Observing an Occupied Site

As an example of the mechanics of an archaeological survey, let's turn our attention to the illustration of a small section of the Assawompset Quadrangle of Massachusetts. The large lake from which the quadrangle takes its name is the largest natural body of water in southeastern Massachusetts (some 2,200 acres) and is now a part of the water reserve of the city of New Bedford. The Cohannet Chapter of the Massachusetts Archaeological Society has the permission of the Water Commissioners of New Bedford to excavate within the reserved areas.

This area was located within the bounds of the original Plimoth Plantations, purchased from the Indians in 1621, and is well documented historically. The Indian inhabitants of the colonial period were known as "pond Indians." They were subjects of the well-known chief Massasoit. Their subchief was a notorious character by the name of Tuspaquin, and their village was located on Betty's Neck (lower left). During the Indian Wars of 1675–1676, part of this band joined the hostile party under King Philip, but a few remained friendly to the English. After the wars, the friendly group returned to their home on the Neck, and in 1694 the General Court of Plimoth set the area aside as a permanent grant to the "pond Indians." The last descendant of this band lived on the Neck until her death in 1928.

Note the strategic location of this village. The land approach is along the narrow beach on the northwestern and southeastern shore of the lake, the way being almost completely blocked by swampy land. Along the northeastern shore the land is high and steep (note the closeness of the contour lines), and a fort was located on the 150-foot heights overlooking The Narrows. In the center of the neck is a fairly large flat area (indicated by the widely spaced contour lines). The highland along the northeastern shore also afforded protection against winter storms. Springs and the lake provided a copious supply of water. The swamps just across the lake probably were full of game, and there were plenty of salmon and trout in the lake. Although it cannot be seen on this small section of the map, water routes led from the lake in two directions. To the north the Nemasket

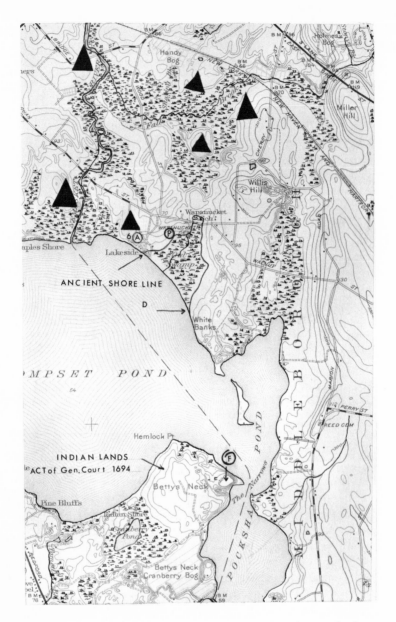

Another section of the Assawompset Quadrangle indicates the location of occupied sites and shows how the early inhabitants of the area took advantage of certain natural features.

42   How to Know Where to Dig

River flows into the Taunton River and thence to the sea at Narragansett Bay, while to the south a waterway leads to the area about Buzzards Bay at the base of Cape Cod. All the requisites for a village of an agricultural people appear to be present.

Now let's cross the lake to the northern shore. At a point marked Lakeside you will note a small circle enclosing the letter A and near it the number 6. This is the location of an Archaic village excavated under my direction and reported under the name of Wapanucket #6. This was a village of relatively early date. While working on this site, we found a number of artifacts (fluted points, gravers, etc.) of Paleo-Indian origin along the lakeshore directly south of the site.

The discovery of these ancient artifacts prompted a detailed geological study of the area that was most rewarding. We found that the lake had a long and complicated history. Briefly, we determined that the present lake was the shrunken remnant of a much larger glacial lake. The swampy areas of the present day were once flooded and were a part of the lake itself. The area known as Owl Swamp was a northern extension or embayment of the lake, and cores taken from the swamp indicated that it began to silt in about 5,000 years ago. The modern shoreline in front of the swamp is a storm beach that was constructed by wind and water action out of material taken from White Banks, which now presents a wave-cut front to the lake. The shoreline of Owl Swamp, therefore, is an ancient shore of the lake. At the location indicated by the circle enclosing the letter P, we discovered the site of a Paleo-Indian village with a covering Archaic component.

Other occupied sites are marked by black triangles. These have not been excavated, so the cultures present and the extent of each site are not yet known. However, the characteristics they possess can be readily seen. Note that each is located on the shoreline of the swamp or ancient lake. One is on an island now surrounded by swamp. All were easily defended, all are on high ground above flood stage. Plenty of drinking water is available, good hunting and fishing abounds, and it is possible to travel by a water route in either direction. This was indeed a most attractive area to aboriginal man.

The area in which Wapanucket #6 and #8 are located is well situated for defense. If we discount the present-day roads that are built across the swamps, we note that the area is entirely surrounded by swamp, the only dry access being from the northeast. This dry land access route is further barred by Willis Hill, where the terrain

Historic site excavation of the John Alden House at Duxbury, Massachusetts, uncovered the foundations of floors on upper and lower levels.

rises to a height of 150 feet and presents a rugged, steep front except for a narrow corridor about the north side of the hill. Other sites probably exist along the Middleboro shore of the lake, as the terrain there offers the favorable features demanded by primitive man.

HISTORIC SITE ARCHAEOLOGY

In recent years historic site archaeology has received wide and well-deserved attention. It is nothing more nor less than the application of archaeological techniques and discipline to various historic sites. The outstanding example is Colonial Williamsburg in Virginia.

Survey Symbols			
Camp or Temp. Village	⌐c⌐	Workshop	⌐ws⌐
Village Site	△ ⌐⌐	Cache	⊕
Paleo (camp or kill site)	Ⓡ Ⓚ	Bedrock Mortar	⌐M⌐
Mound	⌐T⌐ ⌐B⌐	Pictograph	Ⓟ
Shell Heap	⌐s⌐	Cemetery	†
Cave or Rock shelter	⌐	Fortification	Ⓕ
Mine or Quarry	⌐Q⌐	Ford	‡‡

Symbols such as these may be used in plotting features on area survey maps.

Here an entire town of the colonial period has been excavated and restored to much the same condition as it was in pre-Revolutionary times.

Roland W. Robbins and Evan Jones in their book *Hidden America* have made an outstanding contribution to the literature dealing with this subject. At the start of his career Robbins was an amateur archaeologist. His first major undertaking was the excavation of Henry David Thoreau's cabin at Walden Pond in Massachusetts. After this modest beginning Robbins moved on to excavate and restore the First Iron Works at Saugus, Massachusetts. He has since continued colonial archaeology at several sites in New York and Virginia.

Historic site archaeology offers an excellent field for the beginner in archaeology. If there is a colonial site in your neighborhood—an old foundry or dwelling that is documented by early records, for example—you have an opportunity to practice the techniques suggested in this book.

UNDERWATER ARCHAEOLOGY

Another fairly new branch of archaeology has come to the fore with the increasing popularity of scuba diving. Without a doubt many ancient sites are presently under water and are no longer available for conventional archaeology. Salvage attempts, too, are frequently made to recover the treasure of eighteenth-century Spanish galleons wrecked by pirates or storms along the Caribbean and Florida coasts while on their way from the New World to the mother country. Again, this is an application of conventional archaeological techniques to an unconventional atmosphere.

In order to locate an archaeological site in your area, the steps to follow are substantially the same. First, check the available literature for reports or papers in which local sites are located and described. Next, plot these on your survey map using symbols similar to those suggested. In the triangle representing a village site, for example, add the letter P (for Paleo-Indian), A (for Archaic), W (for Woodland), etc. Now check the topography around these known sites. Make a list of the features that recur frequently in their vicinity, note the direction of exposure, proximity of streams or lakes, etc. Then look for these conditions in blank spaces on your map. When you find them, make a field check. This is the only way that archaeologists discover where to look for an Indian site.

4 : What You Will Find

Now that you have located your site, it is a good idea to have a clear picture of what you can expect to find there before getting down to the business of excavation. What you will find depends, of course, upon the culture of its ancient inhabitants. Any single element of a culture is called a *trait*. The sum total of traits found within a culture is the *culture pattern*. In general, traits may be divided into two categories: material traits and nonmaterial traits. The material traits of a culture—tools, artifacts, and other products made by man —are found by archaeologists through careful excavation. They provide us with clues as to the nonmaterial traits—language, social customs, and religious concepts—of their makers. Let's suppose that you find artifacts buried with the dead, for example. You can reasonably conclude that the people who made this burial believed in a life after death. In it the departed would need artifacts similar to those he used in life.

The material culture or artifacts that you would expect to find on a given site will be those made of the least perishable material. In regions with a humid climate, such as the Northeast, the majority of artifacts will be of stone and fired clay. In dry areas on the other hand, especially in the caves and rock shelters of the Southwest, many artifacts of perishable material—baskets, textiles, and wooden objects —have been preserved. Even in the humid areas, perishable materials have been preserved under special circumstances—by charring, for instance. Sometimes perishable material is preserved by the action of copper salts or by similar chemical reactions.

It is important to distinguish between artifacts made by man and imitations that are the work of natural forces. To the archaeologist man-made artifacts reveal many things about the maker. The skill displayed, the technique by which the artifact was produced, the purpose for which it was intended all provide clues as to the level of sophistication of the culture represented. In other words, artifacts reflect the intelligence of the maker and are an index to the kind of existence he lived.

To qualify as an artifact, an object must have been changed or modified by man in some manner in order to adapt it to perform a specific function. Usually, but not always, we know what that function was. In most cases the modification is intentional, but in some instances an object will have been modified only by the work performed with it. Often primitive man would pick up a conveniently shaped stone and use it for a hammer. In this instance the only modification of the artifact will be the scars caused by pounding it against another stone. Often it is difficult to distinguish between the work of nature and that of man. Nature is a great imitator: stone is polished and ground by wind and water action or is fractured by frost.

Obvious tools, such as projectile points, stone axes, or fired clay pottery, are easily recognized. Fragments of these tools, or crudely made tools, are much more difficult to recognize and are often missed by the inexperienced excavator. You must learn not only to distinguish a man-made artifact but also to recognize its characteristic shape, even when only a small portion is present. Man devised several different techniques in the working of stone, and these techniques produced recognizable scars on the material. Although nature often imitates these techniques, it cannot reproduce them exactly.

CHIPPED ARTIFACTS

In some cultures the stoneworker's raw material consisted simply of cobbles of the desired material picked up at random. Others were more selective, preferring to obtain their raw material from quarries, where they detached slabs of stone from the parent ledge. Smaller pieces of the material were obtained by striking a cobble with a hammerstone or by smashing it against a larger cobble. Needless to say, the stoneworker using this technique had very little control over his work. The next step was to select a conveniently shaped fragment and shape it into an artifact by controlled blows. This final work was done by a process called *chipping*.

Chipping is a very ancient technique that was used to change the shape of a stone fragment and to improve its cutting quality. The early American Indians employed this technique in the manufacture of projectile points, knives, and all manner of scraping and drilling tools. The stoneworker first selected the kind of stone that he had learned through experience was best suited to his purpose. This was usually a hard stone that would break with a conchoidal fracture (one having elevations and depressions like those of a bivalve shell); a geologist would call this a cryptocrystalline stone. Flint, chert, quartz, felsite, and basalt were widely used materials.

There are two basic chipping techniques: *percussion*—direct or indirect—and *pressure flaking*. In percussion one stone is chipped or flaked by striking it with another stone. In pressure flaking, an antler tine or other pointed tool is used to apply pressure to the thin edge of a stone by a sudden pushing, twisting motion until a flake is detached.

Some people claim that artifacts were made by dropping cold water on the heated material in order to cause a fracture by expansion. It is possible, of course, to shatter stone by this method, but the action cannot be controlled and fracture will occur along lines of cleavage rather than at a predetermined point. Although this technique may have been used in the quarrying of blocks of stone, it was not used to produce artifacts. It is doubtful that Indians would have preferred such a cumbersome method when a simple blow with a mallet would produce the same result.

Most of the artifacts you will find will be chipped or flaked from stone. As you become familiar with the types found in the area in which you are working, you will be able to identify them according to function—as projectile points, spear points, knives, drills, etc. You will also be able to recognize them as diagnostic, or typical, of a period. Certain types will proclaim their Woodland origin, others will reveal a typically Archaic shape and technique. By their unique design and technique Paleo-Indian types will stand out from the others. You will also learn to recognize the finished artifact from the incomplete or partly worked one, and even small portions of artifacts, broken in use and discarded at the site, will catch your attention.

Of course, a large amount of waste material, the chips and spalls, or fragments, which are the by-product of the stone industry, will appear in your excavations. You may wish to keep some of this material in order to study the technique of manufacture or to determine the various kinds of stone used at the site. Close examination of a flake will often reveal the point of percussion, the spot at which the blow detaching it from the parent stone was struck. If there is a Paleo-Indian level at the site, you will want to retain all of the flakes you

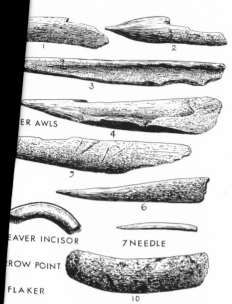

1
2
3
ER AWLS
4
5
6
EAVER INCISOR
7 NEEDLE
ROW POINT
FLAKER
10

Antler tines were used for a variety of purposes. Teeth were set in antler tine or wooden handles and used as awls. Sometimes teeth were drilled and used as beads or ornaments.

shell heaps where the natural lime acts as a preservative. Charring fire is another means of preservation of such artifacts as projectile ints, needles, awls, punches, fishhooks, scrapers, and beads of bone. ounded, polished, or ground surfaces or drilled holes will serve identify artifacts of these materials. Scattered about the refuse pits nd hearths of a village you will find the broken and burned frag- ents of bone from the food cooked and eaten by the occupants. ome long bones were split to obtain the marrow, which was con- idered a delicacy by the Indians. If they are in large enough frag- ents or show a characteristic shape, they can be identified and will urnish considerable information concerning the food habits of the culture.

Shell was often used for making beads, ornaments, spoons, and even such tools as scrapers and hoes. Small shells—periwinkle, for example—became beads by the simple process of grinding the two ends. When recovered from inland sites far removed from their source, shells may often furnish important clues concerning migra- tion or trade routes. Shell beads that I took from an inland site near Brookfield, Massachusetts, have been identified as those of a salt-

Massachusetts, for example, the material used by the Paleo-Indians came from nearly 200 miles northwest of the site, in the Hudson River valley of New York State.

Artifacts can be recognized as such if: (1) there are indications of a regular pattern of chipping that has modified the shape of the object; (2) the shape is similar to other recognizable artifacts; (3) a substantial number of similarly shaped objects are found at the site; or (4) there are indications of use—a battered edge or a polished and ground surface, for example. In case of doubt, save the object until you can get the benefit of expert opinion. It is better to save, check, and discard than to use snap judgment and possibly discard artifacts that may be diagnostic of the site or the period.

PECKED, GROUND, AND POLISHED ARTIFACTS

Another large group of artifacts typical of Late Archaic or Woodland sites is made by a technique known as *pecking* and *grinding*. Such tools as axes, pestles for grinding nuts or grain, and gouges and chisels for woodworking were made by this technique. A pebble or a fragment of material conforming roughly to the size and shape of the finished tool was selected. This was battered or pecked into shape by repeated blows from a hammerstone. You will see evidence of this battering or crushing action in the small pits that cover the surface of the artifact. This was followed by grinding or rubbing on an abrasive surface. Sandstone was often used as a polishing agent. Usually only a portion of the battered surface, such as the cutting edge, will be ground. The rest of the artifact will keep its battered or pecked surface. Occasionally the entire surface of an artifact will be ground so that there will no longer be any evidence of the pecking process. Often the cutting edge will appear to be highly polished, usually by use rather than by design.

It is easy to be misled by the natural grindings and polishing often seen in pebbles that have been subjected to water, wind, and sand action on an exposed beach. Man-made artifacts, however, reveal polish or grinding scars oriented in one direction and not at all angles, as is the case in natural polishing. If you suspect that a fragment has been ground or polished by man, clean off the dirt and hold the artifact to the light so it will show clearly the character of the work. You will soon learn to detect the difference between the work of man and that of nature.

Steatite (soapstone) is a very soft material, but it w
for such artifacts as vessels and pipes.

In some areas during the Late Archaic, soapst
used for the manufacture of vessels for cooking and
for pipes. In the Arctic Coast and Northern areas la
heating and cooking were also made from this mate
very soft and can be scratched with the fingern
scraped fragments of steatite appear at a site, save
carefully. They are an excellent index of the perio
and you may even recover enough fragments to rec
Soapstone is too soft for most purposes, but occasion
or utilitarian artifact will be made of it. Small fragm
(iron oxide) or graphite may be found bearing scrat
on their surfaces. These are paint stones. They are scr
to obtain a powder called pigment, which served as a
Keep these fragments, as they are in a sense an artifact

Recover and preserve all fired clay fragments. T
nostic, or especially significant, and will supply conside
tion concerning the period and derivation of the cult
ments from a vessel may be widely scattered about a
interesting and informative to bring them together. Fr
often possible also to reconstruct the shattered vessel. (
in the Southwest, however, there is such an abundance
(the archaeological term for pottery fragments) that a
save only rim sherds, decorated sherds, or those which
usual shape or function.

Many artifacts are made of bone, antler, or shell an
be recovered at sites where conditions have allowed
preserved. It is surprising how these fragile materials will
resist the destructive forces of nature and remain in re
condition in the earth. Often artifacts of this material are

water mollusk no longer found north of North Carolina. This means either that the shells were obtained by trade from a considerable distance or that they developed when the climate of Massachusetts was somewhat warmer than it is today. Indians left immense shell heaps along the Damariscotta River in Maine. These are mainly shells of the oyster, which, owing to lowered water temperature, no longer exists naturally in the area. As there was altogether too much shell in this deposit to have been transported from a distance, obviously the oysters were taken at this point during a period of much warmer climate than exists at present in Maine.

Indians made artifacts of copper in areas where native copper was obtainable or, in historic times, when copper and brass could be obtained by trade. Projectile points, beads, ornaments, pins, and even an occasional axe or celt (axe-shaped implement) were made from copper and brass. In certain areas artifacts made from meteoric iron, silver, or gold may be found.

A considerable amount of perishable material was used by Indians in the manufacture of artifacts, even though relatively little of it has been preserved or found archaeologically. Under special conditions artifacts of perishable material are found on open sites in humid

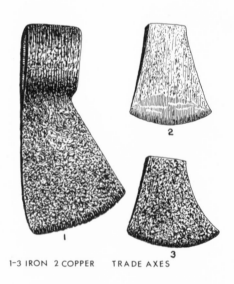

Iron or copper axes and tomahawks were greatly prized by the Indians, who obtained them in trade. When copper beads are recovered, examine them carefully for the cord on which they were strung.

1-3 IRON 2 COPPER   TRADE AXES

areas, but they are much more frequent in the drier areas of the country, especially in caves and rock shelters. Artifacts of wood—dishes and bowls, spoons and ladles, arrow shafts, bows, spear throwers (atlatls), and the handles of stone artifacts—occasionally are recovered. Textiles woven from hair, fur, and vegetable fiber occur, and baskets are fairly common in the Southwest. Sometimes a copper artifact was buried in contact with perishable material, and the copper salts will have acted as a preservative.

Artifacts that have been accidentally charred by fire are sometimes found in refuse pits or near hearths. An excellent example of preservation is the wooden dish I found at the Wapanucket #6 site. It had been lying in a pit filled with charcoal since 2300 B.C. and was in surprisingly good condition.

Trade goods, such as iron axes, beads of glass, or European clay pipes often can be dated historically. They furnish good evidence of trade routes among the Indians.

Natural objects were often found and retained as prize possessions by primitive peoples. If such objects are found on an Indian site, they should be recorded and kept, even though they are not properly artifacts. Crystals of quartz, peculiarly shaped concretions or stones, brightly colored pebbles, fossils, and the like were considered as curiosities or perhaps as fetishes and were preserved in medicine bundles or used as ornaments. From an Indian burial, I once received a sort of pocketbook of birchbark that had been preserved by the mass of copper beads it contained. With the beads were several crystals of quartz that were probably good-luck charms.

In your excavations you will find things other than artifacts that must be recognized and recorded with care. Whenever the natural layers of soil are disturbed by digging a hole, the evidence will remain for centuries unless a later disturbance destroys it. Indians dug holes about their sites for all sorts of purposes: to bury refuse, to build storage pits for vegetable foods, to cook in, or to build shallow hearths, and to dispose of the dead (see chapter 7). The post mold is another important feature. Posts were erected on an Indian site for several purposes, the most common being to form the superstructure of their houses. These molds and the pattern they followed in the ground reveal the house and village plan, suggest how the houses were constructed, and hint at the total population of a given site.

Now that you know approximately what you will find, how arti-

IDEAL STRATIGRAPHIC COLUMN

BISON occidentalis	**ALLEN**	6000 B.P. ONSET OF ALTITHERMAL	
	SIMONSON		
	MESERVE	EXTINCTION OF THE LAST OF THE PLEISTOCENE BIG-GAME ANIMALS RISE OF MODERN BISON	
	EDEN		
BISON ANTIQUUS figginsi	**PLAINVIEW**	PLANO TRADITION	
	SCOTTSBLUFF		
	AGATE BASIN		
	MILNESAND		
	ANGOSTURA	9,500 B.P.	
	PLAINVIEW		
	MIDLAND		
BISON ANTIQUUS antiquus	**FOLSOM**	C-14 LUBBOCK, TEXAS 9,883-10,000 B.P.	
MAMMOTH MASTODON	**CLOVIS**	LEHNER SITE, ARIZ. 11,000-13,000 B.P.	
	SANDIA 2	LLANO COMPLEX	
	SANDIA 1		
		after Mason	

This ideal stratigraphic column shows (center) the cultural variations within the Paleo period, with the levels at which they were found (right) and associated mammals (left). The initials B.P. refer to carbon 14 dating and mean "Before the Present." (Mason, "The Paleo-Indian Tradition in Eastern North America")

facts may be recognized, and something about the various techniques of their manufacture, let's discuss the variations among the artifacts themselves and what these variations mean in terms of time and space. You will also need some means of classifying artifacts so that you can discuss them intelligently with others. In other words, you

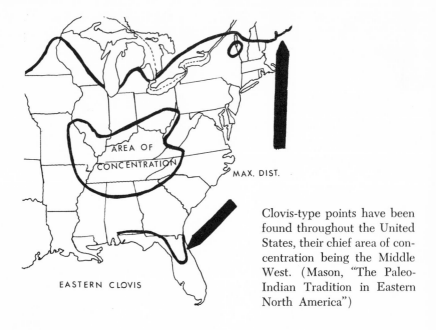

AREA OF
CONCENTRATION

MAX. DIST.

EASTERN CLOVIS

Clovis-type points have been found throughout the United States, their chief area of concentration being the Middle West. (Mason, "The Paleo-Indian Tradition in Eastern North America")

must learn to read the language in which they will speak to you, telling you when they were made and the kind of life lived by the people who made them.

PALEO-INDIAN ARTIFACTS

Artifacts of the Paleo-Indians are recognizable because of the peculiar designs and the technique of manufacture. Essentially the Paleo-Indian material culture consists of a series of double-faced, lanceolate (lance-shaped) projectile points, accompanied by a small number of single-faced scrapers, knives, and gravers and nondescript cutting tools known as utilized flakes.

The most important artifacts are the projectile points, as would be expected of a culture so completely oriented toward hunting as a means of existence. These tools were made by a technique known as a "core and blade industry" that is found in both the Old World and the New. Blocks of selected stone, usually flint or chert, were carefully prepared. From these blocks (or cores) long slivers of stone, called blades, were struck. The artifacts were then made from the blades.

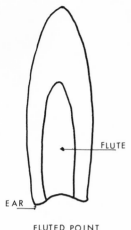

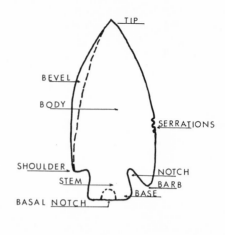

FLUTED POINT   STEMMED POINT

Shown here are the basic parts of a fluted projectile point and of different types of stemmed points. Variations in these parts are important factors in the classification of projectile points.

A chart of the cultural variations within the Paleo period will serve as a useful guide in the following discussion.

The artifacts—including the Clovis and Folsom fluted (grooved or channeled) points, some unfluted specimens, and associated tools —found with mammoth bones in the High Plains and in southern Arizona, are sometimes called the Llano complex. This name is taken from *Llano Estacado*, the Staked Plains of Texas and New Mexico, where several important sites of the complex are located. The term *Plano tradition* has been used to group a number of projectile point forms that are a bit later in time than the Llano complex but are certainly a part of the Paleo-Indian way of life. These points share a tendency toward parallel flaking and are all products of a core and blade technique.

Sandia Points

Sandia Cave, the type site from which the name is taken, is located in the Sandia Mountains of New Mexico. Here, in the lowest level of a dry cave, sealed off by several layers that showed no

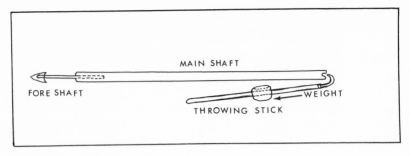

MAIN SHAFT

FORE SHAFT

WEIGHT

THROWING STICK

Before the invention or introduction of the bow and arrow primitive hunters used a spear or javelin. They discovered that they could throw it harder and faster with the aid of a throwing stick, or atlatl. This extension of the arm increased the leverage. After a time a weight was added to the throwing stick.

evidence of occupation, were found the peculiarly shaped projectile points known as Sandia. The next layer above it revealing signs of occupation produced Folsom points and established the priority of Sandia in time. The associated animal life included extinct horses, bison, camel, mastodon, and mammoth. While Sandia points have never been found in strata below Clovis points, on the basis of technique they are assumed to be older. The distribution of Sandia points is presently considered to be restricted to the High Plains area, but alleged specimens have been found in widely separated areas. Two types of Sandia have been recognized and are known as Sandia 1 and Sandia 2.

Except for the Sandia points, Paleo-Indian projectile points are consistently lance-shaped in outline, and have no notching at the base, which is so prominent in the projectile points of other North American cultures. Many of the scrapers are of the snub-nosed variety. Gravers are small tools with one or more delicately chipped points, called "spurs," sharp as a needle in unused specimens. They are thought to have been used for engraving on bone but there is little evidence to support this assumption. Blades sharpened along one or both sides are thought to be knives. Sometimes these knives also have graver spurs. Although no tools were made by grinding, the bases of projectile points are usually smoothed. Probably this was done to limit wear on the binding thongs.

58   What You Will Find

Clovis Points

Clovis points are the typical projectile point of the Llano complex of the Paleo-Indian tradition. The illustration of the stratigraphic column shows them above Sandia, but Clovis may well be contemporary with, or even older than, Sandia. Until further evidence is forthcoming, the precise order in time cannot be determined with accuracy. The first Clovis points were found in 1936–1937 associated with the bones of a mammoth at the Blackwater #1 site, in the area between Portales and Clovis, New Mexico. Points of this type have now been found throughout the United States, although they are rare west of the Rockies. The most important sites from which Clovis-like points have been recovered are shown in chapter 2. The simple map reproduced here shows the distribution of these points in eastern North America. Some specimens have been found in Mexico and in several widely separated places in South America. But most of the present data concerning Clovis points comes from sites located in the American Southwest, particularly at the Lehner and Naco sites in Arizona. At these two kill sites Clovis points have been found associated with mammoth remains. Geological and radiocarbon dating indicate that Clovis spanned a period of from 8,500 to 13,000 years ago.

At the Wapanucket #8 site we have recovered a number of Clovis-type projectile points associated with typical Paleo-Indian gravers, knives, scrapers, and utilized flakes. This appears to have been a dwelling site, at which no remains of extinct mammals so far have been discovered. Two other New England sites where Clovis-type fluted points have been recovered are the Bull Brook site in Massachusetts and the Reagen site in Vermont.

Folsom Points

The Folsom point is restricted to the High Plains of the southwestern United States. A few specimens have been found west of the Rocky Mountains and as far south as Texas and a specimen or two from western Canada. The first Folsom to be found (1926)—and incidentally the first fluted point to be recognized—came from a site near a small tributary of the Cimarron River, a few miles south of the town of Folsom, New Mexico. Underneath 4 to 13 feet of clay and gravel several of these points were found associated with the remains of an extinct type of bison. At the time this important discovery was made the notion of man as a contemporary of Pleistocene animal life was considered improbable.

Since then many Folsom points have been recovered and their association with extinct types of bison has been established beyond all reasonable doubt. A majority of the recoveries have been made from kill sites, but a dwelling site of Folsom hunters that dates back some 10,000 years was found in northeastern Colorado near the Wyoming line. In addition to Folsom-type points this site, called Lindenmeier, yielded snub-nosed scrapers, side scrapers (sometimes called "spokeshaves"), knives, crude chopping tools made from used cores, hammerstones, rubbing stones, beads of hematite (red ochre) and lignite, and associated animal life, largely the bones of an extinct type of bison and camel.

Plano Tradition

Directly above the Folsom point in our table are a number of related points. Taken as a group they have been called the Plano tradition. Because carbon dates are not available for all of these types, the order in which they appear in the table is only an approximate indication of their true chronological order. The Plainview type 1, for example, appears twice, representing conflicting dates. The time range covered by the Plano tradition is immense, spanning the centuries from about 6,000 to 9,000 years ago. During this time great climatic changes took place, the mammoth and mastodon became extinct, and ancient types of bison appeared and passed into oblivion. Although the animal life changed to a considerable extent, the herd-hunting character of the Paleo-Indian culture remained the same throughout its existence. It was the common theme of the entire period east of the Rocky Mountains.

DESERT CULTURE ARTIFACTS

The Desert culture exploited its entire environment. Nothing in the way of food was overlooked by the Desert people. Their artifacts consisted of small projectile points (usually short, broad-bladed points with notches and stems); flat milling stones with pebble *manos* (hand grinding stones) for grinding seeds and nuts; various cutting tools and scrapers of stone; choppers; tools of antler and bone; tubular pipes; and shell beads. Because habitations often were dry caves, materials usually considered perishable and missing from the sites of other cultures (such as baskets, cordage, woven sandals, and objects of wood) have survived. We probably have a more complete inventory of the material culture of the Desert people than of any other equally ancient culture on the North American continent.

CLASSIFICATION OF ARTIFACTS

The multitude of projectile points and other tools made by the cultures that succeeded the three basic cultures just described are so varied that some sort of classification scheme is needed to discuss them intelligently. A classification scheme serves as a means of cataloguing artifacts according to function, shape, area, and chronological position. Such a scheme is an indispensable tool to the archaeologist, especially when he is making comparisons between sites or areas. Bear in mind, however, that this is an arbitrary system—the aboriginal maker did not work from classification charts or blueprints, and the archaeologist can only guess at his intentions. The difficulty with systems of this kind is that there are almost as many as there are archaeologists. Unless a group of classified artifacts can be changed readily from one system to another, great difficulties in comparison will be encountered. You should familiarize yourself with the particular classification system or nomenclature used in the area where you are working and conform to it.

One system has been to assign locality or site names to projectile points. To me it has always seemed unwieldy because it forces you to remember a great many names (often difficult to spell) and to associate them with a particular projectile point shape. For example, it seems odd and confusing to call a point Clovis, after a town in New Mexico, when it is found all over the United States. The system I prefer is the one where projectile points are given names that reflect the geometrical outlines of the different types. It avoids place names completely. In the case of some of the larger artifacts, however, functional names have been used. I have used this system in reporting three sites from which a large variety of artifacts were recovered, and it has proved to be easily applied and understandable.

Projectile Points

In this classification the separation of arrow points from spear points is unimportant, as all sizes are treated similarly and all are projectile points. We like to think of projectile points as being not larger than 3 inches in length. All shapes appear as small as ½ inch; the identical

Type	Culture	Shape	Size
Sandia	Paleo-Indian	Type 1: Rounded outline; lens-shaped in cross section; slight stem on one side. Type 2: Parallel sides; straight or slightly concave base; diamond-shaped in cross section; slight stem on one side.	2–4 in. long.
Clovis	Paleo-Indian	Sides parallel or nearly so; concave base. Fluted usually halfway to tip (sometimes almost to tip). In New England have "ears" at either side of base; in Ohio area have fishtail effect at base.	1½–5 in. long (average 3 in.).
Folsom	Paleo-Indian	Lanceolate outline, sides tapering to base. Base usually concave, marked by central nipple and earlike projections.	1–3 in. or shorter (average 2 in.).

shapes may be a spear, lance, or knife. You can't be absolutely sure of the exact function they filled. Whether or not a given artifact is a projectile point, a hand spear, or a knife depends upon weight-to-length thickness.

	Type	Culture	Shape	Size
	Type 1: Plainview Type 2: Meserve Type 3: Milnesand	Paleo-Indian Plano	Various; some have beveled or nearly parallel sides, convex or concave bases. Stemmed types include Eden and Scottsbluff. All have parallel, or ribbon, flaking.	1–5 in. long.
	Type 1: Gypsum Cave Type 2: Pinto Basin Type 3: Lake Mohave Type 4: Silver Lake	Desert	Various; beveled edges, slightly stemmed, some with basal notching.	1½ in. or longer.
	Corner-removed	Type 1: Early Archaic Type 2: Archaic and Woodland	Type 1: Corners at base removed to form stem terminating in rounded end. Type 2: Corners at base removed to form long or short stem, often quite thick.	Over 1½ in. to 3 in. long.

	Type	Culture	Shape	Size
	Eared	Archaic	Basal points or "ears" formed as result of side-notching and basal reworking, producing more or less concave base.	1–4 in. long. Type 4 often in small sizes.
	Tapered-stem	Archaic	Sloping sides taper to truncated base; may be straight or somewhat convex.	Large and small.
	Side-notched	Archaic and Woodland	Distinct side-notching with truncated base. Blade may be narrow or broad, short or long.	2–4 in.
	Long-eared	Archaic	Relatively broad, with rather slender, outflaring basal points formed by deep side-notching and well-worked concave base.	1–6 in. long. Large sizes in Northeast early Archaic.
	Small-stemmed	Archaic and Woodland	Irregularly shaped stems.	Less than 1½ in. long.

Type	Culture	Shape	Size
Corner-notched	Usually Woodland	Well-defined notches extending obliquely from basal corners.	Large and small sizes.
Small triangular	Archaic and Woodland	Type 1: Sides generally convex; base straight to concave.	Base less than 1¼ in. wide.
		Type 2: Isosceles; base straight to concave.	
Large triangular	Woodland	Sides and base straight to concave; base sometimes extremely concave.	Base over 1¼ in. wide.
Leaf	Woodland	Base rounded from convex sides that converge without shoulders.	3–4 in. long.

Knives

The knife is the most important tool in all Indian cultures. A characteristic trait of all knives, except the ulu (woman's knife), is a serrated (saw-toothed) cutting edge. Serrating often occurs on more than one edge of the implement and is sometimes extremely small. Some knives were hafted (set into a handle), as indicated by stems, while others were simply held in the hand.

A series of large knives was found at the Wapanucket #8 site in Mid-

	Type	Culture	Shape	Size
	Leaf	Early and late Archaic	Relatively broad and long. Usually quite thin, carefully chipped. Symmetrical; sometimes pointed at both ends.	2–6 in. long.
	Ceremonial	Early Archaic	Side-notched and eared.	2½–9 in. long.

dleboro, Massachusetts. They were of the stemmed variety and served to indicate the difficulty of discriminating between knives and spear points. These were probably knives because of the type of wear caused by use. The base and stem shapes of some of these artifacts are similar to those of projectile points and knives found in the Southeast associated with Paleo-Indian artifacts. Their date in Massachusetts has not yet been determined, but they may well be quite early.

	Type	Culture	Shape	Size
	Ulu	Archaic	Semicircular blade with more or less straight back. Similar knives found among Eskimo tools of Alaska.	2½–6 in. long.
	Stem	Archaic and Woodland	Blunt point at one end; different styles of stems resembling those of projectile points. Archaic stems usually ill-defined.	2–6 in. long.
	Flake	Paleo-Indian through Woodland	Flake having one or more edges retouched with minute serrations.	Not over 2 in. long.

Notchers

This is a woodworking tool, probably used in hafting projectile points. It was probably held in the hand with a forefinger grip and used with a sawing motion.

	Type	Culture	Shape	Size
	Graver	Paleo-Indian	Flake having one to three nipple-like points chipped along one edge.	Not over 2 in. long.

Drills or Perforators

The Indians drilled holes in many of their artifacts with these stone drills. They have been classified according to the shape of the base as: expanded, T-base, tapered stem, crescent, side-notched, eared, diamond, and cross-base.

	Type	Culture	Shape	Size
	Eared	Late Archaic	Basal points or "ears" formed by side-notching and basal reworking.	2–4 in. long.

Gouge and Adze Blades

These are woodworking tools used by the Indian carpenter. In areas where the birch tree that provided bark for canoes is not found, canoes were made by the dugout method. The wood was first charred and then removed with these gougelike stone artifacts. The adze is similar to the gouge except that its cutting edge is narrow and the blade has a flat rather than hollowed-out surface.

	Type	Culture	Shape	Size
	Knobbed gouge	Not definitely known	Often hollowed out over entire length, tapering toward upper end. One or more nipple-like knobs on back where lashings cross.	3–10 in. long.
	Plain gouge	Archaic	Hollowed-out portion may extend entire length or end short distance from cutting edge. No provision for holding lashings in place.	3–10 in. long.

Axe, Celt, and Hatchet Blades

This is another group of woodworking artifacts. The larger specimens were probably used in felling trees, possibly with the aid of fire. The smaller ones were intended for less strenuous woodworking tasks. I have no doubt that these were sometimes used as weapons, but this was not their primary purpose. They are usually made from hard, fine-grained, igneous rocks, except for the chipped axe that is sometimes of argillite or sandstone.

	Type	Culture	Shape	Size
	Full-grooved axe	Late Archaic	Relatively thick. Sides taper toward ground cutting edge. Well-defined groove extends around head.	3–10 in. long.
	Celt	Archaic and Woodland	Sides nearly parallel, may flare a bit near cutting edge. Pecked into shape, then ground over entire surface.	2–10 in. long.

Stone Sinkers

Prehistoric man was a fisherman as well as a hunter. Plummets and weights—probably line and net sinkers—have been identified as part of his fishing equipment.

	Type	Culture	Shape	Size
	Classic plummet	Archaic	Symmetrical; shaped like modern plumb bob. Small, well-worked knob on top. Some have pointed base, others nearly round.	3–4 in. long. Some larger.
	Side-notched weight	Woodland	Crudest of all artifacts. Pebble or small core with notches roughly chipped out of two opposite sides.	

Hammerstones or Poundingstones

Throughout the long years of man's struggle for existence he learned a great deal about the use of poundingstones. He discovered that the weight of the poundingstone had a certain relationship to the kind of material or size of the artifact being made. Consequently, hammerstones of all sizes will be found. Only a few of the more recognizable forms have been illustrated.

	Type	Culture	Shape	Size
	Grooved hammerstone	All cultures	Simple cobble of appropriate size; full groove to accommodate thongs for lashing to handle.	2–12 in. long. Some of larger types used for driving wooden stakes.

Spear Thrower Weights

Various names have been applied to these artifacts at different times and in the different areas. They have been called bannerstones by many collectors, who thought that they were some kind of ceremonial object used on a shaft after the manner of the Roman legion totem. Others have called them "problematic" artifacts, which is nothing more than saying that their function is unknown. Recently certain discoveries in burials and in dry caves of the Southwest have shown that these are weights for spear throwers, or atlatls.

Complete examples of the atlatl have been found averaging 2 to 2½ feet in length. The spear thrower is characteristic of the Anasazi culture, but is found commonly all over the eastern United States. Most of the weights are perforated by a hole, ½ to ⅝ of an inch long, running transversely through the stone's midsection. Invariably they are ground and polished and many have fanciful shapes. Perhaps they were not only a functional artifact but also came to have some magical significance to the hunter.

	Type	Culture	Shape	Size
	Wing	Archaic	Various forms with outspreading sides resembling wings. High degree of surface grinding and polishing.	4–12 in. wide, 2–3 in. high.
	Oval	Archaic	Pebble-shaped. Groove often worked along upper longitudinal edge parallel to perforation.	2–3 in. long, 1–1½ in. wide.
	Whaletail	Archaic	Wings extend to points with spread resembling whale's tail. Sometimes grooved around center, rather than perforated.	4–12 in. wide, 2–3 in. high.

Rubbing and Polishing Stones

In the later phases of the Archaic and Woodland times grinding and polishing became an accepted technique of stoneworking. Naturally, the more abrasive types of stone were selected for this use. These tools were also pressed into service for working bone, antler, and wood.

	Type	Culture	Shape	Size
	Whetstone	Late Archaic and Woodland	Relatively slender. Often perforated near upper end, perhaps for thong.	6–8 in. long.
	Sinewstone	Late Archaic and Woodland	Series of narrow grooves on surface (or single broad one) worn smooth by rubbing. Perhaps used in preparation of sinews for bowstrings.	Usually 2–4 in. long.
	Shaft abrader	Late Archaic and Woodland	Specialized tool. Shows one or two deeply worn grooves. Perhaps used in smoothing arrow shafts.	Usually 2–4 in. long.

Scrapers

One of the primitive craftsman's most versatile tools was an artifact with a sharp edge suitable for scraping. The scraping technique, like pounding and grinding, was common to all peoples. Scrapers are found in all areas and in all periods. An artifact may be identified as a scraper if it possesses a cutting edge that shows signs of wear. Many scrapers are fragments of hard stone, and the wear may be insignificant. You will

	Type	Culture	Shape	Size
	Stem	Paleo-Indian through Woodland	Expanding convex blade usually beveled by chips struck off one edge. Definitely worked stem symmetrically placed or offset. Probably used in handle or shaft.	1½–2 in.
	Oval	Archaic and Woodland	Irregular oval form; over-all worn edges.	1–10 in. long. Large sizes called choppers (most frequent in Archaic).

have to examine the suspected artifact closely. *Repeated conformity to a certain shape at a given site is usually a good criterion in determining whether or not a fragment is indeed an artifact. However, the better forms (those which have been modified to adapt them for use or for mounting) are obvious.*

	Type	Culture	Shape	Size
	Steep-edge	Archaic and Woodland	Roughly circular. Top rounded, underside flat. Cutting edge occupies about one-third of circumference; steeply beveled.	½-in. long.
	Shaft	Archaic and Woodland	Usually made from flake or thicker fragment. At least one sharply chipped edge, may be straight or concave. Probably used in scraping down shafts or handles of wood.	Not over 4 in. long.

Agricultural Tools

You would expect to find agricultural tools, of course, only in periods when agriculture was practiced. The triangular hoe was an important tool, judging from the frequency with which it turns up on archaeological sites. It is an irregularly shaped fragment of durable stone, such as basalt, felsite, sandstone, quartz, granite, or quartzite, and commonly has a more or less triangular shape. The manner in which it was hafted to the handle is shown. Another tool was the corn planter, used for making a hole in the earth into which maize (corn) seeds were sown. A similar artifact of wood, called a dibble or planting stick, was used in many areas. Many other agricultural tools were made of shell, bone, and wood, but because these materials are perishable, relatively few such artifacts are found.

	Type	Culture	Shape	Size
	Stem hoe	Woodland	Characteristic crook in stone at stem end, attached to handle. Bit at opposite end thinned by chipping; may be outflaring or spoon-shaped.	8–14 in. long.
	Stem spade	Woodland	Stone slab with thinned blade that may be pointed, rounded, or truncated. Opposite end slightly stemmed for hafting.	8–14 in. long.

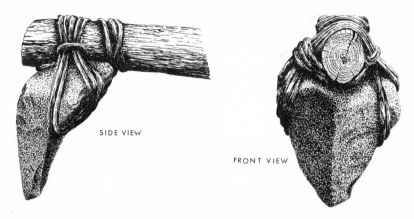

SIDE VIEW

FRONT VIEW

The triangular hoe was hafted by lashing the handle at right angles to the flat dimension of the stone across the oblique or concave base.

Indian women using the dibble, or corn-planter (center, back), and triangular hoe to plant and cultivate corn are shown in this drawing made by J. F. Lafitau in 1774. (Wormington, *Ancient Man in North America*, after J. F. Lafitau, *Moeurs des Sauvages Ameriquains*, Vol. 2, Paris, 1774)

Clay Pottery

Pottery of fired clay was made by most of the later cultures. Its presence marks a very late Archaic or early Woodland site in North America. The variety of styles and forms is so great that only a few can be shown. You should consult the literature on the clay pottery of your particular area for detailed descriptions.

The potter's wheel was never developed by the ancient inhabitants of the Western Hemisphere, so pottery vessels were made by coiling rolls of clay one above the other and pinching them together. There seem to have been two general types of pottery in North America: that of the northern and eastern areas (illustrated by the Eastern Woodland vessels), which reflects an Asian influence; and that of the southern and southwestern areas (illustrated by the Southwest vessel), which appears to have a non-Asian source.

Pipes of fired clay were also made. Most artifacts in this category are plain in design and comprise either tubular or elbow pipes. An example of a more exotic design is also shown.

It is impossible to describe or illustrate here the many hundreds of artifacts of clay, stone, bone, and other materials. In order to arrive at a complete understanding of the artifact categories of any given area, you should obtain and study carefully reports and articles dealing with the specific areas. Familiarize yourself with the artifacts that you can expect to find in your area. Keep and examine any worked stone, bone, or clay that may turn up at your site. You may discover a totally new and significant artifact.

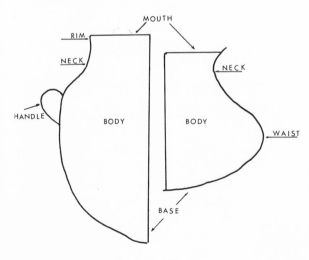

Fired clay pottery vessels of the different regions and cultures vary in shape and surface decoration. The parts of two contrasting vessel forms are indicated.

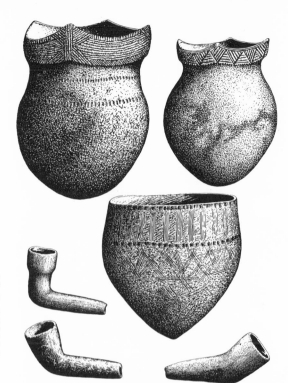

These Eastern Woodland fired clay vessels have cord-marked surface decoration. Early types have cone-shaped or pointed bottoms. The fired clay pipes are late Archaic or early Woodland.

This Hopewell ceremonial pottery vessel was recovered from the Mound City site in Ohio. (Ohio State Museum)

The famous Adena effigy pipe of fired clay is in the collection of the Ohio State Museum (Development Department, State of Ohio)

BURIALS

The burial customs of the American Indian varied considerably from area to area and with the passage of time. Because of the almost infinite variety of burial traits, we must deal with the subject in a very general manner.

Sometimes the body was placed on a platform high enough above the surface to avoid its being molested by predatory animals. Other people made use of caves and crevices in the rock as tombs for the dead. In some areas it was customary to build small funerary houses of wood or stone; in other areas mounds were erected above the burial. Direct inhumation, or burial in the earth, also varied widely. Shallow graves were dug to receive the body, which was often wrapped in bark or some other covering. Some grave shafts are lined with stone, and buried log tombs are not unknown. In other cultures it was the custom to retain the bodies of the dead for some time, perhaps in temporary tombs or on platforms. At intervals a large

This whimsical black-on-white decorated clay effigy vessel from Socorro County, New Mexico, is a striking example of the Anasazi potter's skill. Vessels in the form of goats, sheep, deer, or other animals are frequently found in the prehistoric Southwest. (Photograph courtesy of Museum of the American Indian, Heye Foundation)

grave pit, or ossuary, was dug. In this common grave a large number of individuals would be buried with elaborate ceremonies.

Burial in the earth was sometimes extended, that is, with the body laid out at full length in the grave. Other times it was flexed, which means that the body had been somewhat compressed, with the knees drawn up nearly to the chin, arms folded across the chest or placed beneath the head—perhaps the body was lashed in this position. Or you may come across what is called a "bundle burial," in which the bones of the skeleton are simply gathered together for burial and the skull is usually placed on top with the long bones beneath it. All three types appear in Woodland burials, which were usually inhumations. I have also encountered burials (usually children or infants) deposited in refuse pits. In a few instances parts of a human body may be found, such as trophy skulls collected and buried for some obscure purpose. Occasionally a second skull will be found in association with a complete skeleton.

Burials are often accompanied by grave goods—artifacts for the use of the deceased in afterlife. Among some people red paint was a mortuary color, and various amounts of the red pigment (iron oxide or ochre) occasionally will be found with the burial. Red paint appears in some Woodland burials, and grave goods are common in the early phases of that culture.

Cremation was also practiced by the Woodland people in some areas, but is less common than among the Archaic people. Usually the bodies of a number of individuals were deposited in one huge fire. Later the charred remains were scooped up and reburied in secondary burial pits, often accompanied by burned and unburned grave goods. Red paint was commonly used in these secondary burials. Often cremation burials are difficult to recognize as such, owing to their resemblance to ordinary refuse pit deposits.

5 : How to Plan an Excavation

This chapter might carry the subtitle: "Pothunters, beware!" A pothunter is a person who visits a site in order to find and hoard as many "relics" as possible before being discovered and thrown off the property by the irate owner. Because you are not a pothunter, you are aware that the excavation of an archaeological site must be a carefully planned and controlled investigation in order to yield the all-important records that must accompany any artifacts that you may find.

The purpose of this planning is to place the features and artifacts uncovered on the site in their proper perspective; only then will the site truly "come alive." As you explore with your trowel, you will be able to re-create in your mind's eye the crude lodges that once stood there, and the shadowy forms of those who once called this home will hover about you. The shape, form, type, and material of the tools they used will help to unravel the mystery of their existence—who these people were and when they lived. When your work is completed, you will be able to re-create this fragment of an ancient culture from your records and to report it as living, breathing history. This is scientific excavation.

HOW DO WE START?

After you have selected the area you wish to excavate (chapter 3), you must obtain the permission of the owner of the property on which it is located. Do not approach him and ask point-blank: "Mr. So-and-So, may I dig for Indian relics in your field?" Tell him in some detail what you hope to accomplish and describe how he can make a contribution to scientific knowledge by allowing you to dig. Try to arouse in him an interest in your hobby; if he has children, interest them and you interest the parent. When you do reach an agreement, make certain that there is a complete understanding by both parties.

The property owner must know precisely what you intend to do and how you are going to do it. Be sure that you understand any restrictions he may impose, and observe them implicitly. If there are small trees, for example, ask whether you may cut them, if necessary, or must avoid them. Finally, get his permission in writing, if possible, defining what you may and may not do. Always remember that you are a trespasser with permission. Respect your permission. Be reasonable and treat his property the way you would wish yours to be treated if the situation were reversed.

THE SITE MAP

First of all, you will need a sketch map showing the geography and the topography of the immediate area. Preparation of such a map is a simple matter if you have surveying experience or can secure the services of a surveyor friend. Even if you lack these two assets, you will still be able to prepare a perfectly good map on your own. You will need one of the topographical maps issued by the Geological Survey (described in chapter 3) of the town or county in which your site is located.

From this map make an enlarged sketch (or better still, a photographic enlargement) of the area. Be sure to include the contour lines indicating the height above sea level, as well as swamps, water courses, and other natural features. Include a distance scale indicating that x inches on the map represents y feet on the ground (for example: 1 inch equals 20 feet) and a compass direction for orienting your stake lines, so that you will be able to make accurate measurements.

Another extremely important item to include is a permanent location point, such as a bench mark (indicated by the initials B.M. on the topographical maps); lacking that, include a local land boundary or a road junction. The noting of this permanent or fixed point will enable you to relocate your site even after the disturbance caused by excavating it has disappeared. The topographical map also gives you the height above sea level of the B.M. or road junction, and this you can transfer to the "grid" you will be preparing for the excavation.

I made a sketch map of this type in connection with the excavation of a site known as the Sweet's Knoll Site, in Segreganset, Massachusetts. Notice that the contour lines indicate the elevations and that

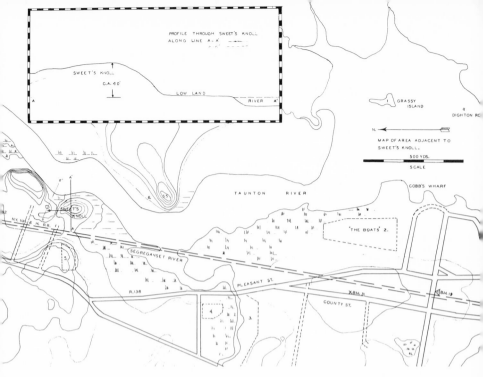

This site map sketched from a section of a Geological Survey topographic map shows the natural and man-made features of the Sweet's Knoll site in Segreganset, Massachusetts. The inset shows the elevation, or profile, of the site.

the tiny numbers within them show the height above sea level. Natural features, such as rivers and swamps, and man-made features, such as roads and railroads, are shown. Also indicated are the locations of nearby Indian sites (The Boats site and unnamed sites 3 and 4). A distance scale (in this case 1 inch equals 100 yards) and a compass direction are included.

Note especially the bench marks (B.M. 19 and B.M. 32). These are circular bronze markers mounted in concrete and placed on the railroad right-of-way by the Geological Survey. They are registered landmarks, protected by law; the railroad may disappear and the road may be relocated, but the bench marks will remain. It will always be possible to relocate this site by measurements from these two fixed points. The inset shows the "profile" of the site—an outline of what it would look like from the side if it were to be sliced in half.

THE GRID

We are now ready to lay out what is known as a "grid" in archaeological terms. All your later measurements will be based on this grid, so it must be laid out with great accuracy.

The basic unit of archaeological excavation is the "square"—a precisely measured plot of ground bounded at each corner by stakes driven firmly into the earth. Ordinarily a grid consists of a rectangle made up of equal sized squares, but as your excavation progresses, the grid may assume an indefinite number of geometric shapes reflecting the size and outline of the area being excavated. Remember that accurate measurements are essential. For example, in measuring from stake to stake, set a nail in the top of each stake and measure from nail to nail.

The size of the square is optional and is governed by a number of considerations. Suppose, for instance, that you are working alone at the site and have no one to help you take measurements. In this situation, your square must be of a size that permits you to hold one end of the measuring tape at a given stake and the other over an object anywhere within the square. A square larger than 6 feet on a side would be too large. If you have one or more helpers, on the other hand, the square can be somewhat larger. The larger the square, of course, the fewer are the stakes needed to lay out a given area.

I happen to be partial to the metric system and use squares that measure 2 meters (or slightly more than 6½ feet) on each side. The grid described on the following pages is based on that size. (It might be helpful to remember that 1 centimeter, or cm., equals 0.3937 inches, and 1 meter, or m., equals 39.37 inches or 3.28 feet.) However, 5-, 6-, and even 10-foot squares have been used successfully.

Think the matter over carefully, decide what size will best meet your requirements, and adopt a standard of your own. If the people working in your area have already adopted a standard size square, it would be best to use the same size in the interest of consistency.

Establishing the Base Line

Having surveyed the immediate locality and determined from the topography and geography the limits of the site and the approximate size of the occupied area, you are now ready to establish the base line. To do this you will need a cloth tape (75 feet, or 25 meters, long), a supply of 26 stout wooden stakes (24 inches long will be suitable), some nails, and an axe or hammer to drive the stakes into the ground. You should also obtain a compass and some sort of field notebook. Both may be purchased from a dealer in surveyor's supplies or at Woolworth's. A regular surveyor's field book will cost between 85¢ and $1.50 (if you prefer the loose-leaf type, between $1.95 and $3.50). Compasses range from 25¢ to several dollars; one of the inexpensive types will serve your purpose.

In deciding where to place the base line, keep in mind the fact that on it you are going to construct a large grid capable of being extended in all directions. It is best to run the base line in either a due north-south or an east-west direction so that extensions can be described easily and without confusion. For example, it is easier to say in your notes "north of the base line" than to say "northeast of the base line." The base line must also be related to some permanent point or mark, which we will call "datum." This point or points, in turn, will be related to the B.M. or other permanent mark used to locate your site on the map.

Some archaeologists like to establish a base line well outside the area to be excavated; they prefer to start excavating in unoccupied territory and to work into the site gradually. Because the actual site location often is difficult to determine, I prefer to try to bisect the assumed site area (that is, divide it in half) with the base line and then develop the grid in the direction indicated by the results of excavation.

In either case, the base line will represent the bases of a selected number of squares, and its length will be some multiple of the size of the individual square. According to the system I use, for instance, the base line represents the bases of 26 squares (since each is 2 meters square, the base line is 52 meters long), so that a letter of the alphabet may be used to designate each stake.

Locating Stake AO

For a datum point, select some fairly permanent object, such as a large rock that cannot be moved readily or a land boundary. Two datum points are better than one, as the position can then be fixed by triangulation or by use of the level or transit. Illustrated are these two methods of measurement.

Triangulation can be accomplished without any instruments

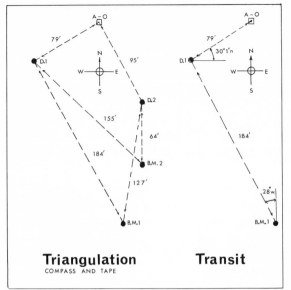

Triangulation
COMPASS AND TAPE

Transit

Location of a third point from datum and bench mark may be made by triangulation with compass and tape or with transit or level.

except a compass and tape. It is based upon the use of two known points to locate a third. Your notebook entry would read:

> From B.M. 1 to D 1 northerly 184′
> From B.M. 1 to D 2 northerly 127′
> From B.M. 2 to D 1 northerly 155′
> From B.M. 2 to D 2 northerly 64′

In this method it is not necessary to measure angles. This is eliminated by making two measurements that can meet or coincide only in two quadrants north or south; thus, if we say "northerly" we arrive at the desired point.

If a level or a transit is available, the measurement can be accurately determined from a single B.M., as it is possible to measure the angle of sight accurately. In this instance the notebook entry would read:

> From B.M. 1 184′ 28 degrees west of north

Next, drive a stake that will become one end of your base line. This is stake AO. Insert a nail on top of the stake in the center.

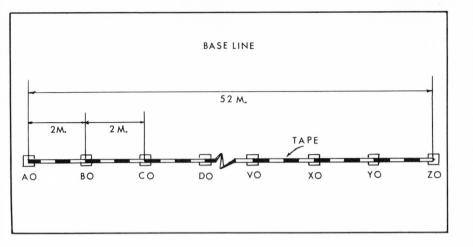

Locate the stakes from AO to ZO at intervals of 2 meters along the base line.

Measure carefully from the datum point or points to this stake. Now if you return to your site after a winter season to find that nature or some vandal has removed your stakes, it will be comparatively simple to relocate datum from B.M. and AO from datum.

Locating the Remaining Stakes

Hook one end of your tape over the nail on top of stake AO and determine the position of the other end of the base line. Use a compass to check direction. Now place a second stake, with its marker nail inserted on top, and label this stake ZO. Keep the tape stretched between AO and ZO stakes. Now you can drive your remaining 24 stakes into the ground to mark off the bases of individual squares along the base line at the proper intervals—in this instance at every 2 meters between AO and ZO.

Again I stress the need for accuracy. Nothing is more confusing when taking later measurements within the squares than to discover that they are in fact not square. Starting from AO, label these stakes BO, CO, DO, etc., all the way to ZO.

The preliminary work of locating base-line stakes has been completed at this site.

Determining the Profile

Before proceeding with the rest of the grid, we have another important item to consider—the vertical, or topographical, relationship of the base-line stakes. The existing surface of the earth between AO and ZO usually is not exactly level. AO may be higher or lower than ZO, or there may be a rise or a depression between them. This is known as a *profile*.

The profile must be measured and recorded. I know of no satisfactory way of making this measurement except by using some sort of level. This is a mechanical and optical device for establishing a perfectly level line of sight from AO to ZO, which will permit you to take vertical measurements on a rod to the surface of the ground.

Several types of leveling devices are available from firms dealing in surveying equipment. Among these are the Abney Hand Level, costing from $15 to $25, and the Farm and Contractor's Level, complete with tripod and rod, costing up to $75, depending upon the quality and accuracy of the instrument (sold by the Frederick Post Co., P.O. Box 803, 3635 No. Hamlin Ave., Chicago, Ill.). Any of these instruments will be adequate for your needs. Of course, the most accurate surveying instrument of all is the Engineer's Transit, costing in the neighborhood of $500 (new)—you may be in luck and know someone who has one and is willing to operate it for you. The standard rod is 12 to 20 feet in length and is marked in either the decimal system of English feet, tenths, and hundredths of feet (surveyors never use eighths or sixteenths of inches), or in metric units.

The simple tripod-mounted level is nothing more than a revolving telescope with cross-hairs and an attached spirit level assembled as a unit and mounted so that it can be leveled by thumb screws. Usually the mount includes a horizontal scale and a vertical scale, marked in degrees and minutes, so that angles in both directions can be measured. The plumb line and bob are shown centered over the nail in a stake.

Set this instrument up over BO. Determine the height (IH) of the instrument by holding the rod vertically in front of the telescope, resting it on the surface of the ground, and noting the point on the rod at which the telescope cross-hair rests. Note this height in your field notes. Next, resting the rod on the ground at stake AO, note the cross-hair reading. Proceed in the same manner to determine the height from ground level at each succeeding stake in the base line.

Assuming that IH at BO is 2 m., the level of the ground is −2 m. at this point. A reading of 0.6 m. at AO would indicate that the level

The profile is determined by setting up a tripod-mounted level over stake BO and taking readings on a rod held at stake AO, then at other stakes along the base line. The readings will give a profile of the height from ground level at each succeeding stake.

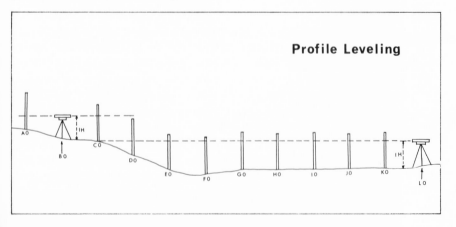

Profile Leveling

of the surface had risen 1.4 m. from BO to AO. A rod reading less than IH indicates a rise in ground level; a rod reading greater than IH indicates a drop in ground level. Your notebook entries would look something like this:

IH at BO	2 m.	(0 for this profile)
AO	0.6 m.	+1.4 above BO
CO	2.2 m.	−0.2 below BO

There are certain difficulties that will be encountered in practice. For example, let us suppose that you have turned the telescope over BO until it points toward ZO only to discover that, although you can see and obtain a reading over CO, you cannot see the rod when held at any of the remaining stakes. Your line of sight passes directly over the top of the rod. When this happens, you must move the level and establish a new instrument position (IP) from which the other stakes can be measured.

The first problem is to establish the relationship between the two groups of measurements. In the illustration the new IH, again 2 m., is such that the line of sight is at O at stake CO. Thus, all measurements taken from this new IP will be precisely 2 m. lower than those taken from the first IP. Now proceed to establish the rest of the profile by holding the rod, at ground, at each stake and recording the height.

Let us assume that the readings at KO, JO, IO, HO, and GO are each 2 m. As IH is also 2 m., this indicates that the ground is level from LO to GO. A reading at FO of 2.3 m. indicates a slight depression, a reading of 1.8 m. at EO now indicates a rise. EO is higher than either FO or GO. A reading of 0.5 m. at DO indicates a further rise, and a 0.0 m. reading at CO indicates that the ground at CO (which is known) is equal to IH at LO. (Note that we have used only half of the base line in the illustration. You would probably make the second IP over ZO in practice.) Your notebook entries would now look something like this:

IH at BO	2.0 m.	(= 0 for this profile)
AO	0.6 m.	+1.4 m. above BO
CO	2.2 m.	−0.2 m. below BO
IH at LO	2.0 m.	= ground or 0 at CO
KO	2.0 m.	± 0
JO	2.0 m.	± 0

IO	2.0 m.	± 0
HO	2.0 m.	± 0
GO	2.0 m.	± 0
FO	2.3 m.	−0.3 m. below LO
EO	1.8 m.	+0.2 m. above LO
DO	0.5 m.	+1.5 m. above LO
CO	0.0 m.	+2.0 m. above LO

When the series of 26 vertical measurements have been taken, you can plot them to scale on graph paper. Now draw a line connecting the several points and you have a base-line profile. You will need to establish a similar profile at other points parallel to the base line and also at right angles to the base line if significant rises and depressions indicate the need.

Constructing the Rest of the Grid

The next step is to erect two lines at a 90 degree (or right) angle to the base line from both AO and ZO. If you are using a level or transit, you can do this simply by setting it up over each stake and swinging the telescope 90 degrees in the desired direction, then driving the stakes at the proper intervals (in this instance 2 meters apart) along the line of sight.

You can obtain the same result without a level by using the geometric solution known as the 6–8–10 triangle. This solution is based on the well-known fact that the square of the hypotenuse (the longer or slanting side) of a right triangle is equal to the sum of the squares of the two opposite sides. In other words, if we have a triangle with sides equal to 6, 8, and 10 units, the angle between the shorter sides (and opposite the longer side) must be a 90 degree angle. (6 squared + 8 squared = 10 squared, or 36 + 64 = 100.)

Measure 8 units (feet or meters, according to the system being used) along the base line from AO toward ZO. If you are using the metric system, the DO stake is the correct position 8 meters from AO. If you are using feet, drive a temporary stake at 8 feet from AO in the base line. Hook the end of one tape on the nail in AO and a second tape on the nail in the temporary or DO stake. Bring the two tapes together at 6 units from AO and 10 units from DO. The point directly below this junction will be in a line at an angle of 90 degrees from AO. Establish this line as you did the base line

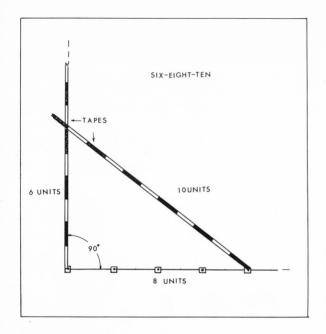

SIX-EIGHT-TEN

←TAPES

6 UNITS   10 UNITS

90°

8 UNITS

The 6–8–10 triangle establishes the sides of the grid extending at right angles to the base line from stakes AO and ZO.

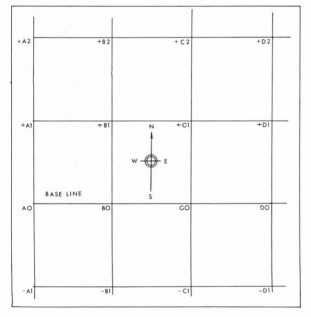

+A2   +B2   + C2   +D2

+A1   +B1   +C1   +D1

N

W ⊕ E

BASE LINE   S

AO   BO   CO   DO

−A1   −B1   −C1   −D1

The original grid (section A) may be extended to the east. The base line may be extended eastward from the original grid (section A) by establishing new grids (section B, etc.), northward by establishing grids +A1, etc., or southward by establishing grids −A1, etc.

by driving stakes along it at intervals corresponding to the determined size of the squares. Repeat the process from ZO.

Extend these lines to any desired length. You can check the accuracy of your measurements by measuring between any opposite pair of stakes on the extensions. This measurement should be 52 meters, exactly the same as the length of the base line.

Number the stakes in the extension lines from the base line A1, A2, A3, or D1, D2, D3, respectively. All that now remains to be done is to stake the interior grid squares. This is accomplished by stretching the tape between opposite pairs of stakes, driving in stakes at the proper intervals, and assigning the appropriate letter and number. You now have a precisely measured rectangle consisting of 26 squares along the base line and x number of squares along the extension lines.

If it becomes necessary to extend the base line in either direction, simply designate the original grid as Section A, and stake a similar section on either side, calling successive sections B, C, D, etc. For example, if the base line runs east and west and you want to extend to the east, establish a new grid and call it Section B.

If it becomes necessary to extend the original grid, or any succeeding grid or section to the north or south, continue the extension lines in the direction desired and label the squares north of the base line +A1, +A2 or +Z1, +Z2; south of the base line label the squares −A1, −A2 or −Z1, −Z2, respectively. In this manner an archaeological grid is capable of expansion in any direction.

Drawing the Grid Plan

Your final task is to draw a duplicate of the grid on paper so that you can plot on it, in its correct position, each feature and artifact found. This grid plan should be drawn on fairly heavy cardboard, as you will be using it in the field, sometimes under adverse conditions. I use a standard 22 × 28-inch cardboard that can be purchased for 25¢ per sheet at any stationery store. A cardboard of this size will permit you to draw 2-inch squares and to represent one-half of a grid with a north or south extension of 10 squares (13 squares × 10 squares). In other words, you will need two cardboards to represent a 26-square grid, 10 squares wide.

Before starting to excavate, locate and plot on your grid plan any natural feature that happens to be present within the grid. Let us

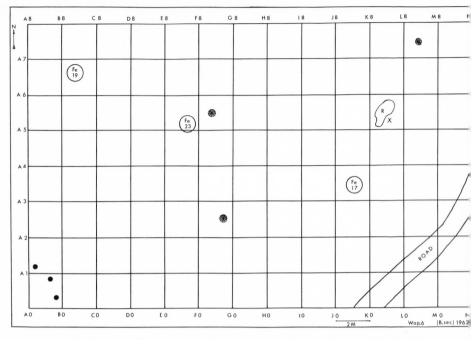

The location of tree stumps, fence posts, rocks, artifacts, and other features should be plotted on the grid map before starting to excavate. No lettering should appear within the squares, as this would interfere with the locations of artifacts and features to be entered as the excavation proceeds.

suppose, for example, that a large rock is present. It is too big to be moved, and the area covered by it will not be excavated. A blank spot will appear on your grid plan unless the rock is shown in its proper location. Again, suppose that a tree stump, which will be removed during excavation, is present. Any artifact or feature near it may have been affected during the growth of the tree or in the process of removing the stump. Your record may indicate an artifact out of context—perhaps it will be an artifact that should be associated with an upper layer, or horizon, yet your record tells you that it was found at a considerable depth. The opposite situation might well be encountered—the artifact that should come from a lower horizon is recorded as coming from near the present surface. Unless you have a record of the stump, there is no explanation for the discrepancy in your record. An old wood road passing through the grid, the rotted posts of an old fence, or an animal burrow can produce similar discrepancies. That is why it is important for you to show all such natural disturbances on your grid plan.

The grid plan and site map will constitute your most important basic records. The care with which they are drawn will be reflected in the accuracy and value of the record you will take.

Because soils play such an important role in archaeology, it is obvious that you ought to know something about them before starting to dig. The following chapter supplies the information needed for participating usefully in the work of excavation described in chapter 7.

6 : What You Need to Know About Soils

Webster defines soil as "the loose material of the earth in which plants grow." So far, so good. But to the soil scientist, soil is more complex than this—it is a mixture of minerals, organic matter, air, and water, which may vary in depth from a few inches to hundreds of feet. All of these elements play a part in producing the various types of soil found throughout the world. And archaeology, as we know, is concerned with retrieving the evidences of human life that have been buried, intentionally or accidentally, in the soil. That is why you will want to familiarize yourself very briefly with a few of the basic facts about soils. Those that have a particular bearing on your work as an archaeologist are: the formation, the profile, classification, and erosion of soil.

HOW SOIL IS FORMED

Soil covers the entire land surface of the earth, with the exception of high mountain areas and polar regions of ice and snow. Its relation to the earth has been likened to the rind of an orange. Unlike the orange rind, however, soil may vary in depth, texture, structure, and color.

Four different agents combine to form soil: (1) parent material (the raw material, such as rock, from which the various elements originate); (2) organic matter (of vegetable or animal origin); (3) climate; and (4) time. The possible combinations of these agents are infinite. As you probably are aware from your own experience, it is impossible to determine exactly where one begins and another ends. It is important to bear in mind that none of these agents alone produces a soil type. Of the four agents, however, climate is the most important.

The Influence of Climate

Climate is the principal factor determining the degree of leaching (removal of elements from the soil by the action of ground water), the profile, and the fertility of the soil. The distinctive characteristics of soils found in certain regions of the world, therefore, are the result of one of these three general climatic processes: laterization, calcification, and podzolization.

Laterization is a process of the hot, humid tropics, in which excessive rainfall and ground water remove all of the elements— except iron and aluminum—from the soil. The remaining iron and aluminum are hardened by the leaching process and by tropical heat. They produce a compacted, bricklike soil with low fertility, called laterite. Laterite occurs, for example, in the southeastern United States and in the equatorial regions of South America.

Calcification is a process of the arid (very dry) grasslands, where there is not enough rainfall to produce leaching. The calcium and magnesium, therefore, have not been leached out of the soil. In addition, decayed grass produces a great deal of humus, which is the organic portion of soil. It is not surprising that these natural grasslands produce the most fertile soils in the world, the soil known as chernozem (or "black earth") being the best example. Soils of this type are found in the corn belt and wheat-producing areas of the United States.

Podzolization is a process of the cool and humid forest regions of the world. In this climate organic matter decays slowly, producing a thin layer of humus with highly leached soil. Soil produced by podzolization usually is very shallow—perhaps only 2 or 3 feet deep—unless it has been added on top of a deeper glacial deposit. The name for these soils, podzols, comes from the Russian words meaning "ash beneath," referring to the layer of soil found just beneath the surface soil. This soil is not fertile. To grow any other crop in it except trees requires a great deal of attention. You will encounter it typically in such areas as northeastern North America and western Europe.

Other Influences

In addition to climate, of course, other factors help to determine the type of soil produced in a particular area. The slope of the land is important when considering the depth of soils. If the slope is adequate but vegetation is scarce, erosion (the wearing away of the land surface by natural forces) can and does remove the topmost layer of soil unless it is checked by proper conservation methods. The parent material determines the texture of the soil as well as the availability of nutrients essential for the growth of plant life. Climate dictates the amount and type of organic material. Unless burrowing animals, insects, and worms are present, the soil becomes so hard-packed that air and water cannot penetrate. Time too is important. The other agents work slowly; most soils are not mature but are in some stage of development. Because erosion works in reverse to time, the stage of a soil's development can be expressed as time minus erosion. A good rainstorm, for example, can remove from a plowed field situated on a slope the amount of soil that all the other agents took hundreds of years to develop.

THE SOIL PROFILE

Every soil has a profile (actually a side view)—a series of two or more layers lying one below the other, like the layers of a cake, and extending down into unbroken bedrock. These layers are known as horizons or zones. Some horizons may be deep, others may be shallow. Each horizon differs from the others in color, texture, structure, and so on. Their arrangement in a soil profile is a record of what has happened to that soil since its earliest beginnings.

The majority of soil profiles have three principal horizons, which are identified by the letters A, B, and C. There are some profiles that have no B horizon; in others both the A and B horizons may have been eroded away. Each of the principal horizons has subdivisions, which are identified as A_1, B_1, etc. A typical soil profile is represented, with letters and numbers identifying the horizons and their subdivisions. This profile is purely theoretical, of course. The thicknesses of the layers bear little relation to the actual thickness of any particular soil type.

The A and B horizons together constitute the true soil, or solum. True soil contains minerals, water, and oxygen. The A_{00} and A_0 horizons are not actually soil, but rather a layer of organic debris— dead leaves, sticks, grass, and roots—on the surface. The A_{00} horizon is made up of dead leaves that have not started to decay. The A_0 horizon contains decayed organic matter that has not yet been mixed

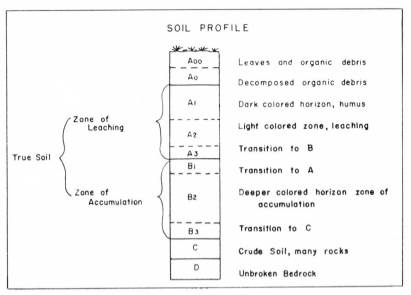

SOIL PROFILE

	Aoo	Leaves and organic debris
	Ao	Decomposed organic debris
Zone of Leaching	A1	Dark colored horizon, humus
	A2	Light colored zone, leaching
True Soil	A3	Transition to B
	B1	Transition to A
Zone of Accumulation	B2	Deeper colored horizon zone of accumulation
	B3	Transition to C
	C	Crude Soil, many rocks
	D	Unbroken Bedrock

This typical soil profile consists of three horizons, A, B, and C. A and B constitute true soil, while C consists of rock rubble. D is solid bedrock.

This section of a soil profile shows the depth of each horizon.

into the A_1 horizon lying just below. This mixing is usually the work of ants, mice, and other insects and small animals.

The A_1 horizon is the first of the true soil horizons. It consists of organic humus and minerals and usually is very dark, almost black, in color. The A_2 horizon is lighter in color and is the zone where leaching takes place, continuously removing both humus and minerals. Leached A_2 horizons are common in the soils of the forested areas in the eastern United States. The transition from the A to the B horizon is not a clear-cut line but a gradual change. Therefore, two zones of transition are shown: the A_2 and the B_1, which are difficult to distinguish from each other.

If the area has been plowed, however, the A_{00}, A_0, and A_1 horizons will be mixed. This mixture will occur as a layer of what is commonly called topsoil. It is brown in color and contains both minerals and humus. There will be a distinct break between this humus-bearing topsoil, the transitional zones, and the exposed B horizon beneath. This break, which could be taken from the A_1–A_2 line, actually occurs at the lower plow marks (A_3–B_1) and is often called the junction.

The B_2 horizon—often called the subsoil—is usually a deeper rusty red or dark gray in color. These colors may result from the accumulations of iron, manganese, and calcium compounds that have been removed from the A horizon by ground water and concentrated here. Because this layer often is extremely hard, it is sometimes called hardpan or a hardpan layer.

Deepest of the three major horizons is the C horizon. It is not actually soil and contains no humus. The C horizon consists of broken rock rubble and is usually lighter in color than the A and B horizons. When the last ice sheet retreated from the northern United States and Canada, it left behind in many places a thick layer of rock and rock fragments. In those areas this glacial till, as it is called, provides a very thick C horizon.

The D horizon is solid bedrock. In many parts of the northern United States and Canada it is buried deep. In other areas it is exposed at the surface.

HOW SOIL IS CLASSIFIED

The three main types of soil—zonal, intrazonal, and azonal—are classified according to the development of the soil profile. Zonal

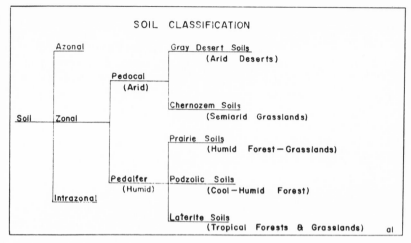

SOIL CLASSIFICATION

Azonal		Gray Desert Soils (Arid Deserts)
	Pedocal (Arid)	
Zonal		Chernozem Soils (Semiarid Grasslands)
		Prairie Soils (Humid Forest — Grasslands)
	Pedalfer (Humid)	Podzolic Soils (Cool — Humid Forest)
Intrazonal		Laterite Soils (Tropical Forests & Grasslands)

Soil types are classified as azonal, zonal, or intrazonal. Azonal and intrazonal soils lack good profile development. Zonal soils, the major type, are widely distributed and have well-developed profiles.

soils (so-called because they have two distinct zones or horizons) constitute the major soil type. They have a well-developed profile, resulting from a definite climatic influence on well-drained land. Zonal type soils are universal—a podzol is a podzol, whether it is found in Canada, the Soviet Union, or the United States—but the azonal and intrazonal types must always be analyzed as individual cases.

Intrazonal soils have only moderately developed profiles because they lack drainage. Soils in marshes, swamps, and bogs are typical of this group.

Azonal soils have been deposited too recently to develop a mature soil profile. Therefore, they have little or no profile development. River delta soils, alluvium deposits (sand, mud, and other sediments deposited by streams), and active sand dunes are typical of this group.

Zonal Soils

The zonal soils are the ones that primarily concern us. They make up the largest and the most universal soil group. As you will notice from the soil classification chart, there are two distinct categories of zonal soils—the pedocal and the pedalfer. The distinction between the two is based chiefly upon the difference in the amount of rainfall they receive.

The pedocal soils are found in the arid regions of the earth. They are the result of the calcification process of soil formation—because there is little or no rainfall, leaching does not occur and calcium accumulates near the surface. The gray desert soil subtype is an example of a soil of the most arid regions—deserts—which can be made fertile if supplied with water, as many irrigated areas in the western United States prove. The chernozem soil subtype, the so-called "black earth," is the most fertile soil in the world. It is formed on the semiarid grasslands. While they are sufficiently dry to hinder the leaching process, these regions still have enough rainfall to produce a good grass cover. The grass, in turn, supplies a great deal of organic matter. When decayed, this matter produces a very thick humus layer in the soil profile.

The pedalfer soils, on the other hand, are found in the more humid regions of the world (in the eastern United States, for example). As you would expect, therefore, they are highly leached. The humus layer of these soils is much thinner than that of pedocal soils because they are covered by forests. The B horizon is a reddish-yellow color, owing to the accumulation there of iron compounds. The prairie soils are found in the transitional forest-grasslands. They receive less rainfall and therefore are less leached than the other two pedalfer subtypes. Low fertility characterizes the podzolic soils that are found in the cool-humid forest regions of northeastern North America. Last of the pedalfer subtypes are the laterite soils of the humid tropics and subtropics, including the southeastern United States. Leaching of the soils in these regions through excessive rainfall and heat has resulted in a concentration of iron that gives these soils their characteristic deep red color.

I have been able to discuss here only a few of the types and subtypes of soil. But they are representative and should give you an idea at least of the many ways in which climate and vegetation influence soil.

HOW EROSION AFFECTS SOIL

As an archaeologist, you will be especially concerned with the aspect of soil formation that has to do with the building up and breaking down of the soil. Building up is the slow process of soil formation. But breaking down is a process of erosion, of wearing away. It may be slow or it may be rapid, depending upon the degree of slope of the land and also upon the character of its vegetation cover.

These two processes make it extremely hazardous to attempt to identify the age of an artifact from the profile and depth of the soil in which it is found. Do not trust these two factors in dating finds unless you can definitely locate a distinct layer that can be identified or an old buried soil profile that can be dated or related to an occurrence known to have taken place. You can make relative statements—when dealing with a single, very limited area—as to which layer is nearer the surface, but the distance of the layer above or below the junction (see the section on the soil profile) has little to do with the age of an artifact. An artifact found on the surface of the ground in one place may actually be much older than an artifact buried some 6 feet (or 200 centimeters) deep in the ground in another place. A lot depends upon the region in which you happen to be excavating. In the northeastern United States where I work, for example, soil formation began as soon as the last ice sheet retreated into Canada, about 10,000 years ago, and the soils there are still in the process of being developed. This makes the relative depths differ much more from the actual ages of artifacts.

Soil has a tendency to "bury" artifacts for various reasons. One of the reasons is that organic material is being continuously added to the surface by insects and animals. When an ant or a fox digs a hole or den, for instance, it brings to the surface materials that subsequently are mixed with the organic matter already there. In this way, anything dropped on the surface—an artifact, let us say— would be effectively covered or buried. Another reason is that erosion often wears away the surface of the ground, thus exposing artifacts that have been lying beneath. Erosion tends to make all land level by removing material from higher elevations and depositing it in lower-lying areas. On sloping ground, surface water is the major agent of erosion. That is why the removal of vegetation— by plowing, burning, or other means—greatly increases the amount of erosion.

When both the "burial" and erosion processes are taken into account, there may be several different results. The situation presented in the accompanying diagram shows the effects of soil buildup

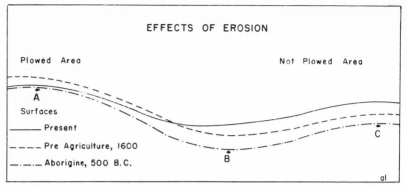

EFFECTS OF EROSION

Plowed Area

Not Plowed Area

A
Surfaces
——— Present
— — — Pre Agriculture, 1600
—.—.— Aborigine, 500 B.C.

B

C

al

The depths at which artifacts A, B, and C are found differ greatly depending upon the amount of soil buildup and erosion and the effects of plowing.

and erosion on the surface of a typical archaeological site. It illustrates clearly why the depths at which an artifact is found may differ greatly, depending upon the varying rates of erosion or build-up.

Let us assume that artifacts A, B, and C were dropped on the aborigine surface (the surface as it existed at the time of the artifacts' manufacture) around 500 B.C. A lies on a small hill, B in a valley, and C on a second hill. During the more than 2,000 years from the time the artifacts were dropped to the beginning of plow-type agriculture (about A.D. 1600), they would have been buried the distance between the pre-agriculture surface and the aborigine surface. B, in the valley, would lie deeper in the ground than A and C, on the hills, because some erosion would have taken soil from the tops of the hills on either side in spite of the presence of trees and grass.

To complicate the situation a bit more, let's assume further that the hill where A rests has been plowed regularly since A.D. 1600 and that the hill where C lies has been kept in woods or in pasture with good grass cover. It is unimportant whether the valley in which B lies has been plowed or not, because it is an area where material has been deposited rather than eroded. The hill where A rests is the result of erosion over a period of some 360 years (1600 to the 1960's). Here erosion has worn the soil down to the level of the artifact—A—that was dropped back in 500 B.C., so that it now rests on the surface. The hill where C lies has not been eroded at the same rate as the other hill, owing to its covering of vegetation, so C remains buried. Artifact B is even more deeply buried than C, because the soil that was removed from A's hill has been deposited in the valley and over B.

All three artifacts, A, B, and C, were deposited on the surface at the same time, yet today one is exposed on the surface and the other two are buried at different depths in the soil profile. I think you will agree with me now that you cannot tell the age of an artifact from its position in the soil profile and from the depth of the soil.

7 : How to Excavate a Site

Somewhere within the mind of every boy lurks an impulse to take things apart. Well do I recall an alarm clock that I once took apart to find out what made it "tick." When I came to put it together again, to my dismay, several parts were left over. For the life of me I couldn't find where they belonged. Thus I learned a lesson that I have never forgotten. Always make sure that you know how the thing was put together before you take it apart.

The excavation of an Indian site is nothing more nor less than taking it apart to discover by whom, when, and how it was put together. There are many kinds of Indian sites. Some have a most complicated history because they were put together by different cultural groups and at different times. Other sites are simpler. Let's start with the simple kind known to archaeologists as "closed sites," which means that they were occupied by only one cultural group and for a comparatively short time.

The site I have in mind is a fishing camp located near the bank of a small stream up which the trout and salmon swam each spring to spawn in the lake. Each year a small group of hunting-fishing-gathering people, whom we call the Archaic people, came to the site for the spring fishing. Each year the old lodges that had blown down during the winter were rebuilt, new fireplaces or hearths were constructed, and new refuse pits were dug. Eventually the surface became pockmarked with post molds (molds or casts left in the ground by decayed or burned posts); refuse pits and hearths were everywhere; and artifacts, together with the chips created by their manufacture, were strewn about.

One spring the people failed to appear. Perhaps the fish did not run, or maybe some unexpected calamity convinced these super-stitious people that an evil spirit had found their favorite fishing place. In autumn the leaves fell and covered the ground. As the years passed, the vegetation took over again. Winds brought soil to cover the abandoned site, and perhaps the river overflowed its banks and contributed a layer of silt. Gradually the surface on which the fishermen lived and left the marks of their presence was buried beneath a layer of soil. The buried surface had become an archaeological horizon. The soil that had accumulated above it is known as the "overburden."

Similar conditions may affect any site unless it has been protected. For example, you would not expect to find severe erosion or plow disturbance in a rock shelter or cave site. Instead, you would find considerable buildup caused by wind-blown soil or by falling material from the rock overhang. Some open sites in the Southwest have been buried deep under wind- and water-deposited soils. This is especially true of some of the very ancient sites that were involved in the geologic and climatic events of the early post-Pleistocene. Examples are the Paleo-Indian sites that were buried beneath 20 or 30 feet of loess.

So far we have been talking about changes that may have taken place at sites where there was only one archaeological horizon or occupation by a single cultural group. This is a rare situation in archaeology. You will find that most sites have been the home of more than one cultural group at various periods in time.

In practice, all sorts of combinations of archaeological horizons, or levels, will be encountered. For example, at a given site you might find a deeply buried Paleo-Indian horizon, a slightly higher early Archaic horizon, a still later late Archaic horizon, and finally, just beneath the present surface, a Woodland horizon. Any two or three of these occupations could have been intermixed. The upper horizon, or possibly the two upper horizons, could have been intermixed and disturbed by plowing. Various subsurface disturbances, such as animal burrows or tree stumps pulled to clear the land, might have produced still further complications.

Excavation techniques must be adapted to the site. They must be selected to produce the maximum result with regard to the particular situation. At a site that is definitely stratified (arranged in layers), excavation by the level method should be used. When archaeological horizons are known to be intermixed, however, this method will not yield the best results and other techniques are called for.

EXCAVATION EQUIPMENT

In addition to the field equipment listed in chapter 3, you will need the following items for the excavation of an archaeological site:

A rounded or pointed shovel, preferably with a long handle. This will be used mainly for the removal of back dirt (soil that has already been removed by the trowel or hoe and is known to be empty of artifacts) and to replace the earth in completed squares. It should not be used in primary excavation.

A pair of pruning shears or root cutters—$2 items at the hardware store.

Several small paintbrushes; perhaps a 1-inch one and 3-inch one will suffice. These need not be expensive—the dime store variety will be adequate—as you will use them only for brushing loose dirt from exposed artifacts, and an occasional loose bristle will not be a problem.

I always carry a number of small tools picked up here and there which I find handy for use on special occasions (you will pick up many useful small gadgets as you become experienced). A few of my gadgets are:

An ice pick, several dental picks given to me by a local dentist, small kitchen knife, pair of tweezers for picking up beads and other small artifacts, a steel file for keeping my hoe sharp, a toothbrush for scrubbing artifacts.

A small screen, which can be made from a couple of pieces of wood and a bit of screen wire. It will come in handy when occasionally a small artifact or beads elude your trowel and you want to search for them through the back dirt.

Small bottles, cardboard boxes, and similar containers. In my digging kit I carry a number of these for the storage of small or delicate artifacts that might become lost or broken.

It is also a good idea to have available some cotton for packing.

An atomizer or other type of inexpensive spraying device is useful. Filled with plain water, it can be used to bring out the detail of a post mold or soil profile that you wish to photograph. Some features are apt to be quite indistinct if the soil is dry but will stand out sharply when sprayed lightly. A wet artifact photographs much better than a dry one.

ORGANIZATION

If only one or two individuals are engaged in the excavation of a small site, no formal organization will be necessary. On the other hand, if a number of persons are to take part in the work, there must be some sort of understanding about procedure and responsibility for records.

Usually one person is designated to act as the director. If possible, this should be someone with previous experience, to whom the group will naturally look for instruction and guidance. With or without experience, the director should be an even-tempered individual who can direct by suggestion rather than by orders. It requires tact to direct the work of a group of volunteers without allowing friction to develop.

The director usually is held responsible for laying out the site and assigning squares to individuals to excavate. He must see that any agreements made with the owner of the property are carefully observed. It is his job to see that each person excavating knows how and what to record and is familiar with the procedure. The director must make certain that each excavator follows the rules and does not become careless when little is being found or excited when something spectacular turns up.

The director generally keeps a progress map of the excavation, entering on it each feature as it is found and assigning to it a number in the sequence. He makes certain that the proper photographs are taken and that the record is complete before the feature is destroyed. Finally, at the close of the season or at the completion of the excavations, the director collects all of the field records, notebooks, and artifacts, which will form the basis of the report. Often he is made responsible for that report and either writes it himself or helps someone else in writing it.

It is usual to appoint or to elect an assistant to the director— someone who will function in his absence or cooperate with him in the general direction of the work. Another good idea is to set up a "dig committee" of from three to five persons, who will draw up a set of rules, assist the director, and help to settle any disputes that may arise.

Make use of any special talents or abilities that may exist within the group. For example, a civil engineer or surveyor might lay out the grid, run the profiles, and do the mapping; an experienced photographer might be assigned the task of making the official photographs; an artist might do the field sketching and illustrate the final report. No one individual can be expected to be an expert in all of these fields.

EXPLORATORY EXCAVATIONS

Exploratory excavation is unnecessary if the entire area of a site is to be excavated. Some sort of exploratory excavation is recommended if there is not enough time or manpower to undertake the complete excavation of the grid or if there is reason to suspect that the site is small and that the finding of the most heavily occupied portion of it will save a lot of unnecessary work. This may be accomplished by either of two methods: test trenching and test pitting.

Test Trenching

This consists of digging a narrow trench, perhaps two feet wide, across the grid. Sometimes two test trenches at right angles to one another are laid out. These test trenches should follow the grid lines so that any records obtained may later be tied in with subsequent records. One advantage of test trenching is that it provides a long, unbroken profile across the grid and indicates the soil distribution over the area.

One of the disadvantages of test trenching is the problem of handling the back earth removed from the test trenches. As you proceed, the back dirt is deposited along one side of the trench. Suppose you encounter post molds along the way and turn to excavate them in adjacent squares. You will soon find yourself surrounded by piles of back earth and must stop excavating to move this out of the way.

Test Pitting

This method consists of excavating a number of squares scattered about the grid. These may be selected because of surface indications or just on a plain hunch. Often the hunch is wrong and nothing of importance is located. The important deposit may be in the next square. The grid is now dotted with piles of earth that must be

Togetherness is the secret of a successful amateur dig. All members of the family, including pets, may participate. This group takes a breather near the base line soil deposit of a sectional excavation.

shoveled back into the test squares if it is not to be in the way of subsequent excavation.

I have learned that most test excavation is a waste of time and effort. Some years ago I was excavating a site with a professional archaeologist. A test trench was laid out and excavated through a promising area nearly 100 feet wide. The trench revealed nothing of interest, and on this basis it was decided that the area was not worth excavating. Later I decided to excavate the area anyhow and found twenty-six Indian burials plus a large number of diagnostic artifacts. The test trench had passed within a few inches of several of the burial shafts without revealing their presence. Had it been started a few inches either to the right or left, it would have uncovered burial shafts within a few feet from its point of origin.

If your site is worth excavating at all, it is worth excavating completely. Do your test digging before selecting and laying out the site. Once you have decided on the site, dig from the base line and let the results indicate to you the direction in which to proceed.

Unless you are engaged in salvage archaeology and the area under investigation is to be dug up immediately by bulldozers, you must plan to return the area to its original condition when the excavations have been completed. With this in mind, store the excavated earth in piles, keeping the several types of soil separated, so that they can be backfilled in the proper order.

To the professional archaeologist with paid laborers at his disposal, this is no problem. A dump area is selected far enough from the grid so that it will not interfere with the work, and the back earth is transported there by wheelbarrow. This technique has many advantages. It permits the exposure of an entire village area at one time, for example. Lodge floors, refuse pits, hearths, and other features can be seen in their original relationship to one another and photographed or sketched in context.

For the amateur, this technique is seldom practical. Not only is labor in quantity unavailable, but his weekend type of operation does not permit him to leave features in place when the site is unprotected. Almost certainly such obvious features as pits and hearths would be destroyed by vandals or relic hunters during the week. Sometimes, of course, you may be forced to use a modified version of this technique. An example would be the discovery of a large feature, such as a lodge floor, occupying a number of squares, when you must expose the entire area for recording and photographing.

A method often used by amateur groups is to start a number of excavators side by side along the base line of the grid. The back earth from the first line of squares is piled on the surface just back of the base line. Having cleared the first line of squares, the backfill will be used to fill the first squares excavated. During the season the digging will advance x number of squares from the base line. When the time comes to close for the season, all of the earth from behind the base line must be carried across the soft surface of the excavated area to backfill the forward squares. This is a sizable and backbreaking job, and you will doubtless note the absence of a number of familiar faces when the time comes to clean up for the season.

SECTIONAL EXCAVATION

Sectional excavation is a method devised by the Cohannet Chapter of the Massachusetts Archaeological Society. Among its advantages is that it is a great labor-saver.

A section of six to eight squares is assigned to one individual—for example, squares FO, F1, F2, GO, G1, G2. Excavation starts along the line FO to GO and proceeds in the direction indicated by the arrow. The earth removed from FO is piled, as shown, to the rear of GO to HO, keeping the loam and subsoil separate. The earth from the second square to be excavated, F1, is used to refill square FO. To keep the soil in the proper order, the loam from F1 is added to the pile back of the base line, but the subsoil from F1 is thrown into the empty square FO. Loam from F2 is then placed on top of the subsoil in FO. Subsoil from F2 is used to refill F1. When the section has been completed, and the excavator is back to square GO, the earth is at hand for refilling the last square without transportation.

If a number of individuals are involved, sections are assigned along the base line. Section A is assigned to one person, section B to another, and so on. Sections, such as C, are left between each excavator. The purpose of this is to allow the individual excavating A or B to turn into the section at his right or left if a feature appears that leads him in either direction. After completing A, the first individual would proceed to excavate C, and so on.

The sectional method of excavation has labor-saving advantages. Subsoil and loam from square FO and loam from F1 are deposited back of the base line, to the rear of squares GO and HO, respectively. Then FO is backfilled with subsoil from F1 and loam from F2. This procedure continues, the last square being backfilled with soils from the two base-line deposits.

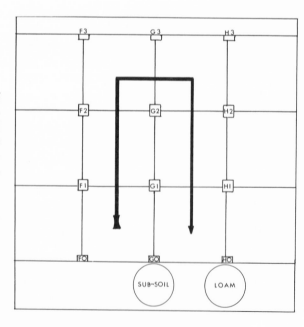

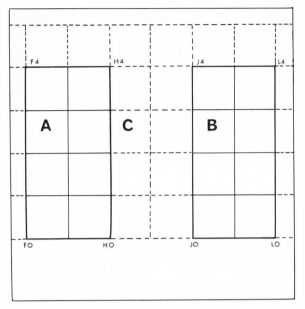

An extension of the sectional method is employed when a number of excavators are involved. Alternate sections along the base line are assigned, so that the excavator of A or B, for example, may work left or right into C if necessary.

EXCAVATION METHODS

The method you adopt for the excavation of a given site will have been determined either by exploratory excavation or by the results obtained in the excavation of the initial squares of the grid.

The site may appear to be stratified in a manner similar to that shown, where two archaeological horizons are separated by a sterile soil layer. You will probably decide to use the level-stripping method in this case.

If the archaeological horizons appear at nearly the same level vertically, the vertical-face method probably will be preferable.

In some instances changes in the character of the site as excavation progresses will necessitate a change in excavation methods. For example, the discovery of the presence of a lodge floor, would suggest a change from the vertical-face to the level-stripping technique, at least in that particular part of the site.

Whenever a feature, such as a refuse pit or hearth, appears, disregard the excavation method you are using and follow the method described in this chapter for excavating features.

ARCHAIC HORIZON
WOODLAND HORIZON
PRESENT SURFACE
PM
PIT
D
S
PM
PIT
D
D
PIT
PIT
D
PM'S
2
1
STERILE

These two diagrams show how stratification may determine the method of excavation. When horizons where features occur are separated by a sterile soil layer (1), the level-stripping method is preferred. Where the archaeological horizons appear nearly level vertically (2), the vertical-face method is best.

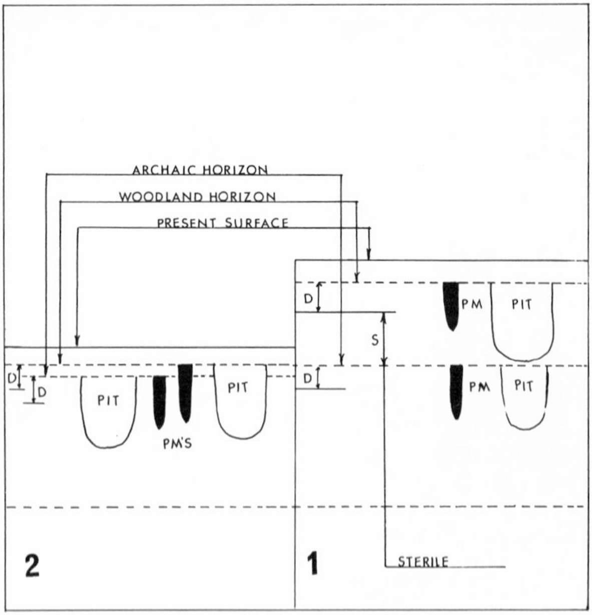

Whatever basic method is adopted, all archaeological excavation is done with the trowel or hoe except in those rare instances when these implements will not penetrate the soil. In this case you may have to use a heavier tool. If you do, you must exercise great care; otherwise archaeological specimens and data will be destroyed without your even being aware of their presence. On soft soil sites the shovel is used only in the removal of back earth that has been excavated with the hoe or trowel and for the refilling of the completed square.

Vertical-Face Method

In this method a square or a section of squares (sometimes the entire grid) is excavated in a horizontal direction, keeping a single face the width of the section and at a predetermined depth from the surface at all times. The blocks of soil that support the square stakes must be left standing, as these measuring points will be necessary for proper recording.

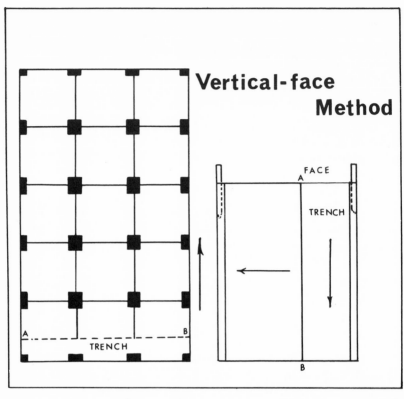

The vertical-face method involves excavating a square or section of squares (or perhaps a whole grid) in a horizontal direction. (1) Dig a narrow trench of the desired depth (possibly 4 feet) along the base line the length of the section or square assigned. (2) Carry this vertical face (A to B) in the direction of the arrow, leaving the indicated blocks of earth standing. Sometimes the blocks may be removed for convenience and the stake replaced at a lower level. (3) If you encounter a feature, abandon the vertical-face method until the feature can be excavated and recorded.

Level-Stripping Method

This is a variation of the vertical-face method. It is used when you want to segregate artifacts and features by arbitrary levels. The levels maintained may be soil horizons, archaeological horizons, or simple convenient depths (for example, 6-inch or 12-inch layers of soil). This method may be applied to sections or the entire grid.

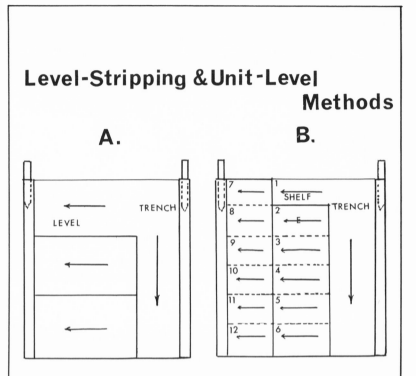

Level-Stripping & Unit-Level Methods

A.

B.

In the level-stripping method (A), artifacts or features are isolated by arbitrary levels. (1) Dig a trench down to the desired level. (2) Proceed in the direction of the arrow, maintaining a vertical face to the established depth, until the entire section has been excavated to the first level or horizon. (3) Start again from the trench and excavate the second shelf, etc. In the unit-level method (B), artifacts and features are exposed completely. (1) Start with the usual trench, at least 3 feet deep. (2) Excavate a shelf of convenient width in the direction of the arrow. The depth of this shelf may be to the soil horizon between loam and subsoil, or it may be to an arbitrary depth (as 6 inches). (3) If you encounter the top of a feature or evidence of a feature nearby, try to locate a definite outline of it by bringing down the immediately surrounding shelves to the same level. (4) If no features appear at level 1, level 2 should be excavated, followed by levels 3, 4, 5, 6, etc., until the shelf has reached the level of the bottom of the trench. Another shelf (levels 7–12) is then excavated in the same manner. This method works well in conjunction with the sectional excavation technique.

The loam (vertical-face method) has been removed and the B horizon exposed. The position of the grid stakes is being checked and measured to make certain that the stakes have not been moved out of place.

Part of the C horizon has been exposed by horizontal scraping. A large area was cleared when the discovery of post molds led the excavators to anticipate the existence of a lodge floor.

Unit-Level Method

This is the method I prefer and use, sometimes with modification, at all of the sites that have been dug under my direction. If the definite outlines of a feature can be found, expose it completely and record it. The unit-level method is abandoned for the moment and the feature excavated. The presence of post molds may indicate a habitation or lodge floor in the area. In this instance a considerable area must be exposed to the level of the tops of the original molds in search of additional evidence. If additional post molds are found and the pattern indicates the presence of a floor, several sections of squares should be taken down to the level at which the feature is appearing.

Record all of the artifacts and features found according to the procedure outlined in chapter 8, including a vertical measurement from the surface for each. Stratification can be checked by a study of artifact types even if there is no visual evidence of cultural horizons. In New England you will seldom find any indication of archaeological horizons except for the presence of artifacts and the tops of associated features. Floors of dwelling places are sometimes discolored by charcoal or other camp refuse that has been trodden into the floor or by the relative hardness within the living area.

EXCAVATING ARTIFACTS

The trowel or short-handled hoe is the tool with which you will do most of your excavating. With it you should carefully scrape the level or shelf being excavated. Do not remove more than a quarter-inch to a half-inch of soil at a time. The object is to locate any artifact that may be present, but in the process do not move it out of position or damage it. Assume that all artifacts encountered will be fragile and may be broken or scarred by too heavy a hand.

You will soon learn the feel of the soil and will recognize the change when your hoe or trowel encounters a foreign object. The moment you feel the contact, stop the stroke and lay down the tool. Do the exposing with a paint brush or a small pointed tool. Many objects will turn out to be nothing but pebbles or broken fragments of burned stone, but it is better to waste time in this way than to damage an artifact. Even an unworked stone may be important at times. If it is burned or reddened by fire, especially if the soil about it is discolored or bits of charcoal are present, it may indicate the presence of a feature of some sort. If careful brushing or probing shows you that more stones are present just beneath the surface, investigate carefully before you start the scraping process again.

If the object should turn out to be an artifact, resist the almost overpowering impulse to pick it up. Let it lie in place, brush it off with the paintbrush, and probe a bit to see if anything more is

Dirt is sifted through a wood-framed screen to make sure that no small artifacts or fragments have been overlooked. (Chicago Natural History Museum)

Careful excavation with a soft brush is the proper method to use in uncovering a broken pottery vessel. (Chicago Natural History Museum)

associated with it. If the artifact should be broken, look for the rest of it nearby. If potsherds appear, locate as many as you can with the brush. Pottery is fragile while wet, so don't be in a hurry. These things have lain here for centuries and a few minutes more will do no harm.

If the artifact is a particularly fine one, or if several artifacts are present in a group, you will probably want a photograph for the record. Keep the working surface flat; don't let it slope from side to side or from front to back of the shelf. Square corners are the rule, with stakes left with sufficient soil to support them. Level surfaces and vertical faces mark the work of an experienced excavator.

EXCAVATING FEATURES

Within the area of a camp or village site, hearths and pits will be encountered frequently. Holes were dug in the ground by the aboriginal occupants for a number of purposes. Vegetable foods were often stored in these holes or pits, which were lined with grass or bark; cooking pits were used in some cultures. Whatever their primary function, pits were finally used in many instances for the disposal of camp refuse of all sorts. I have even found human skeletons in them.

Shallow basins were scooped out to confine the embers of cooking fires. Sometimes these were lined with stone and a large flat stone placed at the bottom as a hearthstone. The charcoal from the last fire burned in them may be present.

An important feature on any site consists of the remains of a structure that may have been used as a dwelling or for ceremonial purposes. We shall have more to say about this type of feature.

Earthworks or fortifications are also features and occur at some sites in all areas. Palisade walls are a common feature in eastern and southeastern sites.

Burials of one type or another may be expected to appear in conjunction with any site at which people lived for any length of time. In fact, there are so many possible features of various kinds that we shall be able to discuss only the more common ones in detail.

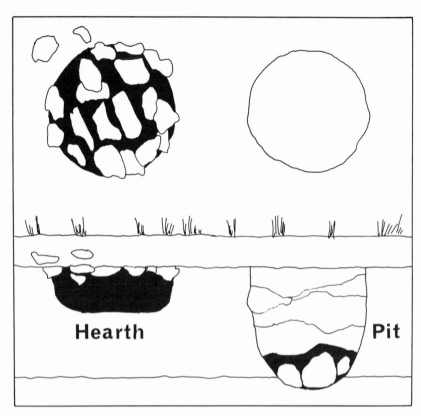

A stone-lined hearth looks something like the drawing on the left. A pit has the general form of the drawings at the right. Its presence will be indicated by a patch of discolored soil.

Hearths

This is a most common type of feature and will be found in one form or another at all sites and in all areas. Probably the first intimation you will have of the presence of a hearth will be fragments of burned and reddened stone. These may be associated with patches of dark soil containing charcoal and/or with reddened areas of burned soil. If you are working on a site that has been subjected to repeated plowing and if the archaeological horizon is within reach of the plowshare, these indicators may have been widely distributed when the top of the feature was disturbed.

The exposure of any of these evidences should be sufficient warning to you to stop scraping the level and to investigate the immediate area for confirming evidence. Leave the stones and areas of discolored soil in place. Using the paint brush and some small, pointed implement, see whether you can locate additional stones or discolored soil. Remember that more stones may lie immediately below the surface you have exposed.

When you have located the top of the hearth, expose it completely by brushing. If it happens to be stone-lined, it will look something like the hearth shown, or it may be simply a shallow basin filled with charcoal and ash.

After the initial record (see chapter 8), the next step is to section or divide the feature approximately in half and excavate one of the halves by vertical exposure of the profile. By this method you can obtain the proper record and obtain a profile picture of the feature. If desired, a carbon sample may be saved (see chapter 10) for dating. Sometimes good charcoal samples will indicate the kind of wood used and thus provide some idea of the plant life of the period and area.

The area immediately about a hearth and within the hearth itself is often a good place to expect artifacts; keep a sharp lookout for them. Cooking utensils were occasionally broken and left in association with these features. Another important potential is the presence of carbonized food remains, which will furnish valuable data concerning the food habits of the culture and may provide a lead with respect to the time of occupation.

Pits

The first indication that you may have of the presence of a pit probably will be a patch of discolored soil. This may be soil darkened by the presence of granular charcoal or other decayed material, or perhaps you will see a small area of red burned earth. Broken stone may also be present. The outline of the top of a pit may be a very distinct ring of black soil standing out sharply in contrast to the surrounding soil, or it may be an indistinct change in the character or color of the soil. The top should be exposed and recorded in the same manner as a hearth is recorded.

These post molds, with associated artifacts, from an Archaic village site have been sectioned and identified for recording purposes. Notice that the working surfaces have been kept flat and level.

Section to obtain a profile as you would in the case of a hearth. Keep one fact in mind, particularly if the site is known to be stratified and the presence of a second and lower occupied horizon is suspected: a pit may penetrate to or through this second horizon. If it does, be on the watch for an intermixing of artifacts. The aboriginal people who dug this pit from the upper horizon may have encountered earlier artifacts that they intermingled with their own, or artifacts of the later culture may have been introduced upon a lower and earlier horizon while the pit was in use.

A pit that was used as a receptacle for camp rubbish may obtain a wealth of information. All sorts of broken artifacts may be present, especially clay or stone vessel sherds; carbonized food remains are often present. The position of the tops of these features may mark an archaeological horizon that is otherwise indistinguishable. Their horizontal distribution can indicate the plan and extent of the occupied area. Be certain that you note all of the implications.

Post Molds

Whenever a post has been driven or set into the ground and allowed to decay or burn there, a record in the form of a mold or cast of the post will remain for an indefinite period, unless it is disturbed by a later excavation. Even if the post or stake has been

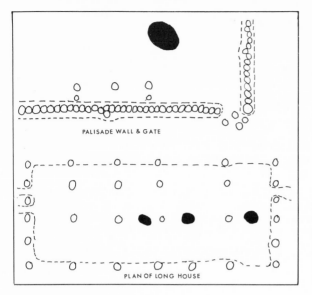

PALISADE WALL & GATE

PLAN OF LONG HOUSE

Post molds more or less evenly spaced may also indicate a structure, perhaps a long house. Several long houses with a palisade constitute a village.

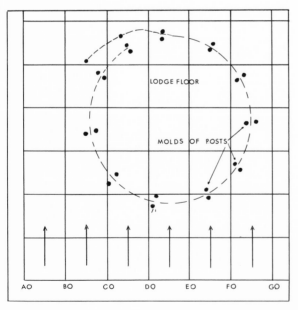

LODGE FLOOR

MOLDS OF POSTS

AO   BO   CO   DO   EO   FO   GO

A circular plan of opposite pairs of post molds suggests the floor of an aboriginal house.

126   How to Excavate a Site

Post molds at the Assawompset #6 site in Massachusetts have been staked out to reveal the contours of a circular lodge floor. Notice the overlap at the entrance.

pulled up, darker-colored soil may have filled the hole and thus left an indication of its presence.

Post molds appear as small, circular, dark spots when scraped by the hoe or trowel. If such a discoloration appears, investigate it immediately. You will encounter many pseudo post molds and must learn to distinguish them from the real article. Such disturbances as animal burrows, small trees, and the like will also appear as circular discolorations. However, animal burrows will wander in vertical profile and usually end in a small chamber or nest. Old trees may be recognized by the presence of side roots and the fact that the mold does not taper to a sharp point or end abruptly in imitation of a cut-off post. Then, too, posts may have been driven or set in the ground by fairly modern occupants. Beware of square molds. This is one good reason for the use of square rather than round stakes for markers. I have known excavators to record their own post molds. Indian posts often occur in pairs or in groups of three or more in close proximity; if part of a structure, the molds will form a recognizable pattern. Perhaps the presence of a pattern will indicate to you the location of additional molds.

After making a record of the location and size of the top of the mold, section it, as in the case of a hearth or pit, in order to learn the shape and length of the mold. At this point you may have to enter in the record: "This is not a post mold but an animal burrow." If you do, just continue to treat the next one in the same way—it may be a post mold this time.

Once you have located and recorded an actual post mold, expand the level or shelf in all directions for several squares in search of more molds that may reveal a pattern. If you simply record the first mold and resume work on the shelf, you may destroy a part of the habitation floor, if present. If additional molds appear, they may form the arc of a circle, a straight line of posts, or the angle of one corner of a rectangle. Continue level excavation until you have the entire pattern of the floor plan or until you are certain that no additional molds are present in the vicinity.

A circular plan, consisting of either single molds or of pairs of molds, may well indicate habitation floor, particularly if the enclosed area is marked by discolored or hardened soil. Look for indications of an entrance or doorway, an interior hearth, a concentration of artifacts or stone flakes. Interior molds may give evidence of supporting posts or interior structures, such as bed platforms.

The floors of aboriginal houses may be circular, oval, or rectangular in outline, with the line of the wall marked by the molds of the posts that supported the superstructure. The perimeter may be marked by single posts more or less evenly spaced, or posts may appear in pairs or perhaps in groups of three or more. When more than two posts are grouped, a repair or replacement is suggested. Pairs of posts may occur in the line or on opposite sides of the line.

In Massachusetts I uncovered seven of these Archaic houses or lodges, comprising a small village. Note the protected doorway created by allowing the walls to overlap. Also note that the line of the wall is marked by pairs of post molds on opposite sides of the line of the wall.

Follow carefully the pattern formed by the post molds. Plot each mold on your site map and mark the position in the ground with a stake. I like to use stakes with brightly painted (orange or red) tops. These will stand out in a colored photograph and can be distinguished from the grid stakes.

You may encounter a straight line of post molds. If these are spaced equally—particularly if the distance between them is con-

The floor plan of a small circular Adena house shows pairs of post molds in the line of the wall. A central hearth has a draft screen attached to central supporting posts. When a stone house, such as this Hopi house in the Southwest, is built in the open, the walls are often constructed with flat slabs of sandstone or volcanic tufa. If more or less protected from the weather in caves or under cliffs, a sun-dried adobe brick could be used.

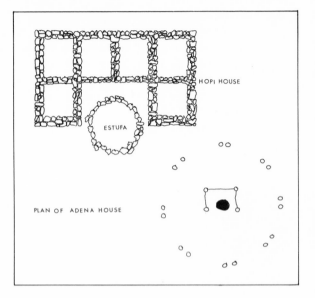

HOPI HOUSE

ESTUFA

PLAN OF ADENA HOUSE

sistently equal to a unit of English measure (feet or yards)—you may suspect an old fence line. This is always a possibility.

Horizontal molds will also show up, representing poles or posts that have decayed while lying on an ancient surface. They may or may not be associated with a pattern of vertical molds. Often they can be recognized as ancient by the presence of projecting stubs, which represent the branches that were lopped off with a stone axe.

Considerable information can be derived from a post mold that is pointed at one end. First, the point indicates that the post was driven and not set in a prepared hole. These molds also can tell you something about the length of house supports or rafters; from them you may be able to deduce the height of the structure from which they came (see plan of Adena house). If a post was driven, it probably did not project out of the ground more than 3 or 4 feet. Indians were not tall people and could hardly be expected to drive an 8-foot post. A taller post would probably have a blunt base and would be set, not driven.

Not all Indian houses were of the pole type of construction. Everyone is familiar with the stone apartment houses of the Southwest (see Hopi house). Often built in caves or under overhanging cliffs, they are typical of the area. The kind of masonry will vary with culture and time. The masonry technique is an excellent indication of the period. Familiarize yourself with the association of technique and culture in the areas in which you intend to work; the time spent will be most profitable.

Usually only the lower portion of the walls will be standing, and the interior will be covered by fallen stone and other debris. Often the wooden roof beams will be found within the rooms and these can be made to yield valuable chronological data (see chapter 10).

Let me hasten to add that the excavation of a large ruin of this type is definitely not an amateur job. Anyhow, the majority of large cliff dwellings and mesa towns are situated on public lands and are protected by federal law, so they are not available for amateur excavation. An occasional small ruin may be found on private property. The purpose of excavating is to establish the culture and the period in which the structure was built. Also the excavator should be interested in reconstruction when it is justified and in preservation in all instances. If you are a beginner, I strongly suggest that you seek the assistance of a more experienced amateur or professional should you discover a structure of this sort, especially if it appears to be undisturbed.

Mounds

Artificial mounds constitute another kind of structure that you may encounter, particularly in the Midwest and Southeast. To the casual observer, many natural mounds closely resemble Indian-built mounds, but the internal structure will reveal their origin. Man-built mounds consist of individual loads of earth brought to the site, often by the basket load from nearby sources called borrow pits. This results in an intermixture of soils within the mound instead of the more orderly deposit of soil layers that would be encountered in a natural mound.

Indians built mounds for many purposes. They served as fortifications; as effigy mounds representing various mammals, birds, and even humans; as burial mounds; or as artificial hills upon which to set a temple.

The excavation of the upper portion of a temple mound may reveal the type of structure that surmounted it and may yield

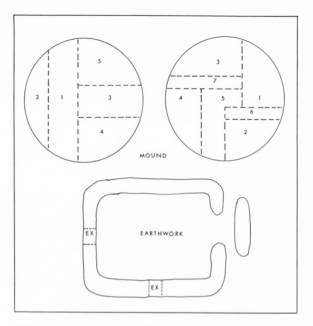

MOUND

EARTHWORK

EX

EX

When investigating an effigy or a fortification mound, select an area that will not damage the appearance of the structure. Cut a slice directly through it so as to reveal a vertical section or profile. This will allow you to record and photograph evidence concerning the method of building the mound. Perhaps the most commonly adopted method of excavating a burial mound is to excavate it in segments, something after the manner of slicing up a cake. Another method is to remove sections directly through the structure revealing several vertical faces for examination.

artifacts that will aid in the determination of the cultural period in which it was built.

Burial mounds are nothing more than exaggerated grave coverings. The primary deposit, or main burial, will usually be found at, or just below, the original surface on which the mound is erected. This may well be a log burial hut, a stone-lined cist, a simple burial pit, a cremation pyre, or some sort of central structure containing a multiple burial. Intrusive burials, often made at a date somewhat later than that of the original mound, may be encountered anywhere within the mound. Your task is to discover and record precisely the history of its construction and the nature of its content. Be on the lookout for indications of any number of successive levels that may indicate as many phases in its construction. These levels may be indicated by a succession of turf lines marking surfaces that have been exposed for some time between stages of construction.

Several techniques have been developed and used in the excavation of mounds. Keep your excavation to a minimum so that you can backfill and repair the damage easily. There is little point in undertaking the complete excavation of fortification or effigy mounds, however. It is far better to preserve them as monuments to a vanished people.

Methods of excavating a burial mound are shown. Both procedures involve the moving of tons of earth and are jobs for a sizable crew under expert supervision. Here again the best possible method is to leave the mound alone and spend your time searching for the living area of the people who built it.

EXCAVATING BURIALS

The excavation of a human burial is one of the most exacting techniques of archaeology. The purpose is to observe and record every detail possible, so that the mortuary customs, religious beliefs, physical traits, and habits of the culture to which the burial belongs may be understood. Particular attention should be given to the deposition and the nature of any grave goods that may be present.

If the skeletal material is sufficiently preserved, a trained observer may be able to determine sex, pathology, cause of death, and other pertinent facts. For example, the following comments were made by a physical anthropologist after examining the remains of a number of individuals that I removed from a burial site in Massachusetts:

"This series of skeletons is large enough so that the characteristics of the Titicut Indians can be reconstructed from their bones. The teeth show rapid wear from early adult life on in most individuals. The dietary of these people was clearly abrasive and wore down the front teeth in particular. Some individuals show dental decay and loss in middle life. The long bones in this population are especially revealing of their mode of life. By and large the muscular attachments of the upper limbs are strong and those of the lower extremities are weaker. This is the kind of musculature to be expected in a people who prefer to travel by boat rather than on foot."

Owing to the similarity between cremation burials and ordinary refuse-pit deposits, the burials are difficult to recognize. The inclusion of well-made artifacts with bits of calcined bone and charcoal would be telltale evidence, especially if red paint is present. The following technique for excavating burials relates to a single direct burial or inhumation, but may be applied with modification to any type of burial (see chapter 4).

A disturbance in the natural layering of the earth will warn you of the presence of a burial. Often the upper portion of the grave shaft will contain charcoal and traces of fire that had been allowed to burn above the burial, probably to discourage investigation by wolves or other predatory animals. Stones and sharp shells were often scattered in the upper grave fill for the same purpose.

The usual refuse pit is round or almost round. If the shape of the disturbance appears as a long oval, you may suspect that a burial is present. In some instances traces of red paint may appear fairly high in the grave shaft, near the surface. Any such disturbance should be treated as a grave until its precise function has been determined.

Locate and measure the plan of the disturbance and note its orientation (direction of north). Clear the overburden from the area for some distance about the top of the grave shaft itself. Then excavate a trench at one side of the disturbance, about a foot from the edge of it and wide and deep enough to work in (2 feet wide by 4 feet deep should suffice). The bottom of the trench should be below the bottom of the grave so that the skeleton, when exposed, will be on a sort of platform.

Never stand on or inside the grave shaft while working. Not only is this most inconvenient, but damage to the skeleton and grave goods is almost certain unless the work of excavation is done from a position outside the shaft. Scrape the earth from the inside of the shaft into the working trench by levels, as indicated by the dotted lines in the profile sketch, watching for signs of the presence of the skeleton. Remember that artifacts may be encountered at any level within the shaft. When you notice the presence of bone, try to determine the position of the skeleton and the direction in which it lies within the shaft. Often the skeleton will lie directly beneath, and in contact with, a dark (black) layer. This is the disintegrated layer of bark that originally protected the body from the surrounding earth.

If you can, locate such key points as the skull, which will be uppermost (higher in the shaft than the associated bones by virtue of its thickness), the elbows, knees, or pelvis. This work must be done with extreme care so as not to dislodge or jar the skeleton in any way. Remember that the bone will probably be soft and can easily be destroyed. Work with a small pointing trowel, brush, or spatula. Once you are certain that you have a burial, it is a good idea to extend the trench all around the shaft so that work can be done from all sides without reaching across the burial. In the process of excavation the skeleton will be left elevated on a sort of platform above the level on which you are standing. You can now work without danger of disturbing either skeleton or grave goods. Start now to take measurements and photographs of the burial itself.

Now that we know how the skeleton lies in the ground and the full extent of the shaft, we are ready to expose it. I like to use such

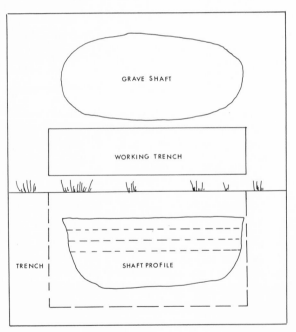

The plan view shows the proper location of the working trench alongside the grave shaft. Standing in the trench, the excavator scrapes earth from inside the shaft by levels, as shown by the dotted lines in the profile view.

This grave shaft was uncovered near Taunton, Massachusetts, on land originally known as the Poole Purchase. Elizabeth Poole and several associates bought the land from the Titicut Indians in 1637.

Excavation of the Poole Purchase grave revealed the remains of a chief accompanied by the trinkets with which the land had been bought—a copper kettle of beans, several iron hoes, a mirror, and glass beads.

Salvage archaeology at Wareham, on Cape Cod, Massachusetts, revealed this flexed burial of a Wampanoag ("White People") man (at left), woman (right), and infant' (indicated by the arrow).

small tools as dental picks, spatulas, teaspoons, and a camel's-hair brush. Start at the center of the burial and work outward.

Expose the central areas first, particularly the rib cage, abdominal cavity, and pelvis. Next expose the long bones of the arms and legs. Start at one end of the bone and follow the length of it with a small knife and brush. Leave the small bones of the feet and hands until last to prevent accidental disturbance of them. Do not attempt to remove the earth from the skull cavities while the skeleton is still *in situ* (in place). Be sure that you leave any associated artifacts in place, leaving little mounds of earth for them to rest on if necessary.

It is difficult for a skeleton to lie about its age. For recording purposes, you will be concerned merely with determining whether the skeleton is that of an infant, a child, a young adult, middle-aged adult, or an old adult.

Infants are individuals up to seven years of age; this can be determined by the eruption of the first permanent molar teeth. A child (seven to fourteen years) is identified by the appearance of the second permanent molars; an adolescent (fourteen to twenty years) when the third permanent molars appear.

A young adult (twenty to forty years) may be identified by some dental attrition, or wearing down of the teeth, the close epiphysis (the uniting of the shaft of the long bone with the joint end), and a partial closing of the cranial (skull) sutures. A middle-aged adult (forty to sixty years) is distinguished by an increasing amount of suture closing, considerable dental wearing, and possibly by some arthritic lipping (distortion) of the spinal vertebrae. An old adult (sixty years and older) is characterized by the loss of many teeth, nearly complete closure of the cranial sutures, and a cindery appearance of the bone.

Sex determination is difficult even for the experienced. Before adolescence it is, for all practical purposes, quite tentative. However, in the adult male the supraorbital ridges of the skull (bony ridge over the eye socket) are usually more prominent than in the female, the projecting mastoid processes (the bone just behind the lower jaw and below the ear) are larger, and the jawbone is more angular.

The pelvic bones are the most reliable sex determinant. The female pelvis is wider and shorter than that of the male, and the pelvic cavity is round in cross section. In the male pelvis the cavity tends to be more triangular in shape. Note in particular the difference in the angle at the base of the pelvis: the angle in the female pelvis is

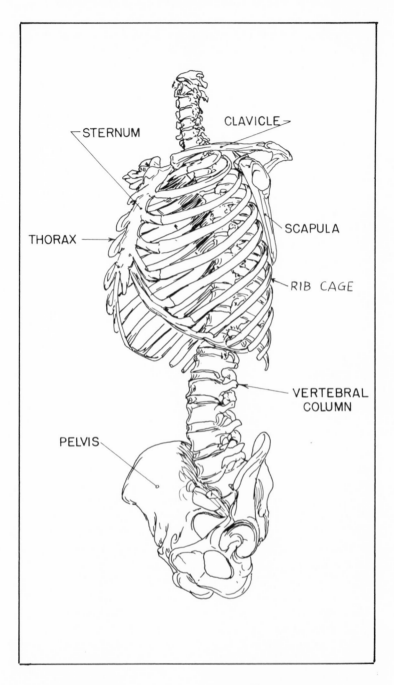

STERNUM

CLAVICLE

THORAX

SCAPULA

RIB CAGE

VERTEBRAL
COLUMN

PELVIS

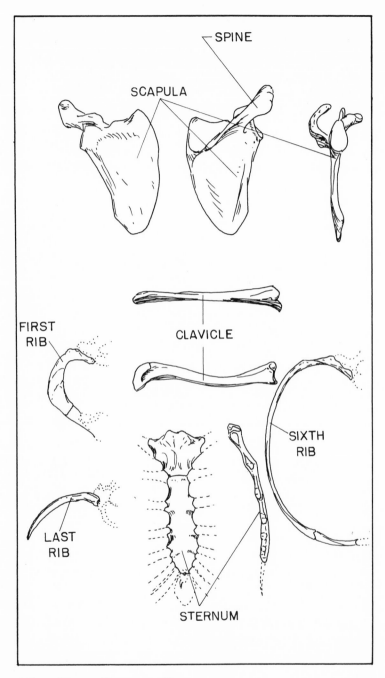

SPINE

SCAPULA

CLAVICLE

FIRST
RIB

SIXTH
RIB

LAST
RIB

STERNUM

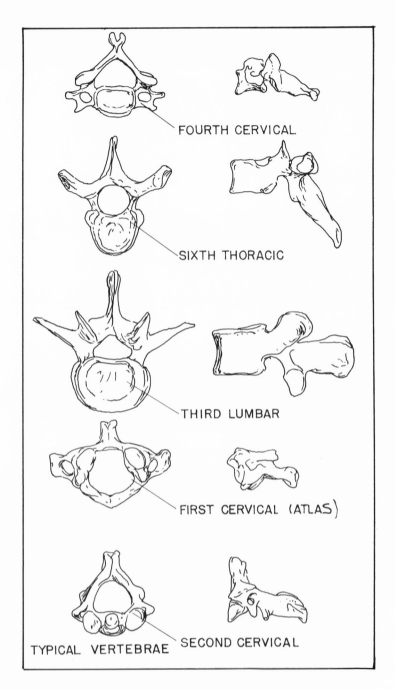

FOURTH CERVICAL

SIXTH THORACIC

THIRD LUMBAR

FIRST CERVICAL (ATLAS)

TYPICAL VERTEBRAE   SECOND CERVICAL

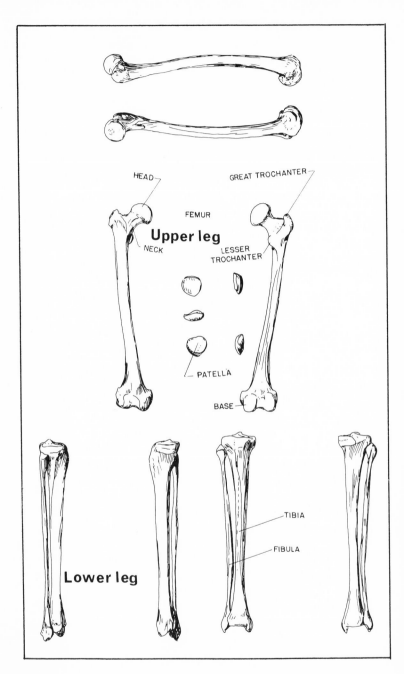

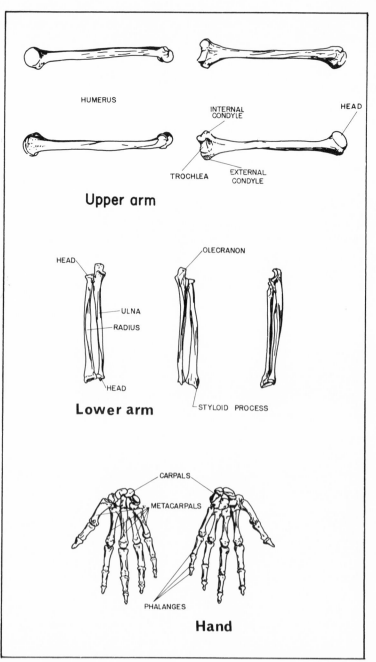

HUMERUS

INTERNAL
CONDYLE

HEAD

TROCHLEA

EXTERNAL
CONDYLE

Upper arm

HEAD

OLECRANON

ULNA

RADIUS

HEAD

Lower arm

STYLOID PROCESS

CARPALS

METACARPALS

PHALANGES

Hand

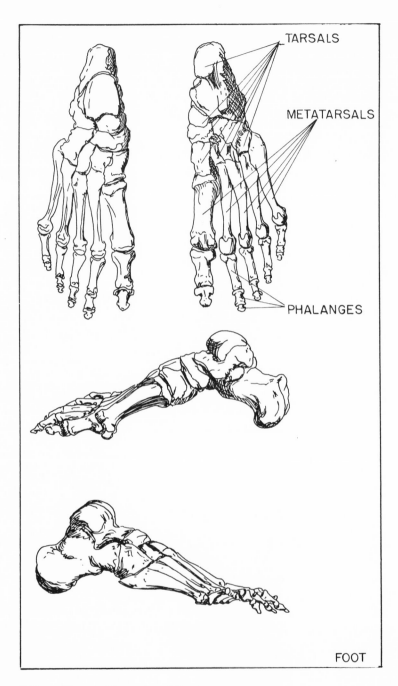

TARSALS

METATARSALS

PHALANGES

FOOT

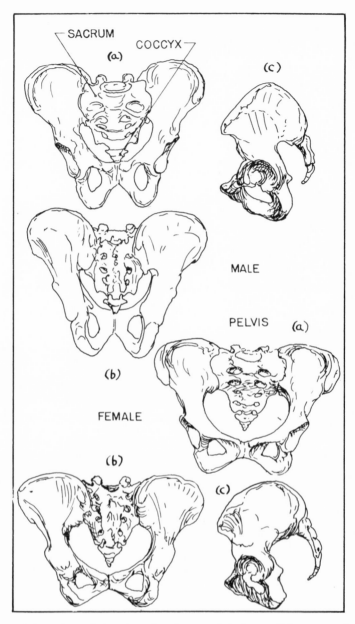

SACRUM

COCCYX

(a)

(c)

MALE

PELVIS (a)

(b)

FEMALE

(b)

(b)

(c)

Adult male and female pelvic bones; (a) front, (b) rear, and (c) side views.

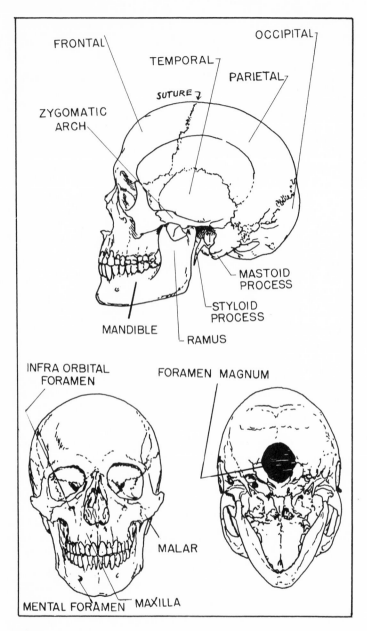

Skulls of young adult human beings.

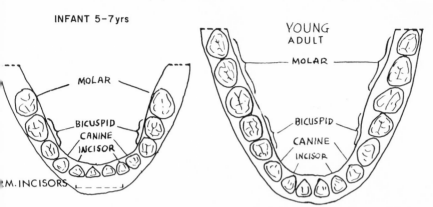

INFANT 5-7yrs

YOUNG ADULT

MOLAR

MOLAR

BICUSPID
CANINE
INCISOR

BICUSPID

CANINE

INCISOR

M. INCISORS

Teeth of infant and young adult.

much less acute than in that of the male. In general, the female skeleton will be lighter in weight and much more slender in appearance. Bear in mind, however, that there are masculine females and feminine males in all races.

Throughout the course of excavation you will be taking careful measurements and photographs. Record the position of artifacts as soon as they are located, in case they should be moved accidentally. There may be stone ornaments, shell or copper artifacts, beads, or even portions of clothing preserved by copper salts. You may notice red or yellow ochre. Pottery vessels may be encountered if the burial is from the proper period. Because the surfaces of such vessels will be extremely soft, they must be treated with great care. A soft brush is the best implement to use in exposing them. Never allow either bone or pottery to be exposed to direct sunlight. Shade it in some way and allow it to dry out very slowly; otherwise it will warp and crack.

In your photography, always use some identification—a lettered card or a small slate upon which you can write in white chalk. Small wooden arrows painted red or white are helpful to call attention to artifacts and special features. Be sure that your records are complete and that you have indicated north. If your sketching is a bit shaky, you can at least draw a stick figure to indicate the position of the skeleton and its component parts. The next chapter will tell you how to record these various types of information.

FLOTATION

For some time, recoveries of seeds and nuts and bones of small mammals, fish, and birds from sites in dry caves in western North America have disclosed the diet of prehistoric groups even before the introduction of agriculture. In areas less favorable to the preservation of such remains, archaeologists have had to rely on guesswork as to the kinds of foods eaten. Now, however, with the application of a new and comparatively simple technique, called flotation, such evidence can be extracted from open sites in other climatic areas.

The fragile remains of prehistory, scattered about once-inhabited areas, concentrated in and about pits or hearths and in habitation floors, are, for the most part, nearly invisible to excavators because of their small size and their ability to assume the coloring of the matrix in which they are found. The field technique of flotation involves the taking of a sample of soil from each cultural feature excavated and one or two control samples as well from an area in which no cultural feature exists, all of which are subject to processing. The processing of a sample consists of two stages: in the field, when it is first collected, the sample is reduced in mass by the removal of the soil matrix; in the laboratory the sample is further reduced, and the organic material is isolated for study.

Field Technique

The materials required for sample reduction are: bags for storing samples, a small wooden tray with a hardware-cloth bottom, and water. The side walls of the tray should be high enough to prevent overwash, and the hardware cloth should be as fine as necessary to allow the passage of soil particles yet retain small seeds and bone fragments. Handles at both ends of the tray are convenient. If water is not available at the site, it must be brought in. At the Wapanucket site a 275-gallon tank from an oil truck was mounted on a small trailer equipped with a pump. A galvanized iron washtub was used for washing, or reducing, the sample.

A given feature sometimes contains different materials, possibly a mass of black colored material at the base and lighter colored materials above. Such a feature is said to contain two components; other features might have several different components. A flotation sample should be taken from each component.

Each sample from a given site should be approximately the same size. A 5-gallon pail for each sample will help to maintain uniformity. A label bearing the feature number or other identification must accompany every sample throughout the process.

The screen operator places the sample in the tray and immerses it in water, taking care to keep the edges of the tray above water. The tray is agitated with a dipping, tipping, seesaw motion, with utmost care so that the fragile remains contained in the mass will not be broken. (This gentler type of reduction is preferable to dry screening as it greatly reduces the breakage of fragile materials, which is typical of dry screening.) The washed content of the try is greatly reduced in bulk by the loss of the fine sand. Whether the water should be replaced with clean water during this process is determined by the nature of the soil and the amount of bulk removed. However, the water should always be changed between samples. After the washing process the sample is no longer suitable for radiocarbon dating.

The washed sample is next emptied into a clean tray, and its identifying label is transferred to the new receptacle. The sample is then dried, either air-dried in a protected place or oven-dried at 250 degrees or less. After drying, the sample is stored (kraft paper bags are appropriate for storage because of their wet strength and slight permeability). Before reusing the screening tray, brush thoroughly to remove any remaining particles.

Laboratory Procedure

The second stage of the flotation technique requires two 18-gallon washtubs, a 6-inch kitchen strainer, a pair of tweezers, and a magnifying glass.

Remove the metal bottom from a washtub and replace it with a 16-mesh bronze screen. The screen should be securely soldered to the upper basal flange. Two lengths of brass welding rod are used to reinforce the screen. Thread the ends of the rods, pass them through holes in opposite sides of the tub, and secure with nuts. Where the brass rods cross at the center they should be bent around each other so as to keep them flush against the screen. Solder the rods together and to the screen at the center. Place the dried sample in this tub.

Fill the second tub about two-thirds full of clean water. Immerse the sample tub in the second tub and rotate with a slight swirling motion to loosen the mass of the sample and to free the lighter organic material it contains from the flakes and pebbles. The lighter material, which will float to the surface, is skimmed off with the kitchen strainer. Place this organic fraction of the sample in a clean tray, lined with newspaper, to dry. If the sample has been thoroughly dried before this step in the flotation process, the heavier organic material—nuts, bone fragments, etc.—will have settled at a slightly slower rate than the pebbles and will, therefore, lie on top of the pebbles. With the aid of a magnifying glass, the heavier organic materials may now be recovered by using tweezers.

Most of the bone fragment will be so small that it cannot be identified except as fish, bird, or mammal bone. Botanical remains will be easily recognizable. The final step is to dry the sample thoroughly, either in the air or in an oven at low heat.

The several organic fractions of the sample will furnish considerable information concerning food preparation habits and plant utilization practiced by the inhabitants of the site. The degree to which the bones are fragmented, ground, or pulverized will tell much about their culinary habits. The diversity of the identified material may furnish clues concerning seasonal diet. Information about the ability of the inhabitants of a site to store foods for use during seasons in which it was scarce may also be acquired.

Since the equipment for flotation is within the means of any group attempting serious archaeological excavation, the technique should be incorporated into every excavator's field method; the results richly justify the effort.

8 : How to Record Data

Good records are the essence of archaeology. They are more valuable than artifacts. Regardless of quality or quantity, artifacts alone cannot tell the story of the people who made and used them. They speak only when accompanied by an accurate record. A record that is too wordy can be pared down, but a record that is incomplete should never be padded out from hazy recollections. Record the evidence as you excavate. Make your record as complete as possible. Check it over to be sure that it is not ambiguous and that you will clearly understand it later.

PRELIMINARY SURVEY RECORDS

Among the most important records in your file are those you keep in the course of your area surveys and field collecting of artifacts (chapter 3). They include your survey maps and preliminary site records.

Survey Maps

Many survey systems have been devised. Some are quite simple; others are much too complicated. Very likely a system already is in use for the particular area in which you plan to work. Find out from the nearest amateur archaeological society or the nearest university with a department of anthropology whether such a system exists. If it does, familiarize yourself with it, and by all means use it. Don't start a duplicate system—there are too many already, and they are most confusing. On the other hand, if no previous system is available, you will have to work out or adopt one of your own.

As a base for your survey, you will need to obtain an index map of the area in which you wish to excavate. This will be furnished by the Geological Survey with the quadrangles you purchase (these

1. Site Name   Wapanucket 16 ....   2.   No. M-22-80

3. Location   East shore Assawompsett Lake - Farm of A.L.Lane ....

Assa. Quad - 70-55,42-55 ....   4.   On contour elevation   78' ....

5. Previous site designations ...... Called Lakeside by Middleboro Arch.Soc. ....

6. Owner   A.L.Lane ....   7.   Address Marion Road,Middleboro,

8. Present tenant   Owner ....

9. Attitude toward excavation   Favorable ....

10. Previous tenants   Present owner has been here about 30 years. Previous owner   or

   tenant unknown. ....

11. Description of site   The site is on the farm of A.L.Lane. A part of the area is under

   ....cultivation and a part is orchard. There is a barn on the orchard area. The orchard

   .... consists of apple trees. ....

12. Area   About one acre ....   13.   Vegetation Brush, trees, cultivated area

14. Nearest water .... on Shore of lake - small spring in orchard near shore.

15. Previous excavation   No archaeological excavation ....

16. Collections (where located)   Owner has a few artifacts - members of the Middleboro

   Arch. Soc. also have some artifacts from the surface. ....

17. Buildings, roads, etc.   Barn and road in orchard ....

18. Cultivation .... See map ....   19.   Erosion   some, particularly along the
                                                                         shore.
20. Photographs (of site) In file .... of artifacts .... none ....

21. Lithic material (local or foreign)   mostly local ....

   ....

22. Published references ....   None ....

23. Possibility of destruction   None at present ....

24. Indian name ....   Unknown ....

25. Associate traits ....   Probably 2 components - Woodland and Archaic

26. Date .... 7/7/53 ....   27.   Recorded By   M.R. ....

Please list artifacts known from this site on reverse.

The information furnished hereon will be considered only for scientific use and will not be made available to
the general public.
1950 Ed.

This type of site survey record is useful for compiling site survey informa-

SITE SURVEY—DETAIL SHEET

(Send in photographs or drawings of material when possible)

CHIPPED BLADES

Triangular Points
Type and Size Large, "isos"
....
....
....

Stemmed Points
(if over 2½" long class as spears)
Show Blade, and Stem Types

Narrow	Round	27
Medium	Ovate	13
Wide	Leaf	45
Ovate	Diamond	2
Lanceolate	Truncated	3
	Corner removed	61
	Bifurcated	1
	Side notched	22
	Eared	3
	Corner removed	45
	Concave	1
	Bossed	
	Fluted	

Knives - same as above, but
with offset blades or stems
....
23
....

Scrapers: Flake	1
Thumbnail	12
Steepedged	3
Stemmed	24

Drills: Bone
Stone (T) Base ___ 3
Others ....

HEAVY TOOLS

Axes or Celts 3 N.G. | No Groove = N. G.
| Part Groove = P. G.
Chipped ___ 1 | Full Groove = F. G.
Pecked ___ 2 | Double Groove = D. G.
Polished ....

ADZES — same as above
5 N.G.

GOUGES ___ 3

SPADES ___ 2

HOES ___ 5

PICKS ___ 2

Others ....

Miscellaneous

Pestles	5
Plummets - Knobbed	2
Sinkers: Perforated	1
Grooved	
Mauls: Natural Stones	
Grooved	
Hammers: Beach Pebble	35
Chipped	
Rubbing Stones	12
Abraders	4

Aesthetic Forms

Gorgets: Shape	
No. of Holes	
Pendants	
Bipennates	1
Pipes: Type	
Material	
Effigies: Subject	
Bird Stones	
Boat Stones	

Vessels - (Sherds) ___ 109

Ceramic: Plain	
Decorated	X
Steatite	none
Worked Bone: Form	
Worked Shell: Form	
Beads: Form	
Material	
Copper: Form	
Fire Sets	
Fire Stones	
Contact Material: Kind	clay pipes - buttons
Red Ochre	X
Graphite	X

Skeletal Material - Description
One skel - fair condition - given to
Peabody Museum, Harvard University
....
Extended burial damaged by plowing.
....
....
....
....

Remarks: Occupied area extends to orchard. If this is ever available it should be excavated
....

tion in a field notebook.

maps are described in detail in chapter 3). Starting with the upper left-hand (northwest) corner, number the quadrangles from left to right, 1, 2, 3, 4, etc., using the abbreviation of the name of the state as a prefix. Continue numbering on the row just below, then the row below that, and so on until a number has been assigned to each quadrangle in the state. In Massachusetts, for instance, there are 52 quadrangles—numbered M-1, M-2, M-3, etc. Each site plotted on the quadrangle has also been given a number, starting with 1. For example, M-22-126 is the 126th site on the 22nd quadrangle in the Massachusetts series. This site number should appear on your site record form as well as on each artifact taken from the site.

Archaeological Site and Survey Records

When you have located the site on your survey map, you will want to visit it and gather more detailed information. Here is the type of information you should obtain. Enter it in your field notebook or on a file card similar to the one shown here.

Owner's name and address. Ownership may change from time to time, so it is a good idea to note down the date on which you obtained the information.

Previous ownership. From a previous owner or tenant you may learn about other collections from the site. You will also want to find out whether the site has already been given a name and number.

Tenant. If the present occupant is a tenant, the owner may be able to furnish additional information. But the tenant is the one from whom you should obtain permission to trespass and excavate.

Description. The physical appearance of the site should be described in detail. Photographs are recommended. The location of the aboriginal (early Indian) site should be determined as precisely as possible. For example, your entry might read: "Small camp site on the edge of the low ground east of the barn." Perhaps there will be evidences of occupation on all disturbed (plowed, etc.) land.

Nearest water. Indians could not store water in quantity and, therefore, would have selected a camp site near a supply of drinking water. Fish, too, may have been important in their economy. If transportation by water was an important factor, a site on or near a navigable stream would have been selected. There is also the possibility that the location of the aboriginal water supply may no longer be readily noticeable.

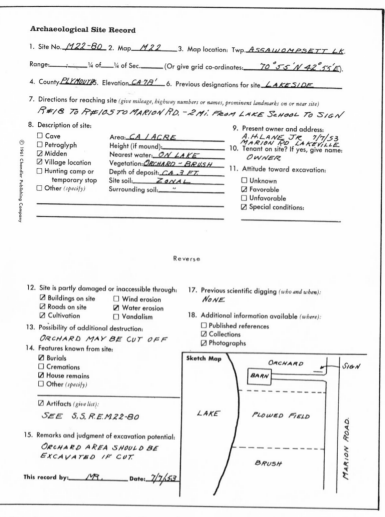

Archaeological Site Record

1. Site No. _M22-80_ 2. Map _M22_ 3. Map location: Twp. _ASSAWOMPSETT LK._

Range:___:___¼ of___¼ of Sec.____(Or give grid co-ordinates:___70°55'N 42°55'E_).

4. County _PLYMOUTH_5. Elevation _CA 78'_ 6. Previous designations for site _LAKESIDE_

7. Directions for reaching site *(give mileage, highway numbers or names, prominent landmarks on or near site)*
R#18 TO R#105 TO MARION RD. -2 MI. FROM LAKE SCHOOL TO SIGN

8. Description of site:

☐ Cave   Area: _CA 1 ACRE_
☐ Petroglyph   Height (if mound)____
☑ Midden   Nearest water: _ON LAKE_
☑ Village location   Vegetation: _ORCHARD - BRUSH_
☐ Hunting camp or   Depth of deposit: _CA. 3 FT._
   temporary stop   Site soil: _ZONAL_
☐ Other *(specify)*   Surrounding soil: ___"___

9. Present owner and address:
A. H. LANE JR 7/7/53
MARION RD LAKEVILLE
10. Tenant on site? If yes, give name:
OWNER
11. Attitude toward excavation:

☐ Unknown
☑ Favorable
☐ Unfavorable
☑ Special conditions:

Reverse

12. Site is partly damaged or inaccessible through:
☑ Buildings on site   ☐ Wind erosion
☑ Roads on site   ☑ Water erosion
☑ Cultivation   ☐ Vandalism

13. Possibility of additional destruction:
ORCHARD MAY BE CUT OFF

14. Features known from site:
☑ Burials
☐ Cremations
☑ House remains
☐ Other *(specify)*

☑ Artifacts *(give list)*:
SEE S.S.R.E.M22-80

15. Remarks and judgment of excavation potential:
ORCHARD AREA SHOULD BE
EXCAVATED IF CUT.

This record by:___MR.___ Date: _7/7/53_

17. Previous scientific digging *(who and when)*:
NONE

18. Additional information available *(where)*:
☐ Published references
☑ Collections
☑ Photographs

Sketch Map

LAKE   PLOWED FIELD   ORCHARD   SIGN   BARN   BRUSH   MARION ROAD.

© 1961 Chandler Publishing Company

Archaeological site record file cards are useful for recording site survey information in abbreviated form.

Area of the site. Determine the extent of the occupied area if possible—it may intrude on a neighboring property.

Physical condition. Is the entire site under cultivation? Are there wooded areas? Is the site subject to erosion or flooding at times of high water?

How to Record Data   153

Previous work. Are there indications of previous archaeological work at the site? If there are, you will want to check up on this work and add the available data to your file.

Artifacts. If you have found artifacts or other evidence of Indian occupation—rejects, burned stone from the aboriginal fireplaces, etc., —make this data a part of your record.

Sketch map. Make a sketch map of the site. Show all natural features as well as the location of all buildings, fences, and so on. Swampy or low areas are important features, as are kitchen midden deposits, shell piles, or refuse pits exposed by plowing. Don't forget to indicate the scale you have used and the orientation (direction of north).

As you gain skill in surveying, you will add many more items of information to those suggested. Some archaeologists like to keep a separate notebook for each site or for those on which there has accumulated considerable data. A convenient method is to make your observations in a field notebook, transferring them later to a form for your file. Printed forms (costing $1 for 60 forms) similar to those illustrated may be purchased (see appendix of *The Archaeologist's Note Book*, Chandler Publishing Co., 604 Mission St., San Francisco, California 94105).

Be sure to include the identification of any artifacts found, so that they can be attributed to the site from which they came. This record will be of paramount importance to you as the types of artifacts begin to have meaning and as you learn to associate them with chronological periods and cultures.

SITE EXCAVATION RECORDS

The records you take during the excavation of an archaeological site are necessarily more extensive and detailed than survey records. Once a grid for the control of excavation has been set up, the control stakes placed in position and properly identified on a map of the site, and the levels measured (see chapter 5), you are ready to excavate and to record your discoveries.

Because excavation and destruction are synonymous, you must keep a full and accurate description of what you observe as the work progresses. This record provides the only source from which a reconstruction of the site can be made. The idea is to keep a daily or hourly narrative of your work: what you found, how you found it, and

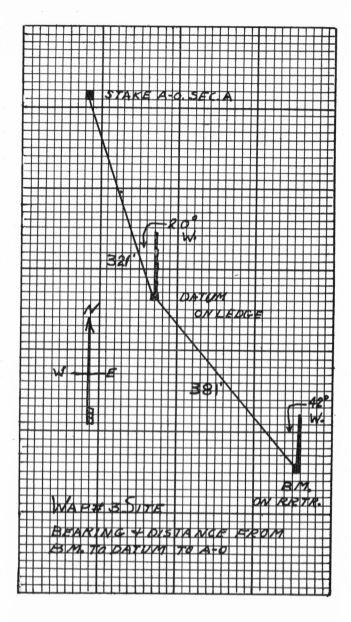

The cross-sectional page of a surveyor's or engineer's notebook provides for proportionate sketching during the course of excavation.

what you thought about it at the time. This record later will be modified or expanded when the time comes to write a site report. Your purpose is to reconstruct the culture of the aboriginal occupants of the site. Every artifact you find, every feature you excavate is an integral part of that culture. Once you remove it from its position in the ground, no one will ever see it again in its original context, as you saw it, except through your notes, pictures, and sketches. An archaeological discovery is only as good as the notes that accompany it.

In the course of excavation, records or notes are made of both natural soil conditions and artificial conditions, such as aboriginal features and the more modern disturbances that may have interfered with them. Again you may prefer to use a notebook. This should be a book with the pages bound in so that they will not fall out and be lost. A surveyor's or engineer's notebook is ideal; one side of each page is cross-sectioned and thus provides a page for proportionate sketching. If you prefer to use individual cards or forms, either in conjunction with, or in place of, a notebook, those illustrated will be most efficient.

Daily Field Record

This field record is designed to keep a daily account of progress as well as to provide a place for general observations. The summary of artifacts and features found, provides a supplementary record duplicating the more specific records discussed on the following pages. This duplicate record will prove extremely valuable if the detailed ones are lost or damaged. Such data as weather and lighting conditions or the number of visitors at the site on a given afternoon may strike you as irrelevant, but it is surprising how often such information is useful. A group of unsatisfactory photographs, for example, may be the result of poor lighting; or a mob of inquisitive visitors may account for a failure to take certain records. Make notes of your own thoughts and observations as you work; in them you may preserve valuable items that no one thought to record.

Feature Record

Indian pits, hearths, and so on, which may be encountered in the course of excavation, are called features. In short, anything made by the occupants of the site—other than their weapons, tools, or artifacts —is a feature. Designate them by a collective term and assign num-

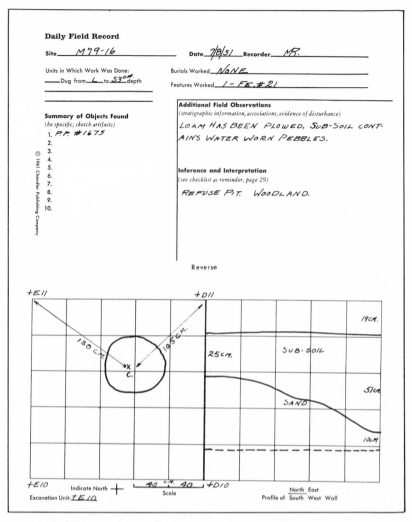

Daily Field Record

Site _M79-16_   Date _7/8/51_ Recorder _MR._

Units in Which Work Was Done:
___ Dug from _6_ to _53 cm._ depth

Burials Worked _NONE_
Features Worked _1 - FE. #21_

Summary of Objects Found
(be specific; sketch artifacts)
1. _P.P. #1675_
2.
3.
4.
5.
6.
7.
8.
9.
10.

© 1961 Chandler Publishing Company

Additional Field Observations
(stratigraphic information, associations, evidence of disturbance)

LOAM HAS BEEN PLOWED. SUB-SOIL CONT-
AINS WATER WORN PEBBLES.

Inference and Interpretation
(see checklist as reminder, page 29)

REFUSE PIT. WOODLAND.

Reverse

+E11   +D11

19CM.

130 CM   105 CM.   25CM.   SUB-SOIL

×X
C.

SAND   51CM.

10CM

+E10   Indicate North +   40 CM. 40 +D10
Excavation Unit: _E 10_   Scale   Profile of South West Wall   North East

The daily field record provides a summary account of progress made during excavation.

bers as a single series. This is better than attempting to determine the function and to keep a record of each type. Assign the designation Fe. 1 to the first feature you find on the site. Make certain that that number appears in all photographs and records. Later when you

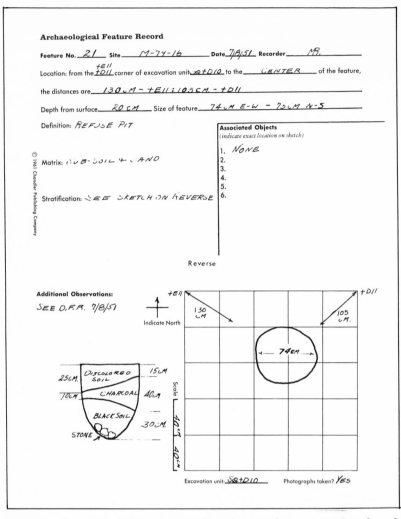

Archaeological Feature Record

Feature No. *21* Site *M-74-16* Date *7/8/51* Recorder *MB.*

Location: from the *+E11 / +D11* corner of excavation unit *2Q+D10* to the *CENTER* of the feature,

the distances are *130 CM - +E11 : 105 CM. - +D11*

Depth from surface *80 CM* Size of feature *74 CM E-W - 75 CM N-S*

Definition: *REFUSE PIT*

© 1961 Chandler Publishing Company

Matrix: *SUB-SOIL + SAND*

Stratification: *SEE SKETCH ON REVERSE*

Associated Objects
(indicate exact location on sketch)
1. *NONE*
2.
3.
4.
5.
6.

Reverse

Additional Observations:
SEE D.F.R. 7/8/51

Indicate North

+E11

+D11

130 CM

105 CM.

74 CM

25 CM. DISCOLORED SOIL 15 CM
70 CM. CHARCOAL 40 CM
BLACK SOIL 30 CM
STONE

Scale

40" — 40 CM

Excavation unit: *2Q+D10*   Photographs taken? *YES*

In the archaeological feature record, series numbers are assigned and recorded for archaeological features uncovered at each site.

write your report, you can determine the function of the feature and assign another number to it if you wish.

As soon as you notice anything indicating the presence of a feature—a sudden change in the color of the soil or perhaps a deposit of charcoal or collection of burned stones—the recording process begins. Assign a number, enter it on the feature record, and write it on a card (or perhaps a small slate) that will appear in your photographs.

Determine the approximate center of the feature and take measurements from two adjacent stakes. Also take a vertical measurement from the present surface of the ground to the top of the feature. Note the position of the top with regard to the soil layers. Your record, for example, might read: "Top of feature 107 was first noted at a depth of 2 inches [or perhaps 5 centimeters] below the bottom of the loam in yellow subsoil."

The layering and total content of a feature are important and should be noted and sketched as the excavation proceeds. The presence and location of ash, charcoal, discolored soil, burned or unburned stone, and artifacts that appear to be associated with the feature should be noted and sketched as the excavation progresses,

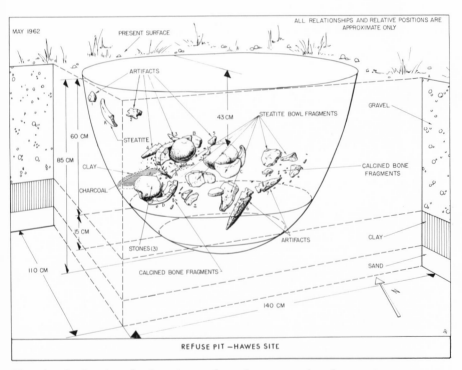

The sketch showing the layering and total content of a feature is an important part of the record.

including measurements indicating horizontal and vertical positions.

The diameter of the top of a feature should also be a part of the initial record. When taking horizontal measurements, be sure to hold the tape level or, in the case of a vertical measurement, at a right angle to the surface. Sloppy technique can cause many errors.

You will probably find that you are hampered by the possession of only two hands and that you must either ask someone to help or use a mechanical aid, if measurements are to be accurate. A simple device developed by Rei Heino of the Massachusetts Archaeological Society's Cohannet Chapter will prove extremely useful. The following paragraphs and accompanying drawing describe this device.

Using the Cohannet Line. The component parts of the Cohannet Line may be purchased at any hardware store. They consist of two 20-penny nails (surveyor's pins may be substituted); a spring-type plastic or wooden clothespin; a small, lightweight plumb bob (aluminum is preferred); and about 10 feet of chalk line.

Two holes must be made through the top of each arm of the

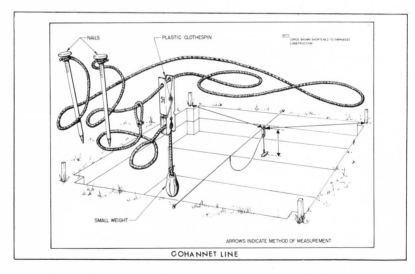

COHANNET LINE

The Cohannet Line is a simple mechanical device for making exact measurements of a feature's location. It is set up so that the plumb bob is suspended directly over the center of the feature.

The location of all artifacts and features must be carefully measured, then recorded.

clothespin for the passage of the chalk line. In the case of a plastic clothespin this is accomplished by heating a small nail and pushing it through the top of each arm so that the hole in one will be slightly higher than the hole in the other. The purpose of having the holes offset is to cause the plumb line to form a right angle with the one arm of the pin. Make another hole at the base of the arm in which the lower of the two previous perforations has been made. The upper end of the plumb bob line will pass through this hole.

Now cut two lengths from the chalk line. One 6-foot piece will form the horizontal line; the second, a 4-foot piece, will be the vertical or plumb bob line. The lengths of these two lines may be varied according to the width of the squares being excavated. Fasten one end of the longer line to a 20-penny nail, pass it through the holes at the top of the clothespin arms, and fasten the free end to the second nail. Next, pass the shorter line (plumb bob or vertical line) through the hole at the base of the clothespin and secure to the plumb bob. Tie a loop in the free end around the horizontal line so that it can slide. Coating the lines with wax and placing a dab of cement on the knots will help. Paint a red dab on the end of the clothespin in the vertical line of the plumb bob. This will serve as a measuring point.

This device is so simple to use that the following description is unnecessary. However, it is perhaps just as well to be on the safe side and include the explanation. Care in setting up the device will pay off in accurate measurements. Push the nails into the ground on opposite sides of the square, as shown. The horizontal line thus becomes an extension of the present surface of the ground above the feature or artifact to be measured. Move the clothespin along the horizontal line to a point directly above the point to be determined. Release the pressure of the clothespin on the vertical line. Slide the free end along the horizontal line to take up the slack and adjust the vertical length so that the plumb bob is suspended directly above the point to be measured. Both hands are now free to handle the tape, and an accurate measurement can be taken from the corner stakes of the square to the artificial measuring point (red dab) on the clothespin, which will be directly above the true point. In this way errors due to an accidental angle of the tape are eliminated. Vertical distance or depth from the present surface of the ground can also be measured accurately from the horizontal line.

Set up the Cohannet Line just as soon as the center of a feature can be determined. Adjust the measurement point to the center, and leave in place as the excavation proceeds. The tip of the plumb bob will serve as a convenient and permanent center from which to measure any artifacts or other objects that may be included. If the center of the feature should shift, that fact will be noticeable immediately and you can then correct the record. You may have several lines in use simultaneously in order to mark the location of artifacts that must be removed in the process of excavation.

Archaeological Stratigraphy Record

The stratigraphy, or natural arrangement, of the various types of soil in all excavated squares should be a part of the record. When you have completely excavated the square, clean the four vertical faces and make a sketch to show the position of soil horizons or layers (chapter 6) complete with measurements.

The upper horizon will consist of loam or topsoil (sometimes called the overburden). In a cultivated area the lower horizon of the loam will be a false horizon created by plowing. The second layer may be subsoil, colored yellow or brown by acids from the topsoil. Perhaps the third layer will be sand. Layers of different soils—clay,

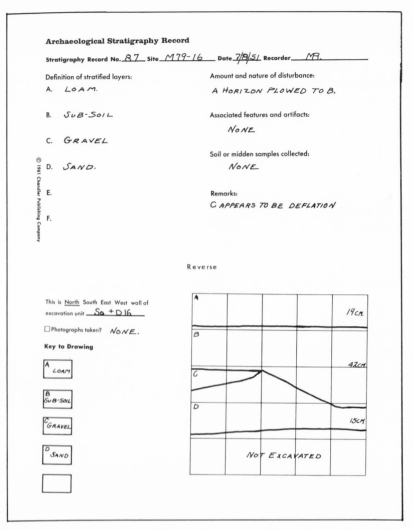

Archaeological Stratigraphy Record

Stratigraphy Record No. _87_ Site _M79-16_ Date _7/8/51_ Recorder _MR._

Definition of stratified layers:

A. _LOAM._

B. _SUB-SOIL_

C. _GRAVEL_

D. _SAND._

E.

F.

Amount and nature of disturbance:

A HORIZON PLOWED TO B.

Associated features and artifacts:

NONE

Soil or midden samples collected:

NONE

Remarks:

C APPEARS TO BE DEFLATION

© 1961 Chandler Publishing Company

Reverse

This is <u>North</u> South East West wall of
excavation unit _S0 + D16_

☐ Photographs taken? _NONE._

Key to Drawing

A
LOAM

B
SUB-SOIL

C
GRAVEL

D
SAND

A

B   19CM.

                                           42CM

C

D   15CM

NOT EXCAVATED

The archaeological stratigraphy record contains a description and measurements of the soil types in the horizons of all excavated squares.

silt, fine sand, coarse gravel, or a buried layer of old topsoil—may be encountered at any depth.

Describe these layers accurately and measure them so that they

How to Record Data   163

will match up with adjoining sections of the soil profile or outline (chapter 6) that will turn up in adjacent squares. For example, your notes might read: "Encountered a layer of coarse sand containing many small pebbles (pea size to egg size), rounded and smooth, at a depth of 5.5 inches (19 cm.) from the present surface. This layer was 20 inches (51 cm.) thick at Stake +D11 and 10 inches (25 cm.) thick at Stake +E11—see Stratigraphy Record #56, Profile of S.W. wall, and Daily Field Record for July 8, 1951." When the stratigraphy is complicated or diagnostic (especially meaningful), a useful aid will be a photograph that includes signs and arrows calling attention to the various types of soil. In such cases, a note in the archaeological stratigraphy would be made to tie in with the archaeological photo record.

Artifact Record

Each artifact should have its individual record card or entry in the field notebook. Take the usual three measurements—two horizontal and one vertical. Entries should be made noting the type of soil in which the artifact was found and the position of the artifact in the ground (whether it is horizontal, point up, or point down). Note any associations between a specific artifact and other objects, artifacts, features, animal burrows, and so on. Make an outline drawing of the artifact in the record or, if too large, make a miniature sketch with the dimensions indicated. Mention the material from which it is made; if it is broken, note that fact. Assign an artifact number. Whether or not you place this number on the artifact at the time of excavation is not too important as long as there is sufficient identification to insure proper association with the record at a later time. Some archaeologists prefer to place an artifact in a paper bag and write the number on the bag. If the artifact was taken from a feature, make certain that the feature number is given. In the case of diagnostic artifacts, a photograph of the artifact in its original position should be a part of the record.

Archaeological Field Catalog

The record of the total number of artifacts found is a duplicate record in a sense. However, it can be extremely useful if you ever have the misfortune to lose or damage an artifact record. It should

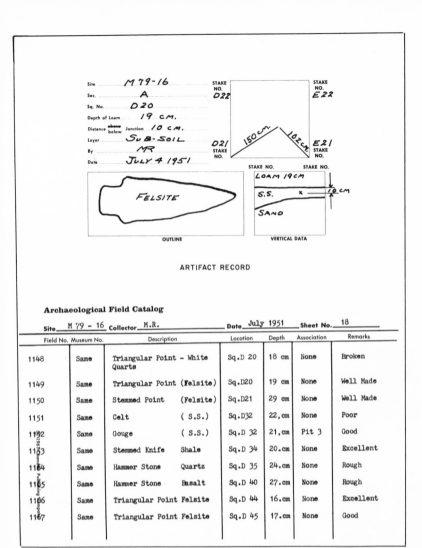

Site ..... M 79-16
Sec. ..... A
Sq. No. ..... D 20
Depth of Loam ..... 19 CM.
Distance above/below Junction ..... 10 CM.
Layer ..... SUB-SOIL
By ..... MR
Date ..... JULY 4 1951

STAKE NO. D22   STAKE NO. E22
D21 STAKE NO.   150 CM.   102 CM.   E21 STAKE NO.
STAKE NO.   STAKE NO.

LOAM 19CM
S.S.   10 CM
SAND

FELSITE

OUTLINE

VERTICAL DATA

ARTIFACT RECORD

Archaeological Field Catalog

Site M 79 - 16   Collector M.R.   Date July 1951   Sheet No. 18

Field No.	Museum No.	Description	Location	Depth	Association	Remarks
1148	Same	Triangular Point - White Quarts	Sq.D 20	18 cm	None	Broken
1149	Same	Triangular Point (Felsite)	Sq.D20	19 cm	None	Well Made
1150	Same	Stemmed Point (Felsite)	Sq.D21	29 cm	None	Well Made
1151	Same	Celt (S.S.)	Sq.D32	22, cm	None	Poor
1152	Same	Gouge (S.S.)	Sq.D 32	21, cm	Pit 3	Good
1153	Same	Stemmed Knife Shale	Sq.D 34	20. cm	None	Excellent
1154	Same	Hammer Stone Quartz	Sq.D 35	24.cm	None	Rough
1155	Same	Hammer Stone Basalt	Sq.D 40	27.cm	None	Rough
1156	Same	Triangular Point Felsite	Sq.D 44	16.cm	None	Excellent
1157	Same	Triangular Point Felsite	Sq.D 45	17.cm	None	Good

Each artifact has its description and measurements recorded on its individual artifact card or record. Assign an artifact number, make an outline sketch, and enter all pertinent details (material, associated features, type of soil in which found, etc.). The archaeological field catalog serves as a duplicate record should the artifact record be lost or damaged.

include the number of the artifact, a description of it, the location or number of the square from which it was taken, the depth at which it was found, and any associations noted.

Archaeological Burial Record

No description or archaeological recording procedure would be complete without mention of the excavation of human burials. I am not unduly squeamish, but I happen to feel that human skeletal remains should not be regarded in the same light as other relics of the past. There is something incongruous—if not immoral—in removing a human skeleton from its final resting place if the remains are destined to become part of a private collection of artifacts and relics. If the bones are in such poor condition that little, if any, information of a scientific nature can be determined from them, it is better to leave them *in situ* after you have completed your record. On the other hand, if the skeleton is in good condition and could be of value to a physical anthropologist in his study of pathology and race, it should be excavated properly. Do not overlook the fact that there may be laws regulating the excavation of human remains in the area in which you are working. It is your responsibility to find out what these laws are and how they may affect your investigations.

In case you are not familiar with the techniques of excavating a burial, I suggest that you report the presence of such a feature to an expert in this phase of archaeology. Let him remove and preserve the remains. Be content to observe, make your field record, and take your photographs. This is the best way to learn the technique and to become proficient in an important aspect of archaeological excavation.

Often a burial is in danger of destruction if it is not removed. If this is the case—and an expert cannot be immediately contacted—you must perform the task yourself. Proceed with care, make an accurate record, and preserve the skeletal material from breakage. Then place the material in the safekeeping of someone who will make proper use of it. Such remains, when accompanied by proper records, will be received gratefully by any physical anthropologist and will not injure your record as a serious amateur.

In excavating a burial, your purpose will be to record every significant detail possible. Artifacts, features, or anything that appears to be associated with it should receive your careful attention. A great

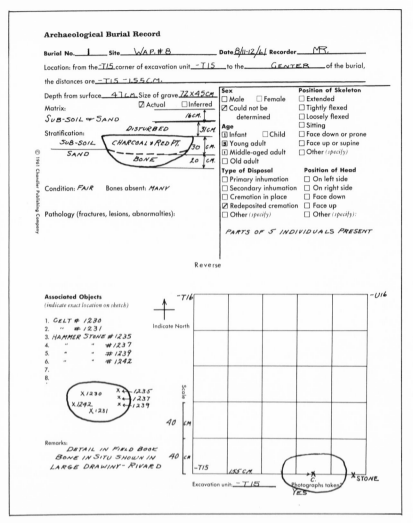

Archaeological Burial Record

Burial No. **1** Site **W.A.P. #8** Date **8/11-12/61** Recorder **MR.**

Location: from the **-T15** corner of excavation unit **-T15** to the **CENTER** of the burial,

the distances are **-T15 -155 CM.**

Depth from surface **47 CM.** Size of grave **72×45 CM**

Matrix: ☑ Actual ☐ Inferred

SUB-SOIL & SAND 16 CM.

Stratification:
DISTURBED 31 CM.
SUB-SOIL CHARCOAL & RED PT. 30 CM.
SAND BONE 20 CM.

Condition: **FAIR** Bones absent: **MANY**

Pathology (fractures, lesions, abnormalties):

© 1961 Chandler Publishing Company

Sex
☐ Male ☐ Female
☑ Could not be
  determined

Age
☐ Infant ☐ Child
☒ Young adult
☐ Middle-aged adult
☐ Old adult

Type of Disposal
☐ Primary inhumation
☐ Secondary inhumation
☐ Cremation in place
☑ Redeposited cremation
☐ Other (specify)

Position of Skeleton
☐ Extended
☐ Tightly flexed
☐ Loosely flexed
☐ Sitting
☐ Face down or prone
☐ Face up or supine
☐ Other (specify)

Position of Head
☐ On left side
☐ On right side
☐ Face down
☐ Face up
☐ Other (specify):

PARTS OF 5 INDIVIDUALS PRESENT

Reverse

Associated Objects
(indicate exact location on sketch)

1. CELT # 1230
2. " # 1231
3. HAMMER STONE # 1235
4. " " # 1237
5. " " # 1239
6. " " # 1242
7.
8.

X 1230   X ← 1235
         X ← 1237
X 1242   X ← 1239
   X 1231

Remarks:
    DETAIL IN FIELD BOOK
  BONE IN SITU SHOWN IN
LARGE DRAWING - RIVARD

-T16   **-U16**

↑ Indicate North

Scale

40 CM

40 CM

-T15   155 CM

Excavation unit: **-T15**

STONE

Photographs taken? **YES**

All significant details about a burial, including associated artifacts and features, are entered in the archaeological burial record.

deal of valuable information concerning the burial customs of a people can be realized from such records (see description of types of burials in chapter 4, and of excavation techniques in chapter 7).

Archaeological Photo Record

General Subject __M- 22-80__ Photographer __M.R.__ Date __7/7/53__ Camera __Reflex 4__

Roll or Pack No.	Exposure No.	Subject	Looking toward	Negative catalog No.
60	1	View from Barn looking toward lake.	East	65
60	2	View from lake toward barn	West	66
60	3	View from Marion Road	East	67
60	4	Orchard from plowed field	North	68
60	5	Sign by road	North	69
60	6	Plowed field	East	70
60	7	Closeup of artifacts found in plowed field 7/7/53		71
60	8	Stone axe from Orchard		72
60	9	Artifacts found by Mr. Lane exact spot ubknwon		73

The archaeological photo record identifies all photographs taken of the site. These may include serial and ground photographs taken during the preliminary site survey as well as those of work in progress and of individual artifacts or features.

Archaeological Photo Record

The purpose of taking archaeological photographs is to provide a permanent record of archaeological finds. Before taking a picture, therefore, make certain that identification marks, artifact markers, square numbers, feature numbers, orientation arrows, and the like are in place within the field of the camera. Do not rely upon your memory to recall all of these details, or you will end up with many pictures that you will be unable to place. Artistic composition is helpful, of course, especially if the pictures are intended for later publication or showing to a nonscientific audience, but it is not essential. Concentrate upon the record rather than the artistic quality of your pictures. Relative size of objects may be indicated by including a scale or some object the size of which is obvious. Remember to include in your record the aerial photographs taken in connection with your preliminary survey.

Artifacts and hearth are well identified in this archaeological photographic record. Note the site and feature number markers, scales, and direction indicator.

ARCHAEOLOGICAL PHOTOGRAPHY

Photography plays an important part in the recording of archaeological data. After a feature has been excavated and destroyed, nothing is more frustrating than to discover that some important detail has been overlooked in the recording. Good photographic coverage may supply the missing information. But this is not the only function of photography in archaeology. You will also want good black-and-white photographs for your final report and colored slides to illustrate the talks you will be called upon to give later on.

What Camera to Choose

Cameras and auxiliary equipment are always a part of the archaeologist's tool kit. Perhaps you are asking yourself: What sort of a camera should I have for this work? The answer to this will depend upon the answers to two more questions: What kind of a picture do I want to take? How much can I afford to invest in photography (including camera, film, and processing)?

You will want a camera that will make clear, sharp pictures, in color and black-and-white, under a variety of lighting conditions. It should focus accurately and easily, be rugged yet not too bulky to carry. Good cameras are available at prices ranging from $25 to $500. All cameras can be used for taking pictures, just as all pencils can be used for drawing sketches. The end result will be governed by the ability of the person using the tool. Study the camera you have decided upon and learn to use its capabilities.

To choose between the various types of cameras, we must know what each one will do for us. There is the old, reliable box camera, for instance, known and used by almost everyone at some time or another. Pictures with a box camera must be made with good lighting and under ideal conditions. The action is slow and the subject cannot be closer than 8 to 10 feet. A general view taken with a box camera may appear to give a satisfactory picture, but a close examination of the negative from, and enlargement of, it will tell a different story. The picture is never really sharp and clear, but tends to be grainy or fuzzy. The box camera is too clumsy to carry and use. Obviously, it is not ideal for our purpose.

The Kodak or folding camera is more convenient to carry and is also a little more expensive (from about $15 to $100). Some cameras of this type are simple to use—and are not much more efficient than the box camera. Others are more complex, have fine lenses, good action, and will accept auxiliary lenses for close-up work. They use a medium-sized ($3\frac{1}{2} \times 3\frac{1}{2}$ in. or $3\frac{1}{2} \times 5$ in.) roll film. This means that picture will not have to be enlarged too much and you need not worry about the size of the grain in the negative. Many excellent models are available, both new and secondhand. A camera of this type will serve your purpose very well.

Even better is the twin-lens reflex camera, the Rolleiflex type. This is an extremely popular camera and ranges in price from $20 to $300. It is equipped with two lenses, one located above the other. The upper, or viewing, lens provides a full-sized image that is reflected upward by a mirror on ground glass. The lower lens actually takes the picture. These cameras usually take twelve $2\frac{1}{4} \times 2\frac{1}{4}$-inch pictures per roll of No. 120 film, which gives a good-quality negative at reasonable cost (black-and-white film from 35¢ to 50¢ per roll, color from $1.25 to $1.50). The cheaper models of this type of camera have certain disadvantages. They lack a most important feature—close-up focusing. For close-up focusing with these cheaper models, therefore, you will need two additional auxiliary lenses, one for each lens of the camera. When using these close-up lenses, another problem—called parallax—will arise. This means that at close range the upper, or viewing, lens will not see precisely what the lower, or picture-taking, lens will see and you must allow for this error. A final disadvantage is that most cameras of this type (check with your photo supply dealer for possible exceptions) do not accept a wide-angle or telephoto lens. Despite these disadvantages, however, it is an excellent camera for the archaeologist.

The camera that I consider best of all is the single-lens reflex type (priced from $20 to $200). Most of these cameras use 35 mm. film, which gives you 20 or 36 pictures per roll. Some of the latest models use No. 120 film. This camera makes use of a mirror to reflect the image upward to the eye. With this camera, however, you can see the image directly through the taking lens, and you see precisely the picture you will take, regardless of whether you are close to, or far away from, the subject. Auxiliary lenses must be used for closer work —3 feet or less—but there is no parallax problem. Most of these cameras have removable lenses and will accept both wide-angle and telephoto lenses. If you must be content with one camera, this is it.

A good "second camera" for your kit is the press-type (costing from $25 to $500). I like to keep my single-lens reflex loaded with color film and depend upon my press camera for black-and-white pictures. In spite of its bulk and weight, this is the best camera for all-around use when you want maximum picture quality. It uses either roll or cut film of various sizes and produces negatives from which either contact prints or enlargements may be made. It is not simple to operate, but if you will take the time to learn how to use it, you will be well rewarded by the results.

We might say just a word about the Polaroid Land cameras (about $145 to $160) with their ability to produce in a matter of min-utes a finished picture in black-and-white or color. Black-and-white film costs about $2 to $4, color film about $5. This camera has one disadvantage—it does not make a re-usable negative—but copies of the picture can be made. Pictures taken with this camera will serve as a good check on exposure time and composition for a larger, more expensive color shot.

Although it cannot be classed as an archaeological necessity, I carry a third camera of the stereo type (about $25 to $80). This camera has two lenses operated by a single release and takes 16 pairs of pictures on a 20-exposure 35 mm. roll. The lenses are spaced horizontally apart at about the distance between the eyes, producing a pair of pictures at a slightly different angle from each other. When seen through a viewer, the transparencies provide a remarkably life-like, three-dimensional reproduction of the scene or object, with a depth of perspective unobtainable by a single lens. These slides are excellent for recalling the actual appearance of archaeological features. One disadvantage is that stereo pictures must be shown in a hand-held viewer, as there is no good method of projecting them on a screen.

When all is said and done, however, photography should be considered as a necessary accessory to—not a substitute for—the written record. The quality of a field excavation often is revealed by photographs of the digging activities. The reader of a report is bound to assume that workers who are careful and methodical in their excavation techniques are equally careful in their interpretation and study. The reverse is also true. Photographs revealing slovenly, haphazard field techniques brand the project as the work of poorly trained or careless archaeologists.

9 : How to Preserve and Restore Your Finds

Some people feel that an ancient object should look old. They say that the dust and grime of centuries should not be removed under any circumstances. They claim that any attempt to clean and restore the object is nothing short of cheating. I agree—if this were done in an effort to deceive. But there is no deception if the object is restored simply to show how it appeared before it was ravaged by time and the elements. In fact, I prefer to restore the specimen so that it will look, as much as possible, the way it did when it was used by the original owner.

Before embarking on any cleaning or preservation project, be sure that you have correctly identified the material with which you are dealing. It is important to understand the changes that deterioration has caused, or may cause in the future, so that you can apply the proper treatment. It is always a good idea to proceed with caution. Often what appears to be dirt turns out to be something else—paint, for instance. Many a good specimen has been ruined by too vigorous cleaning.

CLEANING

Unpainted hard stone objects may be washed safely with warm soap and water. For all other materials, dry cleaning is preferred. When a specimen is thoroughly dry, most of the dirt can be brushed or blown off. In stubborn cases, however, a liquid cleaning agent may be used sparingly.

Before cleaning specimens of such materials as antler, shell, wood, glass, iron, porous stone, and pottery, check to see if salt is present. If it is, remove it by soaking the specimen in fresh water. In the case of fragile pottery make certain that it is absolutely dry and

173

hard prior to soaking. This is important because, upon drying, salt in solution will recrystallize inside or on the specimen. This action creates internal pressures that may split the specimen or cause the surface to flake off.

How to Check for Salt

Soak the specimen in fresh water (in the case of pottery, use one of the sherds). Remove the specimen and add to the water a drop or two of silver nitrate, which may be obtained at any drug store or chemical supply house. If salt is present, the water will become cloudy.

If salt is present let the specimen soak in fresh water for about an hour, then make a second salt test. Repeat this procedure until a negative salt test results. When checking clay pottery, this procedure must be watched carefully in order not to destroy the sherd. It is better to have some salt present than to destroy the specimen in the process of restoration.

Liquid Cleaning Agents

Depending upon the material with which you are dealing, water, alcohol, acetone, ether, or gasoline are good cleaning agents. If the material permits, dip the specimen in the liquid until it is covered

Table C. Use of Liquid Cleaning Agents

Cleaning Agent	Material of Specimen
Water	Turtle shell, gold, stone
Alcohol	Wood, glass
Acetone	Antler, horn, ivory, shell, amber, copper
Gasoline and Ether	Grease or similar organic dirt is best removed by these agents. But be sure that they will not injure the specimen.

Can usually be completely covered without danger: Antler, horn, ivory, shell, wood, copper, glass, silver, stone.

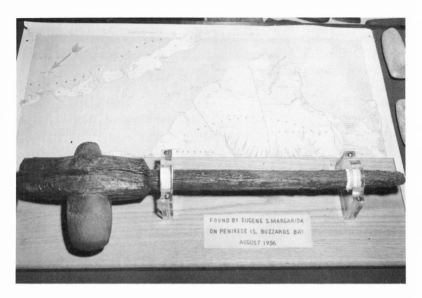

This Indian axe was found buried in a tidal flat off the Massachusetts coast. The arrow (upper left) shows the location of the find. The axe was preserved in a celluloid-acetone solution and is now in the Bronson Museum, Attleboro, Massachusetts.

completely. Otherwise, dip a cotton swab or very soft brush in the liquid and apply. If you have any doubts about the effect of a given solution, try it on a small area of the specimen where damage will not show too much. Better still, try it on some less valuable material of the same type.

PRESERVING

The celluloid-in-acetone solution is the most valuable material known to the archaeologist. You will find many uses for it in the laboratory and in the field. The solution was first used in the restoration work on the material from Tutankhamen's tomb in Egypt about 1927. Since that time it has been employed by archaeologists the world over.

The Indian axe reproduced here provides an example of the use of the celluloid-acetone solution. This specimen was buried in a tidal flat and so was saturated with salt water. Thus, it was in an excellent state of preservation.

A Portuguese fisherman from Fall River found this remarkable artifact. He was out fishing in Buzzards Bay one day and was so unfortunate as to run out of bait. As the tide was low and he was close to Penikese Island (one of the Elizabeth chain), he went ashore to dig bait on the clam flats. This island is government property and was used as a target for practice bombing runs during World War II. The fisherman had no right to be there, of course, so he was digging fast to get the bait and leave before anyone noticed him. All of a sudden his clam hoe brought up this primitive-looking axe. It was hardly recognizable, being covered with mud and seaweed. How he was able to distinguish it from a stick of driftwood, I'll never know, but he did. As he told me later, he reasoned from his knowledge of wooden boats that wood must be kept wet to prevent splitting. So he did the very thing an archaeologist would do under the circumstances—he packed the whole thing in wet seaweed and an old blanket. If he had simply put it in the boat and rowed back to Fall River, or kept on fishing in the blazing sun, there would have been nothing left but the stone axe-head by night. As it was, he preserved it and brought it to me in such condition that I was able to save it. The Bronson Museum purchased the artifact from him and I went to work. I treated that thing like a new baby. As a result, we have one of the very few complete Indian axes in existence.

A small metal tank with a close-fitting cover was constructed and the axe was placed inside. The initial treatment was to remove salt by repeatedly soaking the artifact in fresh-water baths. A quantity of high-test pure alcohol sufficient to remove the water content was required for the next series of baths. During the following ten weeks the specimen was continuously immersed in baths of 190 proof alcohol until about 10 gallons of the precious fluid had been used. The next step was to eliminate the alcohol by repeated baths of Zylol over the ensuing five weeks. Zylol is eliminated by immersion in acetone. The final step was to feed small scraps of celluloid to the acetone bath until the wooden portion of the specimen was completely filled by the hardening material. In all, about twenty weeks passed before the specimen could be removed from the solution and allowed to dry and harden. As no cracks appeared after several weeks of slow drying, the preservation was deemed complete.

The celluloid-acetone solution is unsurpassed for strengthening

Table D. Preservation of Various Materials

ANTLER
(ornaments, flaking
tools, projectile points)

Condition will depend upon the relative acidity of the soil from which the specimen was taken.
1. Check for salt and remove if present (*see* "Preserving," pages 175–176).
2. Immerse in thin celluloid-acetone solution until air bubbles stop rising.
3. Remove, dry.
4. Repeat process twice.

BABICHE
(hide cut into thongs)

Becomes brittle and stiff with age.
1. Treat with warm Vaseline, rubbing in sparingly with a cloth.
2. Remove surplus Vaseline with dry cloth.
3. Repeat treatment two or three times, about a week apart.

BALEEN
(whalebone)

Becomes brittle, edges fray with age.
1. If warped, immerse in boiling water and press gently into the original shape.
2. Make a thin solution of gelatin by dissolving a small amount in hot water and immerse object.
3. Dry, then immerse in formaldehyde (4 oz. or 8 oz. should be sufficient; obtainable at any drugstore).
4. Remove and dry thoroughly at room temperature.

BONE
(awls, needles, fish-
hooks, beads, scrapers,
projectile points)

Subject to cracking and splitting if allowed to become dry or if exposed to strong light while still wet.
1. Check for salt and remove if present.
2. If in good condition, wash in warm soapy water. Rinse. Dry slowly at room temperature.
3. If too fragile to wash, strengthen with celluloid-acetone solution.

BUCKSKIN
(tanned deerskin)

See Babiche.

FEATHERS	Become brittle and bent with age. 1. If bent, straighten by holding in a stream of hot water from faucet or in steam (from spout of boiling kettle). 2. Strengthen by spraying with celluloid-acetone solution.
HAIR	Becomes dry and brittle. Human hair often turns a reddish-brown with age. 1. Brush on a small amount of lanolin or Vaseline.
HORN (spoons, ornaments)	Some objects of horn from the West Coast may be inlaid with shell. Dissolve resins in which they are imbedded with acetone or alcohol. Remove the inlay, immerse in celluloid-acetone solution to preserve, and later restore to object. 1. Wash with warm soap and water. 2. Immerse in celluloid-acetone solution.
IVORY (weapons, ornaments, various tools)	Subject to much warping and cracking. 1. *Do not* clean with water—it may cause further splitting. Clean with an ordinary typewriter eraser, then rub with a cotton swab. 2. Immerse in celluloid-acetone solution until air bubbles stop rising.
LEATHER	Will be hard and brittle. 1. Soak in warm Vaseline or lanolin bath (prepared by heating the material until liquid). 2. Remove from bath. Cool, then rub in surplus Vaseline or lanolin. 3. *Do not* use oils or grease, which cause an acid reaction and will injure the specimen.
RAWHIDE	*See* Leather. If painted, rub Vaseline on the unpainted side (parfleches from the Plains are often painted).

SHELL (ornaments, spoons, hoes, beads)	1. Check for salt; remove if present. 2. Immerse in thin celluloid-acetone solution. 3. Kitchen-midden shell (recovered archaeologically from refuse heaps or pits) will crumble if allowed to become very dry. 4. Place in a bath of about 5 per cent by volume gelatin dissolved in hot water. 5. While still wet, remove dirt with a soft brush. 6. Place in a second bath of the same strength for about an hour. 7. Remove and immerse directly in formaldehyde bath (10 per cent by volume in water) for an hour. 8. Remove and dry at room temperature.
TURTLE SHELL (rattles from the Eastern Woodlands)	1. Clean with soap and water. 2. Dry slowly at room temperature. 3. Rub in a little Vaseline to restore gloss.

II. MATERIALS OF VEGETABLE ORIGIN

BIRCHBARK	Apt to be cracked and brittle. 1. Celluloid-acetone will improve condition but will not make more pliable. This solution should be sprayed onto the bark. 2. Immerse in beechwood creosote (should be available at a chemical supply house). 3. Dry. Then paint with formaldehyde.
RESIN (gums, pitch, bitumen)	Often used by the Indians as adhesives. Gums will dissolve in water but not in alcohol. Almost all resins will dissolve in alcohol but not in water. Pitch, or bitumen, will not dissolve in water or alcohol. Celluloid-acetone is a good preservative.

Table D. Preservation of Various Materials (cont.)

WOOD
(may be preserved by charring or contact with copper. Often preserved in very wet soil or under extremely dry conditions.)

Wooden objects are liable to be split and warped. Under alternately wet and dry conditions wood deteriorates rapidly. Charred objects of wood sometimes occur at archaeological sites. If collected from damp soil, pack in damp material, such as moss, and keep damp until the preservation process.

1. Check for salt and remove if present.
2. Immerse in bath of pure alcohol (25 per cent) and water for at least two days (a week is better).
3. Repeat alcohol bath with 50 per cent solution and water for at least two days (a week is better).
4. Repeat in bath of alcohol (75 per cent) and water for at least two days (a week is better).
5. Repeat in bath of alcohol (95 per cent) and water—two days (a week is better).
6. Transfer without drying to 100 per cent bath of Zylol (Xylene, obtainable at drug or chemical stores) for at least two days.
7. Transfer without drying to 100 per cent acetone for two days.
8. Add strips of colorless celluloid to acetone bath until mass becomes stringy. Allow to set for two days. If evaporation is rapid, add acetone to keep in solution.
9. Remove and allow to dry at room temperature.

III. MATERIALS OF MINERAL ORIGIN

AMBER
(ornaments, beads)

A fossilized resin; will dissolve in alcohol, acetone, benzol, etc.

1. Clean with soap and warm water.
2. Carefully apply a thin coat of celluloid-acetone with a brush. *Do not immerse.*

COPPER
(beads, weapons,
ornaments, gorgets,
pins, celts)

Will be either so badly corroded that little of the original metal is preserved, or will be covered with an unsightly patina or tarnish that must be removed.

Badly corroded:
1. Check for salt; remove if present.
2. Immerse in celluloid-acetone solution.
3. Repeat if necessary.

Slightly corroded:
1. Clean in solution of 15 parts Rochelle salts (sodium potassium tartrate), 5 parts caustic soda, 100 parts water. (Salts and soda are obtainable at any drug or chemical store.) Soak for two hours. Rinse in clear cold water. Brush with a stiff brush. If the specimen should become coated with a layer of red oxide, it will readily come off in brushing.
2. *Alternate treatment.* Immerse in a bath of 10 parts of acetic acid (obtainable at drug or chemical store) in 100 parts water. Allow to soak until green corrosion is replaced by red oxide. Rinse in clear cold water; then brush.
3. If the object appears too bright, allow to stand at room temperature until a slight tarnish appears.
4. Coat with celluloid-acetone solution.

GLASS
(beads)

1. Check for salt and remove if present.
2. Immerse in alcohol. Remove and dry.
3. Coat with celluloid-acetone.

GOLD
(ornaments)

1. Wash with soap and warm water. Take care not to scratch the surface. A 10 per cent solution of ammonia in water or a weak solution of hydrochloric acid (obtainable at any drug or chemical store) will remove stubborn stains.

2. Wash thoroughly with soap and warm water after using either of the above solutions.
3. Coat with celluloid-acetone solution.

IRON
(weapons, particularly
trade axes or
tomahawks)

Badly rusted so that little original metal is present:
1. Check for salt; remove if present.
2. Boil in strong solution of caustic soda or carbonate of soda in water.
3. Dry quickly in artificial heat (electric heater, oven, etc.)
4. Soak in celluloid-acetone solution.

Slightly rusted:
1. Remove most of rust with a steel brush, holding the object under water while working.
2. Place on a layer of granulated zinc (obtainable at a chemical supply store) in an iron or porcelain dish. Cover with more granulated zinc until the object is completely buried.
3. Add a 10 per cent solution of caustic soda in water until zinc is completely covered.
4. Allow solution to simmer gently on low heat for at least four hours. When removed from the solution, iron will be covered with a black deposit.
5. Repeat the above process if necessary.
6. Dry immediately in hot oven.
7. When cool, paint with celluloid-acetone or immerse in solution.

LEAD

Seldom needs any treatment. If tarnish or corrosion appears, remove by brushing.

PETROGLYPHS AND
PICTOGRAPHS

Petroglyphs are carvings or inscriptions on rock surfaces. Pictographs are scratched or picked drawings on rock surfaces, often painted with red ochre or cinnabar. Often covered with lichens.

1. If in color, do not pull or scrape off lichens, as pigment will stick to the plant. A weak solution of ammonia or carbolic acid (obtainable at drugstore) will soften the lichens. They can then be brushed off without injuring the painting.
2. Carefully brush away dirt.
3. Spray the entire surface with celluloid-acetone solution. This will bind the pigment to the rock surface. It will also protect the surface from further disintegration for a period of time.

Note: Do not attempt the above work unless the surface of the rock is dry. Often several days of hot summer weather are necessary for the rock to dry thoroughly.

SILVER

Badly tarnished:
1. Soak in a 50 per cent solution of ammonia in water, then in a 10 per cent solution of formic acid (obtainable at any drugstore) in water for at least two minutes.

Slightly tarnished:
1. Soak in a 5 per cent solution of formic acid in water for two minutes. Remove tarnish with a cotton swab dipped in this solution. Use a glass or porcelain dish for the bath, never a metal container.

STONE

Porous stone objects may contain certain salts that will recrystallize in dry weather, sometimes flaking off the surface.
1. Check for salt; remove if present (may take some time).
2. Wash with soap and warm water.
3. Immerse in celluloid-acetone solution.
4. Dry at room temperature.

Hard, fine-grained stone:
1. Wash with soap and warm water.

Birchbark embroidered with moose hair in delicate tones of green and blue, the work of Naskapi Indians during the eighteenth century, has been carefully restored and is now in the Bronson Museum.

porous materials. Used with a soft brush, it makes an excellent waterproof, airtight varnish. Cut down on the acetone content, and you have a strong, flexible cement. This solution will give you an excellent writing surface for numbering specimens. When sufficiently thinned, it can be used as a spray in an atomizer; be sure to clean the atomizer with clear acetone after use. The solution is sold under various trade names (Duco cement, for example, which you can purchase at Woolworth's or any hardware store), or you can make it quite simply and inexpensively in your own workshop.

How to Make Celluloid-Acetone Solution

1] The basic requirement is a sheet of clear celluloid about two feet square. Scrap celluloid can sometimes be obtained from a manufacturer of celluloid products; or old photographic negatives may be used—remove the emulsion by immersing in hot water.

2] Cut the celluloid into small pieces—½-inch squares are about right.

3] Place a cupful of cut-up celluloid in a quart preserving jar. Add about a pint of acetone. Cover tightly, then shake the jar vigorously. Unless the mass of celluloid is broken up quickly, it will take a long time to dissolve.

4] Allow the celluloid jelly to stand for 30 minutes. Then turn the jar upside down, then right side up, repeating until the celluloid is completely dissolved, and the solution appears to be consistent throughout.

Even if only a slight amount of moisture is present in a specimen, it will cause a white deposit to appear when the celluloid-acetone solution is used. This is especially noticeable when using the solution in the field, where it is difficult to dry an object thoroughly. If such a deposit appears, you can remove it easily with a cotton swab dipped in pure acetone.

A WORD OF WARNING: Use this solution only where there is plenty of ventilation—have at least one window open—as it gives off toxic and explosive fumes. Do not store a large quantity of it and do not use in the presence of an open flame—the solution is highly flammable, even explosive, until the acetone has completely evaporated.

REPAIRING

At various times you may have to undertake the job of replacing broken segments of an object or of putting together an object consisting of several parts. To fasten together parts of broken stone implements, for example, celluloid-acetone is very useful. To obtain a good cement, allow some of the mixture to stand for a few minutes in an open container. You can also use any good prepared adhesive, such as Duco cement.

1] Always remove old cement or glue from broken parts with clear acetone before proceeding with repairs. Do not attempt to scrape off old cement, as this will also remove some of the original materials along with the cement.

2] Apply cement to broken edges of parts to be joined together. Allow the cement to become tacky and press the parts firmly together.

3] Bind the parts with string or tape until completely dry.

4] Use clear acetone to remove excess cement.

5] If small parts are missing, fill in with plastic wood or plaster of Paris (which hardens rapidly and must be used right away). To make clear that the object is a restoration, you might prefer to use material of a different color for the restored parts. Mark the specimen as restored (a corresponding note should appear in your catalog).

6] To keep the parts of the repaired specimen in contact with each other, place them in a small box filled with sand.

RESTORATION OF CLAY POTTERY

"Pottery," famed archaeologist Nelson Glueck has declared, "is man's most enduring material." Its discovery, preservation, and restoration represent a singularly rewarding achievement for the amateur archaeologist. From the shape and decoration of the pottery and from the composition of the clay itself, it is sometimes possible to deter-

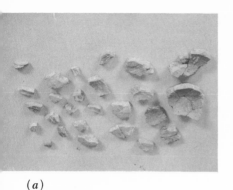

(a)   (b)   (c)

How to Restore a Clay Vessel

(a)   Fill a small, low-sided box with clean sand for holding sherds and
parts of the vessel together during the matching and drying
processes. Spread out the sherds on the worktable. Keep them in
the order in which you packed them in the field.

(b)   Select rim sherds and reconstruct as much as possible of the rim
of the vessel. If the rim is complete, you have one important
dimension. If it is not, put together what fragments you have.
Check the curvature carefully to make sure that the opening is
not distorted.

(c)   Do not attempt to reassemble the body all in one piece. Match the
sherds that belong together and cement them so that you have
several continuous sections of the body of the vessel. When the
sherds have been cemented together there may be gaps or open
spaces (you may also wind up with some sherds that simply do
not fit anywhere).

(d)   To fill the gap, cut a piece of screen wire to the approximate shape
(it need not fit exactly). Place it about midway between the inner
and outer surfaces; hold in place with a drop of celluloid-acetone
cement. With the screen wire securely cemented in place, mix a

mine the period in which it was made. Once this has been established, the culture of the site at which the pottery was found can be
pinpointed.

The fragments of clay pottery found at an archaeological site are
known as "sherds" or "shards." Sherds recovered in dry regions, such
as the Southwest, usually will be hard, with clean, sharp fractures

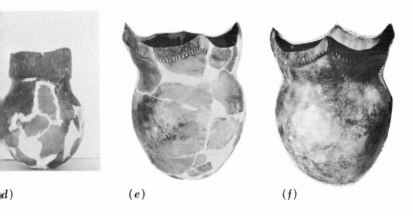

(d)   (e)   (f)

small portion of Cast-stone or plaster of Paris. (Cast-stone may be obtained from a dental supply house. It dries much harder than plaster of Paris and does not shrink as much in drying.) You will have to work fast as the plaster will harden rapidly. Smooth around the edges of the screen wire to hold it firmly in place. Fill the inner surfaces, then carefully apply to the outside surface (a pallet knife, obtainable from an art supply shop, is useful).

(e)   A different type of vessel is shown with plastering completed. Before the plaster hardens, continue any decorative designs from the original sherds or copy the surface markings of the body sherds. Use a flat wooden paddle with a plain surface. You can whittle a small paddle (about ½-inch wide by 6 inches long) or if the surface is cordmarked, wrap a piece of twine with approximately the same size twist about the paddle to simulate the body marking.

(f)   To color the plaster, apply a coat of wall-size; paint with artists' oil color to match the original color of the vessel. Apply a final coat of celluloid-acetone to protect the vessel from moisture, or spray with artists' fixative if the former material produces an objectionable luster.

(breaks). Those found in the damp soil of more humid forest regions, such as the Northeast, are apt to be soft; the surface along which the break has occurred will be ragged, therefore more difficult to match together.

If you have recovered approximately 50 to 75 per cent of the sherds belonging to a pottery vessel, go ahead and try a full restoration. If you have only a few sherds, put as much as you can of the vessel together—do not attempt a full restoration because it will only result in creating a false impression of the original.

Before You Begin

1] Clean all dirt from the sherds with a soft brush. Take special care to see that the fracture surfaces are clean—a grain of sand can distort the curvature and result in a poor restoration. If the sherds tend to flake during brushing, harden them with the celluloid-acetone solution.

2] Check for the presence of salt; remove if present, provided the sherds are sufficiently hard to allow soaking. If the salt is present in any amount and is not removed, it will recrystallize and flake off the surface of your restored vessel.

How to Restore a Clay Vessel

Restoring a pottery vessel is similar in some ways to putting together a jigsaw puzzle, except that the vessel is three-dimensional. Not only must the fragments match perfectly along the fracture surfaces, but they must also be joined so that they follow the correct curve. Also, there will probably be some missing pieces in this puzzle. If you use celluloid-acetone to cement the sherds together, you can brush on pure acetone to soften the cement so as to permit a realignment to correct any slight curvature error. The series of illustrations shows the step-by-step procedure to follow in the restoration of a clay vessel.

10 : How to Date Archaeological Finds

Earlier chapters have already exposed you to some of the contributions that the other sciences have been able to make to archaeology. Now let's find out how the archaeologist calls upon the other sciences for the assistance they can offer in the way of special techniques. Obviously, no single individual can hope to be expert in all of these techniques. As an aspiring archaeologist, however, you should be aware of what the other sciences have to offer, what questions they may be able to answer for you, and what limitations they may possess.

Other sciences have made valuable contributions in establishing the time sequence—date or chronology—of a prehistoric site. "How old is it?" is one of the questions most frequently asked of, and by, the archaeologist.

GEOLOGY

The science of geology—the study of the earth, its formation, the various ages through which it has passed, and the natural forces that have governed its development—offers a number of approaches to chronology, or dating. Dr. Kirk Bryan and Dr. Ernst Antevs have done outstanding work in the study of the relationship between geologic events and man. The brief chronological scale in the second chapter shows what geologists believe to be the progression of geological events in North America and their relationship to archaeology. If it can be shown that certain archaeological evidence is directly associated with these geological events, we may establish their place in the timetable, i.e., their date.

One widely used method is known as the *geomorphic-stratigraphic technique*. This has to do with geological stratification (or layering) of the soils and such geomorphological features of the earth as stream terraces, deltas, kames (hills, ridges), and the like. Let's suppose that an archaeological deposit is found within a stratum (or layer) and can be shown to be related to some geologic event, such as a volcanic eruption or a glacial advance, which in turn can be placed in the geologic chronology of the area. The archaeological deposit can be dated with relative accuracy. This technique applies with greater accuracy in the case of an open site than it does in the case of a sheltered site, such as a cave deposit. It is often difficult to show the relationship between strata inside and outside of the cave.

If one of the components, or occupied levels, at a given archaeological site has been covered by a volcanic deposit, and if the geologist can furnish the date of the volcanic eruption, we can be sure that the archaeological material is older. But how much older? In certain caverns it has been shown that the debris of human occupation was left stratigraphically—in a layer or layers—above a marine deposition (material deposited by retreating waters) for which the geologist can give a relative date. Thus we know that the archaeological material is younger than the marine invasion. But how much younger?

This method of dating archaeological deposits can be tricky. The geologic date for a given stratum, varve (layer of silt deposited in a glacial lake), or stream terrace may be relatively accurate. The validity of the archaeological date, however, is only as good as the evidence relating the archaeological material to the stratum in which it was found. While it is possible that a modern sardine can might be found embedded in a soil profile of considerable antiquity, to assume a Pleistocene date for the sardine can would be ridiculous. Geological dating of archaeological material, then, is a matter for experts and is of considerable significance to the archaeologist.

Geological techniques are also of value in locating the sites of ancient man, as well as in dating them. In chapter 3, I spoke of the geologic procedure followed in the study of the Lake Assawompset area in Middleboro, Massachusetts. It enabled us to discover the ancient shorelines of the modern lake and to find there a Paleo-Indian site. Without the benefit of this geological reconstruction of the terrain we would not have searched for a site at that particular spot.

Another useful branch of geology is *petrology*. It is the study of the structure, origin, formation, and distribution of rock. Rock or stone is the raw material of primitive industry, and a knowledge of its properties and of its source is essential in a study of that industry.

The ancient worker in stone at times seems to have been quite selective in his demands. At many Woodland or Archaic sites the bulk of the stone artifacts were made from local varieties. On the other hand, particularly at Paleo-Indian sites, the flint or chert used often came from quite distant sources. Evidence of the importation of flint from the New York area into New England 200 miles away exists, for example, at the Wapanucket #8 site in Middleboro. The use of nonlocal material at a site is a clue to either migratory movements or to trade contacts with distant areas.

DENDROCHRONOLOGY

The work of Dr. Andrew E. Douglass, director of Steward Observatory at the University of Arizona, demonstrates a most interesting connection between astronomy and archaeology. In his study of sunspots and their effect upon climate and weather, Dr. Douglass became involved in the study of the effect of weather upon plant life in Arizona.

Arizona is a particularly favorable area for such a study. In its comparatively dry climate trees and other plant life react to variations in the amount of moisture. A tree can be said to keep a diary in which it records all of the events that occurred during its lifetime. Each year the tree adds a new layer of wood, or growth ring, over all its living parts—trunk, limbs, and twigs. In good growing years, when rainfall is plentiful, these annual growth rings are broad. In poor years, when the rainfall is inadequate, the rings are narrow.

Using sections taken from the trunks of living specimens from the area, Dr. Douglass found that the number of rings and their comparative growth corresponded precisely with sunspot activity observed for that year. For example, sunspot activity, as recorded by astronomers, appears to occur in cycles. Every eleven years there is a marked increase in the frequency of sunspot activity. The tree rings reflected this condition nicely. This cyclical record of sunspots has been recorded for a period of some five hundred years, except for an interval of seventy-five years between 1650 and 1725 when there was a lull in sunspot activity. The astronomical record agreed with the record kept by the trees with uncanny accuracy.

The initial procedure in this tree-ring study, which is called *dendrochronology*, is to establish a master chart. Starting with sections cut from living trees, the master chart was constructed. It cov-

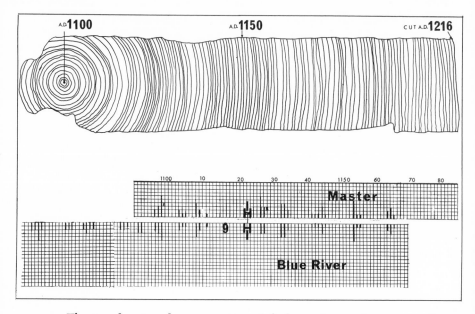

The top drawing shows a section of fir beam from a house ruin. Rings indicate the birth of the tree at about A.D. 1100. It was cut and used about A.D. 1216. Note the periods of relatively heavy rainfall (marked by wide rings) and the periods of drought (marked by a number of successive narrow rings). Beneath that is a section of chart from a beam taken from a ruin at the Blue River site as compared with the master chart for the area. Note the agreement of rings that locate the sample chronologically.

ered the last few hundred years, or about the limit for trees living in this area. It was then necessary to turn to more ancient trees, which had been preserved in the old roof beams of ancient Indian dwellings of the area. With the help of this mute testimony, Dr. Douglass was able to extend his master chart backward for an additional period to about 200 B.C.

In this manner the study of sunspots, climate, and weather came to date the construction of the ancient houses of the Anasazi people from which the roof beams were taken. This has now become a common means of dating by archaeologists within areas where datable wood is available. In more humid areas, such as eastern North America, wood of sufficient antiquity has not been preserved and master charts are not available.

The tree-ring technique of dating is a complicated procedure and must be done by experts. Master charts are available at most universities and museums in the areas where dendrochronology is a practical procedure. If you work in an area where tree-ring dating is practical, it might be interesting to experiment with this method of dating.

To prepare a sample for dating, cut a section about two inches thick from the sample beam. Sand the sample until it is extremely smooth. Then polish and wax it to bring out the details of the annual growth rings. Now compare it with the master chart. At some point it will match perfectly. This will establish the date of the section. If the center and last growth rings are present, they will furnish the life span of the sample.

The date of the last growth ring indicates the date of the death of the tree from which the sample is taken but not necessarily the date when it was used by the Indian. In Arizona, for example, a tree might have been preserved for some time before it was actually used by the housebuilder.

POLLEN ANALYSIS

Another dating technique, which comes to us from the field of paleobotany, is *pollen analysis*. The microscopic study of the pollen obtained from the local plant life will sometimes yield valuable information concerning the climatic changes and progression of the area.

Flowering plants and trees produce large amounts of pollen or seed annually. Under favorable circumstances this pollen will accumulate in neighboring lakes, ponds, or bogs. The layers of wind-blown organic and inorganic sediments are built up slowly over the years, and the pollen in them will be preserved to furnish a continuous record of the type of plant life that existed during the formation of the deposit. Particularly favorable conditions for the deposition of these sediments existed in the multitude of shallow ponds, lakes, and bogs that were created in the wake of the last glacial retreat. Pollen analysis, therefore, is especially favored in formerly glaciated land areas. It is also possible to obtain samples for pollen analysis in those unglaciated areas where proper conditions favored the deposition of sediments.

This technique has been widely used in Europe, where a fairly

Histogram of Pollen

SAMPLE	ACER MAPLE 5 10	ALNUS ALDER 5 10 15	BETULA BIRCH 5 10	CARYA HICKORY 5	CORYLUS HAZELNUT 5	FAGUS BEECH 5 10	LEDUM LABRADOR TEA 5	OSTRYA HORNBEAM 5	PLANTAGO PLANTAIN 5 10	PINUS PINE 5 10 15	PYRUS ASH 5	QUERCUS OAK 5 10 15	TSUGA SPRUCE 5 10 15	ULM ELM 5
1 0–30 CM.														
2 30–60 CM.														
3 60–90 CM.														
4 90–120 CM.														
5 120–150 CM.														
6 150–180 CM.														

This histogram of pollen shows the manner in which the results of a pollen identification and count are recorded. The presence of pollen from plantain, a weed that usually accompanies agriculture in this area, indicates the beginnings of farming in the upper portions of the core and its absence in earlier times. Labrador tea, present in samples 5 and 6, now grows only in colder, more northerly areas of New England. The presence of elm in sample 2 and its absence in sample 1 show the prevalence of the disease that has practically eliminated the elm in the Northeast.

accurate sequence of dates has been established. As yet there is no correlation between European and North American sequences, so it is inaccurate to assume exact dates from American samples. While it is of considerable value in the Americas, pollen analysis can furnish only a relative chronology in the area.

The technique of securing proper samples or cores for pollen analysis is a difficult one; the recognition of species from pollen grains and the counting of the identifiable pollen is a task for the specialist. The botanist can assist the archaeologist by determining the species of certain seeds and plant remains recovered from the refuse pits and middens of a site. Such identification will help to establish the relationship between the culture and its biological environment and will provide a hint as to the climate of the period during which it existed.

If they can be associated directly with the activities of the occupants of a site, identifiable wood samples furnish another good index of climate and period. In most areas it can be assumed that dead wood did not last too long and that it was used by the Indians soon after it ceased to live.

In addition to giving an idea of chronology, the recognition of pollen from some plant known to have been cultivated by ancient man or a sharp rise in the count of pollen grains from some of the weeds known to accompany the practice of agriculture may furnish a valuable clue to the period of occupancy. The uses of pollen analysis in archaeology and in geology are still in the experimental stage. The development of more reliable chronological tables, their relation to world-wide events, and improvements in the sampling and counting methods may be expected in the near future.

CARBON 14

For some years the measurement of the amount of disintegration of radioactive elements has been used as a measure of elapsed time. For example, uranium 238, which breaks down into lead 206 over a period of billions of years, can be used to determine the age of the oldest rocks on earth. Archaeologists, however, are interested in more recent eras; accordingly, they need a shorter yardstick.

Experiments at the University of Chicago in 1931 revealed the existence of an unknown radioactive source high in the atmosphere. Later investigation showed this source to be carbon 14. This isotope is produced when cosmic rays from outer space collide with the gases of earth's atmosphere. These collisions generate neutrons, some of which strike atoms of nitrogen, causing them to disintegrate into carbon 14.

The radioactive carbon is a comparatively short-lived isotope. Its half-life—meaning the time required for half the carbon in any sample to break down into the stable carbon 13—originally was calculated at 5,568 years. Later calculations have produced different figures, including 5,750 and 5,700 years, but some laboratories still use the original determination. Of course, the carbon 14 will not have disappeared entirely after the half-life is doubled; rather, after 11,400 years (using the 5,700-year determination), one-quarter of the original amount will remain, and after 17,100 years, one-eighth will remain, and so on. Carbon 14 checking now covers a range of more than 40,000 years.

Cosmic rays

O

Neutron$+ N^{14} =$Proton$+ C^{14}$

Intake ceases

−5,568yrs.
Dis.=7.8 per gr.per min.

Radioactive Carbon (c^{14}) Cycle

Plants and animals take in sufficient radiocarbon to maintain an equilibrium with the atmosphere during life. The disintegration rate during life or immediately after death is Dis. $= 15.6$ per gram of weight per minute. After the organism's death, the intake of radioactive carbon ceases and the disintegration rate increases progressively. At approximately 5,568 years it has decreased by one-half, or Dis. $= 7.8$ per gram of weight per minute. Thus, the measured disintegration rate of radioactive carbon will reflect its age since the death of the plant or animal from which it came. These figures are based on the original half-life of C-14, which is still in use by some laboratories.

Though present only in tiny amouts (there are a trillion regular carbon atoms in the atmosphere for every atom of carbon 14), the radioactive carbon is pervasive. Every living organism, vegetable as well as animal, ingests or inhales carbon 14. This means that every living organism is slightly radioactive. When the organism dies, it ceases to take in carbon 14, and that which is present begins to disintegrate. The disintegration can be measured in terms of emissions per gram per minute. The emissions decrease according to a known curve. The lower the number of emissions the more time has elapsed since death occurred. Laboratory measurements are made by Geiger counters from a prepared sample of carbon 14 over a period of standard runs, usually forty-eight hours. Modern organic material averages 15.6 emissions per gram of weight per minute. At half-life the emissions would average 7.8 per gram of weight per minute. The result is reported as an average between two extremes, expressed as a ± number of years, with a probability of 66⅔ per cent accuracy. For example, a sample submitted from a Massachusetts site yielded a date of 4,720 ± 140 years ago. This means that the organism from which the sample was taken died between 4,580 and 4,860 years ago or between approximately 2,580 and 2,860 B.C.

Before radiocarbon dates could be accepted as accurate measurements, it was necessary to establish the validity of two basic assumptions upon which the procedure is based—that the atmospheric C-14 is uniform throughout the world and that its presence in the atmosphere has been constant through time. To test the correctness of these assumptions, C-14 tests were conducted on samples of organic material of known date. Wood from Egyptian tombs and from the American Southwest that had been dated by dendrochronology were selected and the resulting C-14 dates were in substantial agreement with those previously determined by the older technique. Some few tests, however, did not agree, but it was assumed in these rare instances that the disagreement was the result of faulty technique or contamination of the sample. At that time the oldest dated wood from America was only about 2,200 years old (about 200 B.C.).

In 1958 several bristle-cone pine trees were discovered in Inyo National Forest in the White Mountains of eastern California that extended the range of the chronological chart considerably. Seventeen of the trees carried the ring count back more than 4,000 years (to 2,000 B.C.). Samples of the wood were submitted to two radiocarbon laboratories (Yale University and the Geochronological Laboratory of Arizona). The results of these tests, published in *Radiocarbon*, a professional journal, in 1966, revealed significant differences between radiocarbon dates and true dates. The tests showed that radiocarbon dates are within 200 years of true dates over the past

2,000 years but that radiocarbon dates older than that are much too young. The deviation increases linearly to about 6,000 years ago, at which point the error is about 1,100 years. It then decreases to become correct again at about 10,000 years.

Minze Stuiver of the Yale Laboratory has proposed the following formula for correcting radiocarbon dates falling between 2,300 and 6,000 years ago: T(true time) = carbon 14 years $\times$ 1.4 − 900. Using this formula to correct the radiocarbon date from Massachusetts mentioned above:

$$T(\text{true time}) = 4,720 \times 1.4 - 900$$
$$T(\text{true time}) = 5,708 \pm 140 \text{ years ago or } 3,708 \text{ B.C.} \pm 140$$

Thus, the sample would have come from an organism that died between 3,568 and 3,848 B.C., indicating an error of 988 years too young.

In order to obtain good samples for radioactive carbon dating and thus to obtain reliable dates, several factors must be taken into consideration. The following directions for obtaining datable carbon 14 samples are suggested by one of the most reliable commercial laboratories (Krueger Enterprises, Inc., Geochron Laboratories Division, 24 Blackstone Street, Cambridge, Massachusetts).

Materials Suitable for Carbon 14 Analysis

Nearly all material containing carbon is potentially datable from an analytic viewpoint. Certain materials high in carbon content have proven to be most reliable for dating and are frequently available on archaeological sites.

Charcoal. The high carbon content and the ease of obtaining clean samples make charcoal the most desirable and reliable material in most cases.

Wood. Wood or other cellulose material from plants is an excellent material for dating.

Peat. Provides excellent material for dating soil horizons or geomorphic features.

Shells. Marine or nonmarine shell material provides good carbon for dating. It is easily cleaned but large samples are necessary.

Bone. This material is low in carbon and requires large samples. It is difficult to analyze, but will provide good dates.

Paper, parchment, cloth, etc. These are typical of the many vegetable or animal products which will yield good dates if sufficient material is available.

Table E. Sample Size Required for Carbon 14 Analysis

Type	Desired Size	Minimum Size
Charcoal	8 to 12 grams	1 gram
Wood	10 to 30 grams	3 grams
Shell	30 to 100 grams	5 grams
Peat	10 to 25 grams	3 grams
Bone	50 to 200 grams	5 grams
Carbonate	30 to 100 grams	5 grams

Inorganic carbonates. Calcium carbonate, caliche, or other inorganic precipitates may provide dates which cannot be obtained from other materials.

Other materials. These include atmospheric or dissolved carbon dioxide, leaves, pollen, nuts, hydrocarbons, organic liquids, animal tissue, soils containing carbons, and many other carbon-bearing objects.

Age limitations. Nearly all materials younger than 40,000 years can be readily dated. Slightly older materials may offer qualitative dates under ideal conditions.

If sample material is abundant, collect more than the required amount. It is always desirable to have enough material for a duplicate sample.

What Does a Carbon 14 Date Mean?

The most important consideration in collecting samples for carbon 14 dating is the true meaning of the "date" that will be obtained and how it may be linked to the problem under investigation. Many potentially suitable samples will give clues as to whether or not they will provide useful dates. The measurement of carbon 14 concentration in a sample merely gives some measure of the time that has elapsed since the carbon was formed. The following general conclusions about certain samples can be made.

Wood. The carbon in wood is fixed at the time the plant grew. Each ring of the tree is of different age and will so date. Therefore, to date the death of a tree, the outermost rings or small twigs or branches are best. We still get only the date at which the tree died rather than the date when the woody material was used in construction, in a fire, or in artwork. The possibility of "fossil" wood being used must be considered when sampling. While such situations are rare, they can only be detected in the field by those doing the sampling.

Charcoal. The foregoing considerations apply also to charcoal, as the carbon remaining in charcoal is the original carbon in the fuel. Fortunately, dead wood for fires is seldom preserved for more than a few years in most areas, but "fossil" wood may have been used if it could be found. Charcoal from fires made with peat will date not the fire but the much older peat.

Shell. Shell samples may also be either contemporary or "fossil" in relation to the event you wish to date. If the shells were obtained from living animals by the Indians, they will date from the time they were collected. If the shells were obtained from beach litter by the Indians, they will probably be somewhat older than the culture using them. Radioactive carbon derived from a marine shell yields a slightly older date than the actual date of the death of the shellfish. This is because the carbon was derived from dissolved, rather than from atmospheric, carbon dioxide. Shells in the water absorb some of this older carbon 14 and thus give a much older date than the shell deserves.

Always try to date an event by dating materials known to be associated physically with that event. It is only by careful field work that you can be sure the material was formed at the same time the event occurred; in other words, that it did not exist for many years previously and was merely used in conjunction with the event.

Carbon 14 dates often are given with the initials B.P. (Before the Present). Commonly used as a convenient date is the year 1950. Thus a C^{14} date of 4250 B.P. would indicate 4250 years before 1950 or, historically, 2300 B.C.

Contamination: Inherent and Introduced

Inherent, or natural, contamination exists in many carbon 14 samples and cannot always be avoided. It may be in the form of more recent rootlets or lichens (perhaps still growing), organic debris that has been added since the sample was formed, insect alteration, or bacterial action, etc. In brief, any natural process that may have added carbon in any form since the sample was presumably isolated can cause inherent contamination.

Carbon-dating laboratories will have techniques to remove most of these contaminants, but it is wise to consider these factors when selecting samples. If you suspect any such contamination, inform those doing the laboratory work of your suspicion.

Introduced contamination may result from poor sampling practices or sampling difficulties. It may be caused by: unintentional mixing of two portions of similar samples; wind-blown organic debris collected with the sample; dirty or oily tools; wooden or plastic tools; excessive handling; poor packaging; use of preservatives; use of bristle brushes for cleaning; or similar carelessness. It can be avoided only by careful, painstaking work.

Obtaining, Handling, and Shipping the Sample

When you know that a sample may be used for carbon 14 dating, exercise care in obtaining the sample from its original environment. If possible, only metal or glass should come in contact with the sample. The tools and containers should be clean and free from all organic material, greases, lubricants, preservatives, etc. I recommend removing samples with clean metal trowels or spatulas and placing them directly in new aluminum foil. Wrap the foil around the sample, and place the sample in a glass or metal container.

Fill the container with crushed aluminum foil, *but not straw or paper*, and seal it. Once a sample is sealed in this fashion, pack the container for shipment with paper or straw to protect it. *Do not handle the specimen at all if possible and never use any preservative.* If the sample has to be cut from a larger piece of material, use especially clean metal tools. The cuttings should be caught directly on aluminum foil and wrapped as above. If a piece of the sample should drop on the ground, throw it away. Your dates will come out better if you observe these precautions.

The Krueger Enterprises, Inc., will process your carbon 14 samples as reasonably as any commercial source at the following prices:

Table F. Approximate Cost of Carbon 14 Analysis

Number of Samples Submitted Per Year Under Contract	Cost Per Sample (Approx.)
1	$160
2–10	$150
11–30	$140
31–50	$130
51–100	$125
101 or more	$120

Occasional users of radiocarbon dates will be charged at a rate varying with the number of samples they have already submitted during the calendar year. The first sample will cost about $160, the second through the tenth, $150 each, etc., in accordance with the above table. Address your inquiries to Mr. Harold W. Krueger, Technical Director.

If your sample has a potential importance of interest to archaeology in general—such as providing a date for some event of archaeological significance—one of the geochronological laboratories operated by a university may be willing to check it for you. However, do not send such a sample to a university laboratory without first contacting the proper party, explaining the nature of your sample, how and where it was obtained, and what you believe it to date. If your sample is requested after such an explanation, you will probably have to wait a year or more before the sample is processed. This delay is caused by the great demand for carbon 14 dating and the backlog that exists at all reputable laboratories.

SPECTROGRAPHY

Often it is desirable to determine the composition of certain metallic specimens. By destroying a very small portion of the object by burning, it is possible to observe the pattern of lines that appear in the spectrum and to determine from them the metals of which the object is made. For example, a metallic object recovered from an archaeological site may have been made by the aboriginals from local material, or it may have been obtained in trade. The spectrographic analysis will often indicate the native or European origin of the material.

Obviously, we have not mentioned all of the instances in which the other sciences have rendered valuable aid to the archaeologist. Archaeology is a rapidly expanding field and many new and as yet undiscovered techniques will be worked out that will assist the archaeologist. One of the newest schools of archaeology, underwater archaeology, is drawing heavily on the techniques of diving and underwater existence and on the wealth of information collected by oceanographers.

The archaeologist in his never-ending quest for knowledge is using all of the available disciplines to expand his ability to interpret the past. You may have some special knowledge that will enable you to make a valuable contribution to the science.

11 : How to Write a Site Report

The final report is the goal of all of your work. With the passing of time, data accumulated in the field becomes unintelligible —and artifacts without accompanying data are worthless. In a nutshell: without a final report, a site has been destroyed to no purpose. So write a final report while the data is still fresh in your mind.

It is all too easy to find an excuse for putting this off. "I am no writer," "No one will publish my writing," "This site is not of sufficient importance"—all of these are timeworn excuses that have been used by both amateur and professional. Don't fall into this trap.

Your local archaeological society will be glad to get your report as a contribution to its bulletin. In fact, if this is your first attempt at writing a report, the editor will be happy to assist in its preparation and with the illustrations. If your site is of more than local importance, perhaps one of the national publications will accept your report. If you are writing for a particular publication, read their instructions to authors and examine one or two articles that they have published. Many scientific papers are preceded by an "abstract," a device to give the reader a preview of the content of the paper. This allows the reader to select the articles in which he has particular interest without wasting time on articles outside his field. In scientific literature the "abstract" takes the place of the "blurb" or description found on the paper cover of a book.

Even if your report is not published, it is the one step that translates the potential value of the artifacts you have recovered into something tangible. A report, filed with the artifacts and other data, puts the stamp of scientific purpose on your work and justifies the excavation of the site. It fulfills the moral obligation that you assumed when you undertook the excavation.

Writing style is a personal thing. You will develop your own. Don't attempt to copy someone else; use the other fellow as a model but avoid the pitfall of trying to imitate his style. The best approach for a novice is to read a number of site reports and to make an outline of the general pattern followed. Note how the writer distinguishes between the factual evidence and his conclusions. Pay particular attention to the manner in which he has used tables to bring out the detail and how he has chosen his illustrations. Follow his conclusions with care and note how he has made use of his evidence to justify his thinking.

You will probably notice that scientific reports are often the subject of disagreement. This should not prevent you from expressing your own thoughts in print. The mere fact that someone comments on your work is an indication of its importance. Everyone, including yourself, may profit by these criticisms. I have learned a great deal from reading the critical reviews of some of my own reports. This is the way in which the science advances. The fact that a given conclusion can be proven to be incorrect is an indication of progress. State your evidence clearly, draw your conclusions, and let the chips fall where they may. Even those who disagree with you will admire your perseverance and applaud your efforts. Here is a suggested sample outline.

INTRODUCTION

Your readers will be interested in learning how you happened to select this particular site. Did you simply find surface evidence of Indian occupation, or did you find some historical evidence that led you to examine this particular site? Perhaps the topography or the geography led you to conclude that here was a likely spot. I once located a fortified Indian site by tracing a reference found in an ancient land deed. A certain bound established in 1674 was said to bear a certain relation to the "northeast corner of the Injun fort." A few hours of surveying and a 10-foot trench revealed the unmistakable outline of the palisade wall. This kind of information will make an excellent opening for your report by exciting the reader's interest in the first paragraphs.

If information furnished to you led to the discovery of the site, be sure to give credit for that fact, and express your thanks for the assistance. This is a good place also to introduce yourself and your fellow workers and to express your thanks for whatever assistance you received in excavating and reporting the site. Remember, too, that you are indebted to the owner of the property on which your site is located. Here is a good opportunity to thank him publicly and to compliment him for his contribution to the science.

You might explain in the introduction why you excavated this particular site. Was it undertaken in order to amplify available information concerning a period or a specific culture? Or were you perhaps searching for confirming data of a certain kind? Explain the facts of the situation clearly.

THE SITE

The next step is to describe the site in detail. First, locate the site with regard to the geography of the area. Be specific. Use maps. Refer to state, town, section, county, or whatever political designations are used locally in such descriptions. Put yourself in the reader's place and pretend that you want to find this site. Mention roads by name or routes by number and give distances. Specify permanent markers such as these rather than the name of the present owner— Farmer Brown may not be living there next year.

Now that you have described the area in general terms, give particulars concerning the site itself. Describe the topography in some detail, mentioning such natural features as bodies of water, swamps, hills, springs. Indicate whether the land was under cultivation, was wooded, or open.

Finally, accurately locate the area excavated, if possible giving distances and bearings from some permanent bound or geodetic survey marker. These precautions will permit the area you excavated to be pinpointed precisely and without difficulty in the future, should the need arise.

HISTORY

Here is where you will wish to relate the salient facts about the past history of the site. When was this land first obtained from the Indians? What, if any, important events occurred here? What use has been made of the area in historic times? Historic events may have affected the data that you obtained and may explain some of the problems encountered. Possibly some of the natural features were changed during historic occupation. If so, this is the place to call attention to the fact.

METHODS OF EXCAVATING AND RECORDING

This section should include a complete description of the methods you used in the excavation and the manner in which you kept your records. Such a description indicates the scientific authenticity of your report and inspires the confidence of the reader in your work.

ARTIFACTS FOUND AND ACCOMPANYING DATA

You have now completed this preliminary section of your report. Now comes that section in which you will make a factual statement about the artifacts you found and the accompanying data.

Make certain that every bit of evidence is reported, whether or not it happens to reflect favorably upon your own conclusions. Include all of the evidence seen even though it may not seem important to you at the time. Be careful to separate fact from fiction—include only what you found and how you found it. Reserve your conclusions for the closing section of the report.

This is the most important part of your report and should be subdivided as follows:

Stratigraphy

Describe the stratigraphy, or the way in which you found the various soils distributed vertically and horizontally. Be sure to mention any disturbances you encountered that may have affected the evidence you are about to present. Such things as rodent burrows, uprooted trees, cultivated areas, or surface disturbances of unknown origin should be noted and shown on your site or grid map.

Features

Describe the hearths, refuse pits, storage pits, and similar features found at the site. It is not necessary to include an illustration of each feature as long as typical examples are shown. Any departures from the normal should be illustrated. If burials are included among the features, it is best to seek the assistance of a physical anthropologist for an expert appraisal, which, with his permission, should be quoted verbatim.

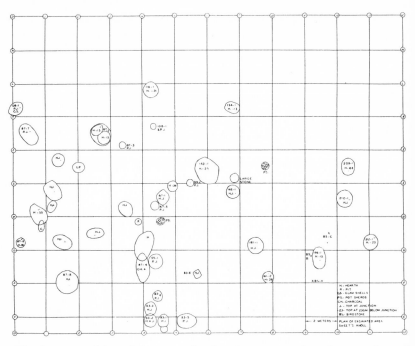

The location of hearths, pits, and other features is plotted on a plan of the excavated area.

Artifacts

A description of the artifacts found at your site constitutes one of the most important sections of your report. Describe clearly the objects themselves so that the reader will be able to compare them with similar artifacts in his own collection and with those from other sites. You should also give their vertical and horizontal positions and state the material from which they were made.

The usual method is to divide the artifacts into general categories —stone, bone, clay, textiles, metallic objects, etc.—and then proceed to a more detailed description under these headings. The largest of these categories commonly consists of artifacts made of stone.

Stone Artifacts. Classify all the stone objects according to the system in use in the area of your site. Then subdivide them into three subgroups: chipped artifacts, polished artifacts, and rough stone artifacts.

The chipped artifacts subgroup includes all objects made by the process of flaking or chipping, such as projectile points, knives, scrapers, drills, etc. Polished artifacts are objects made by pecking and polishing, such as axes, celts, gouges, atlatl weights, ulus, and pestles. Rough stone artifacts include such very roughly made objects as notched weights and hammerstones. Under these headings describe the various stone artifacts in detail, using illustrations (either accurate drawings or photographs) to emphasize the many variations.

Perhaps the most convenient manner of showing vertical distribution or stratigraphic position is by means of a table similar to that shown. The various kinds of stone material used at the site may be shown by the second table illustrated.

Clay Pottery. If present at your site, clay pottery should be described in very exact detail and should be illustrated with clear, accurate photographs or drawings. These artifacts are often important indications of time or period. Be sure to mention such items as temper (materials mixed with clay to prevent cracking during firing), decorative designs, shapes, etc.

Bone Artifacts. At some sites the bone artifacts form a rather substantial portion of the total recoveries. Classify them according

ARTIFACTS FROM SWEET'S KNOLL M-39.-SE-71 M.A.S. STANDARD CLASSIFICATION SYSTEM

	PROJECTILE POINTS							OTHER ARTIFACTS											DRILLS								
	LARGE TRIANGULAR	SMALL TRIANGULAR	SMALL STEMMED	LONG EARED	EARED	CORNER-REMOVED	SIDE-NOTCHED	CORNER-NOTCHED	TAPERED STEM	TRUNCATED	DIAMOND	STEMMED KNIVES	STEMLESS KNIVES	SCRAPERS	PESTLE	SPEAR	ATL-ATL WEIGHT	BIRD-STONE	PLAIN BASE	CRESCENT BASE	T-BASE	HAMMERSTONES	CHOPPER	PLUMBAGO	CLAY POTSHERDS	UNCLASSIFIED	TOTAL
		1 3 4 5 6		2 3 4		3 7 1		4 5 7																			
LOAM	3	1	1	1																				1			7
JUNCTION.	12	2	6	4			1	1		1	1	2		1	2	2	1	1			1	1	1	2	X	22	74
0 – 5 CM.		2		1	17		2		1				3		1				1	1	1		X	2	35
5 – 10 CM.			1	20	1	1	1	1	1		1	1	3	*1	1		2		1		5	42
10 – 15 CM.		1		2	1	1		1	2	2	1	1	1	1		*1		3		7	27
15 – 20 CM.	1	1		1	1										1	2	1		8
20 – 25 CM.	1	1		1			1							1		1	6
25 – 30 CM.														1			1
TOTAL	15	2 3 5 7 2	56	3 2 1 2 1	5	1 2 1	2	1 3 3 2	1	4	7	5	1	1	2	1	2	1	2	11	1	5	X	37	200

*PART OF ONE ARTIFACT

The stratigraphic position of artifacts found at a site can be shown in tabular form.

ARTIFACTS BY TYPE	ARGILITE	BASALT	FELSITE	FLINT	GRANITE	JASPER	PLUMBAGO	QUARTZITE	RED OCHRE	SANDSTONE	STEATITE	
CHIPPED STONE												
POLISHED STONE												
ROUGH STONE												

This table is useful for recording stone artifacts by technique (type) and material.

to use if you can; even if you do not know their use, describe them in some detail.

Textiles. A most interesting and informative type of artifact if present, even if they are trade goods rather than of native manufacture.

Wooden Artifacts. Artifacts of wood are sometimes present, particularly if they have become charred, and thus sterilized, by fire. I have found wooden dishes of respectable antiquity on Archaic sites.

These are only a few of the various categories of artifacts. A study of your material will probably suggest additional subdivisions for your report.

With the completion of this section of the report, you have covered the factual data that should be presented. Review it carefully. Make certain that you have reported the truth, the whole truth, and nothing but the truth, both in your text and in your illustrations. Don't be redundant. Make certain that you have described and illustrated the typical examples of both artifacts and features and that you have called attention to any departure from what is normal at this particular site.

COMPARISONS

Your next step is to search the literature carefully for examples with which you can compare your data. Do not confine yourself to the reports of other sites in the immediate area. Check what has been

SITES	PROJECTILE POINTS												OTHER ARTIFACTS								
TRIBUTION AT EIGHT ATIFIED SITES IN TERN MASSACHUSETTS PTED FROM BULLEN ANTIQUITY VOL.14NO.1.	LARGE TRIANGULAR	SMALL TRIANGULAR	SMALL STEMMED	LONG EARED	EARED	CORNER-REMOVED	SIDE-NOTCHED	CORNER-NOTCHED	TAPERED-STEM	TRUNCATED	DIAMOND	TOTAL PROJECTILE POINTS	SEMI-LUNAR KNIFE	STEMMED KNIFE	STEMLESS KNIFE	CHOPPER	GOUGE	PESTLE	STEATITE SHERDS	GRAPHITE	CELT
) EATON, TEST 7, UPPER.	6							1				7								1	
TER'S COVE, UPPER.	28	5	2			2		3				40								2	
:THS SWAMP, UPPER.	67	27				2						96							x		X
EAKED HILL, UPPER.	7											7									1
IFF SHELL HEAP, UPPER.	6											6									
MANN, UPPER.	12	4										16									
IGLE, UPPER.	1							1				2								1	
) EATON T. 4, UPPER.								3				3									
ETS KNOLL, UPPER	15	13	32			4	2	2	2	1	1	72						1		4	
MANN, FIRST POTTERY								2?				2?						1		1	
TER'S COVE, 1ST POTTERY							2					2									
) EATON, 6, 1ST POTTERY							2					2									
GLE, FIRST POTTERY			X									X?									
TER'S COVE, MIDDLE	5	18	11			6						40		1	4						
GLE, MIDDLE		4	9			5						18									
D EATON, T6, MIDDLE		1	8			1						10									
ETS KNOLL, MIDDLE		6	24	3	5	3	4	1	1	1		48		1						1	
IFF SHELL HEAP, LOWER		1				31	1					34									
THS SWAMP, LOWER						35		1		2		38									
EAKED HILL, LOWER						11						11									
GLE, LOWER						2				1		3									
D EATON, T4, LOWER						6						6	1								
TER'S COVE, LOWER						17				2		19	3	1							
MANN, LOWER						60						60									

SITES	OTHER ARTIFACTS										POTTERY							COMMENTS
	PIPE	SCRAPERS	SPEARS	ATL-ATL WEIGHT	BIRD-STONE	DRILL-PLAIN BASE	DRILL-CRESCENT BASE	DRILL-T BASE	HAMMERSTONES	UNCLASSIFIED OBJECTS	VINETTE TYPE I.	EARLY INTERMEDIATE	LATE INTERMEDIATE	LATE PREHISTORIC, 1.	LATE PREHISTORIC, 2.	HISTORIC	TOTAL ARTIFACTS	SWEET'S KNOLL, UPPER = LOAM, JUNCTION, & 5CM. OF SUB-SOIL; MIDDLE = 5 TO 25CM. SUB-SOIL. HOFMANN-MIDDLE & LOWER COMBINED IN LOWER. CAPE COD SITES, UPPER & LOWER REFER TO COLOR ZONES. OTHER SITES, UPPER = LOAM, MIDDLE = NEXT 13CM.
) EATON, TEST 7, UPPER.																X	8	GUN-FLINTS & BRASS ARROW
TER'S COVE, UPPER.													X	S			42	2 CHIPS OF ENGLISH FLINT
:THS SWAMP, UPPER.	1													X	S*		97	GUN FLINTS-MUSKET BALLS
EAKED HILL, UPPER.															17*		8	*ALL SHELL TEMPER
IFF SHELL HEAP, UPPER.															17*		6	
MANN, UPPER.													X				16	
IGLE, UPPER.												X	S				3	
) EATON T. 4, UPPER.											S	X	S				3	
ETS KNOLL, UPPER		1	1			1	1	2	2	22			X	X			107	ALL MINERAL TEMPER
MANN, FIRST POTTERY											X		S				4	
TER'S COVE, 1ST POTTERY											X						2	
) EATON, 6, 1ST POTTERY											X						2	
GLE, FIRST POTTERY											X							
TER'S COVE, MIDDLE										2							47	
GLE, MIDDLE																	18	
D EATON, T6, MIDDLE																	10	
ETS KNOLL, MIDDLE		4		2	1	1			9	15							82	
IFF SHELL HEAP, LOWER												X*					34	*ALL MINERAL TEMPER
THS SWAMP, LOWER											S	X					38	ONE COLLARED SHERD & 2
EAKED HILL, LOWER																	11	ADZES
GLE, LOWER																	3	
D EATON, T4, LOWER											.						?	
TER'S COVE, LOWER																	23	
MANN, LOWER																	60	

The relationship between artifacts and pottery found at several different sites can be shown clearly and simply in a table such as this.

reported from distant sites, particularly if you have evidence of migration or trade from other areas. For example, on the Assawompset site in Massachusetts, certain chipped artifacts bear a striking resemblance to those reported from as far away as Tennessee.

Probably few will agree with your assumptions, but no one will question your right to call attention to suspected relationships. Make it clear that these are *opinions*, not *facts*, and you are on safe ground. Perhaps you may find it simpler to express these facts in tabular form, as shown in the illustration, where I have attempted to show the relationships between artifacts recovered from a site known as Sweet's Knoll and a number of other sites in the area.

CONCLUSIONS

Here you may draw conclusions from the evidence reported in the earlier sections of your report. Of course, these conclusions must be logical assumptions based upon factual evidence. If contradictory evidence exists, call it to the attention of the reader, don't just ignore it. If there is an explanation, give it; if not, acknowledge that you are aware of the discrepancy.

As your conclusions develop, you will probably want to refer to statements contained in other reports you have read. By all means make such references whenever they are pertinent, but be sure that you acknowledge the source clearly so that it can be checked. This may be done within the body of the text in parenthesis, in a footnote, or in a bibliography at the end of the report. Be specific in these acknowledgments: give the name of the publication, volume, number, and date of issue, and take care to quote the name of the author correctly. If you are writing for a specific journal, note the manner in which the bibliographies of articles in that publication are set up and make yours conform to that style. If you wish to quote someone at length, it is ethical to obtain their permission regardless of whether or not the article is copyrighted.

Make your conclusions as full and complete as the evidence warrants. Try to give the reader a complete picture of the people who occupied the site. What kind of house did they live in? What kind of food did they eat and how did they obtain it? Perhaps you can tell something about their nonmaterial traits from the material ones that you found. How did they bury their dead, and do the grave goods suggest something of their beliefs in the life after death? Were they in contact with other primitives in the area, or do trade goods suggest white contact? When was the site occupied, as indicated by carbon dating, pollen analysis, or simply by culture content? In short, your conclusions should contain all that you have learned from your work at this site and from the comparisons that you have made with the work of others.

12 : Historical Archaeology

The pursuit of historical archaeology, once neglected in this country because the sites of the colonial period seemed so "new," is becoming increasingly popular. The excavation and restoration of pre-Revolutionary Williamsburg, Virginia, is a classic example of historical archaeology, but opportunities abound for less elaborate digs. The site of an old mill, a foundry, or a simple dwelling may yield valuable information about earlier periods in American history, supplementing and on occasion correcting the written record.

It is commonly—but incorrectly—assumed that any qualified archaeologist is competent to excavate, analyze, and report on a historical site. Of course, many of the techniques described in the preceding chapters on prehistoric archaeology are applicable to historical archaeology. However, the two types of sites differ greatly, as do the problems they pose and the skills and the knowledge that are required to solve them.

Where the prehistorian deals with cultures that, for the most part, are not documented, the historical archaeologist has available a wealth of written evidence to help him identify artifacts, determine their sources, and establish their dates. As a result, while the prehistorian relies primarily on his powers of deductive logic and on comparisons with the evidence (also undocumented) of other sites to interpret his finds, the historical archaeologist may spend less time in the field than in the library, searching for clues in land records, wills, and contemporary letters, diaries, and newspapers, as well as in formal histories. The historical archaeologist, moreover, must deal with a more complex cultural pattern, since colonial society was an amalgam of many different cultures. Old World ideas, traits, and artifacts were imported, borrowed, improved, and adapted by the New World settlers. The historical archaeologist should know something of the ceramic arts of several European nations, the history of clay pipes, the evolution of the bottle, and the

213

many varieties of the lowly button. All of these subjects, and many more, are grist for the mill of historical archaeology.

LOCATING HISTORIC SITES

Most Indian sites are found by observing the geographical and topographical features and selecting those that best met the need of the Indian (see chapter 3). The search for historical sites, however, properly begins at the local library or county courthouse. From these and similar sources one may learn where to search for the material evidence that will confirm the presence of historical remains. However, the written record must not be accepted too literally. Altogether too much hearsay and too many unwarranted assumptions are contained in these records. For example, a building reported to have been constructed in 1650 was recently moved to a new location. Beneath this structure the foundations of another building appeared. Greatly to the surprise of the excavator, the

Foundation of Whaler's Tavern, Wellfleet, Massachusetts, late seventeenth century-early eighteenth century. The plan indicates a two-room, two-story structure, with a lean-to on the rear, a central chimney, and cellars beneath. (Plimoth Plantation Photo)

second foundation was found to be that of a building erected in the early eighteenth century. Obviously, the earlier 1650 building had either been moved to the site from another location or its vintage was not as early as had been reported. The intent of the historical archaeologist should be not only to confirm documented evidence, but to amplify and correct it.

In those areas of America in which original settlements were made, particularly along the eastern seaboard, numerous sites exist that have a long history of successive occupation. Before the earliest level of occupation is reached, the successive levels above it must, of course, be excavated. The topmost level, for example, might indicate not only a modern structure but one that in later years had been altered or enlarged. On the second level a colonial structure might appear, a structure that had been burned and was, perhaps, replaced by the modern structure of the first level. And beneath the colonial structure, evidence of Indian culture might be found. In the effort to reach the earliest level of occupation, there is often a regrettable tendency to dig quickly through the more recent horizons, paying little attention to their content. Research should start with the uppermost level so that when the digging is complete, the archaeologist will know the complete cultural history of the site. In your preparatory research, both at the library and in the field, become familiar with the entire history of the site and learn to recognize the artifacts of each historical level. Don't be content to scan only those documents relating to the sixteenth century; examine with equal care the records of more recent times.

Having located the site you intend to excavate, you must now make another decision. How extensive a job can you undertake? What is your ultimate goal? Do you plan only to excavate the site, study the artifacts, and write a report? Or do you intend to reconstruct whatever is present as a permanent illustration? It is always a good rule in archaeology not to attempt more than you can reasonably expect to accomplish. Unlike prehistoric sites in which a restoration is seldom intended, many historic sites are excavated for precisely that purpose. Most amateurs, however, have no such ambitious intentions. In either case, keep in mind that colonial buildings are usually associated with various outbuildings, with surrounding stone walls, fences, and gardens. Your work will not be complete unless all of these adjoining features are at least located and described.

LAYING OUT A SITE

Most of the procedures described in chapter 7 can be adapted to historical archaeology. With few exceptions, similar tools are used, and the methods need only minor adaptation. The pits look much the same, only their content differs. Post molds probably indicate a fence line rather than the outline of a house. Old brick or fieldstone walls often mark the location of buildings. If, by chance, you come across a Christian burial, it is best to leave it *in situ,* but don't neglect to record its presence and location. Photographic records are most important at all stages of excavation. The Cohannet Line (see page 160), fully as useful in this type of archaeology, is often used by professionals.

The Probe

One new tool, the probe, is indispensable, and is perhaps the most important tool historical archaeologists use. The probe is made from a steel rod from ⅜ to 1 inch in diameter with a T-bar handle welded across one end. The other end should be tapered slightly with a small concavity in the end to recover traces of ash, brick, shell, or whatever material may be encountered. Two probes are valuable, one about 3 feet in length for use on shallow sites and another 5 or 6 feet long for deeper probing. With experience, one learns to tell with uncanny accuracy the kind of soil into which the probe is inserted and to identify objects encountered within it. In hard dry or clay soil it is sometimes difficult to insert the probe, particularly the longer instrument. A slight rotary motion will enlarge the hole and decrease the side friction. Practice to get the feel of the probe in the soil; learn to cease your downward thrust instantly when an object is encountered. The probe is used at all stages of excavation, both in the preliminary location of walls, pits, or paved areas, and later to find the position of corners in a foundation wall and to determine the approximate size of encountered objects. Probes are also useful in determining the character of suspicious looking depressions or other surface anomalies.

The probing of a site should not be done in a hit or miss manner. Such procedure may succeed in locating some unsuspected feature but, if so, it will be at the expense of much wasted time. It is much more satisfactory to proceed in an orderly and well planned pattern. Construct a small rectangular frame of wood or metal about

Cellar of a farmhouse, about 1660, at the Allerton Site, Kingston, Massachusetts. (Allerton was the treasurer of Plymouth Colony.) In the upper left corner the cellar intersects an earlier hearth that belongs to a house built about 1635. (Plimoth Plantation Photo)

5 feet square. Subdivide the area within the square by cross wires placed at 6-inch intervals around the perimeter. Solder the wires together where they cross. Place the portable grid in the corner of your 10-foot grid; insert the probe at the intersections of the cross wires. Each of these small squares will be represented by a similar square to scale on your master plan. Record the depth at which the probe meets an obstruction in the soil. The spacing is kept small so that little will be missed. If you are following the line of a wall, the plan will develop on your plotting board, showing the direction of the wall as well as any changes in direction or deviations that may be present. If the wall happens to be of fieldstone, it is probable that some of the upper stones will have been displaced and your wall will appear as a series of bumps. However, most archaeological features form a recognizable pattern and are easily recognized as man-made features.

Electrical Devices

Various electrical, electronic, and magnetic devices, used to pinpoint objects or features of interest on historical sites, are being marketed. Most of these devices, however, are too expensive, too complicated to operate, and require too much expertise and theoretical knowledge to be suitable for amateur use.

The Metal Detector

The most common and least expensive detecting device is the metal, or "mine," detector. Such an instrument can be purchased at low cost from an army surplus store or at a slightly higher price from the manufacturer. Their use is limited to the detection of metallic objects or possibly mineralized stones. They are not recommended for use in locating a site as they are very indiscriminate in their indications. A beer can will produce as much excitement for a metal detector as will an ancient flintlock gun. You can have a lot of fun with this device and you may locate old coins and the like, but serious amateurs will not want to waste time and effort in digging up random cans, rusty nails, and iron-bearing rocks. We have attempted to use the metal detector on prehistoric sites but with little success and with much wasted time.

The Proton Magnetometer

At the other extreme in detecting devices is the sophisticated proton magnetometer, which takes advantage of the fact that the magnetic properties of soils are altered by exposure to high temperatures. For example, the clay of which bricks are made has different magnetic qualities from that of the surrounding soil. This property is known as thermoremnant magnetism. Still another phenomenon— a chemical change of the ferromagnetic parts of the soil in the presence of organic matter—increases the magnetism of unfired soils, such as those found in cellar holes containing refuse.

The proton magnetometer has made possible the measurement of these phenomena. Although the process has been used with marked success on historic sites in both Europe and America, the technique will doubtless be further improved and may become even more important in the future. The equipment is costly and demands a high degree of competency for its operation and interpretation.

Removing fill by 6-inch levels from a 7-foot 1790 trash pit. The site is at the rear of a shoe store in the business district of present-day Plymouth. (Plimoth Plantation Photo)

Only professional archaeologists, with rather large budgets, are likely to be able to take advantage of this device.

The Resistivity Meter

Yet another electrical principle being used to locate underground objects is resistivity. In simple terms, the resistivity meter consists of a source of electricity and a meter that records electrical impulses. Variations in the resistance offered within an electrical circuit to the flow of current control the amount of flow. Two metal probes called electrodes are inserted in the ground at a measured distance apart and a small current is passed between them. Two additional probes, spaced at the same distance apart, are used to indicate potential changes in the circuit. The amount of electricity that flows from one probe to the other depends upon the resistance between them, and varies with the amount of moisture present and the composition of the soil. Obviously, many readings must be taken to establish the norm for a given location under specific moisture conditions before anomalies caused by the presence of foreign objects can be recognized. Resistivity meters cost as little as $150. However, for the amateur, the results obtained and the time required to experiment and to learn to interpret the indications of the meter do not warrant the expenditure.

The Dowsing Rod

And finally, you can have a lot of fun—and you might even find something—by trying your hand at dowsing. Professional archaeologists, as well as amateurs, have been experimenting recently with this ancient method of divining the location of underground water and ores. Traditionally, dowsers have used forked branches as indicators, but sticks, rulers, and rods of various sorts also have been put into service. For example, Ivor Noël Hume, director of the Department of Archaeology at Colonial Williamsburg, reports in his book *Historical Archaeology:*

> Metal-detecting equipment other than government surplus varies in price from about $120.00 to $500.00 which is quite expensive, particularly when one may well be able to achieve the same results with a couple of bent wire coat hangers. This simple device,

which must, I suppose, be classified as archaeological dousing, has been thoroughly tested under all sorts of conditions and there remains no doubt that two pieces of wire, each bent at a right-angle and held lightly in each hand, will cross when they pass over metal. This is by no means a new discovery; it has been used by plumbers and electricians both in the United States and in Europe for years as a means of locating the course of buried pipes and cables. It is only recently, however, that the archaeological potential of the "tool" has been appreciated.

Dowsing rods held in the proper position.

Having experimented with dowsing myself, I can testify that it does seem to produce results for some people under some conditions. You can make rods of the sort that I used with two lengths (about 4 feet each) of the bronze rods used by welders and two lengths of copper tube (about 8 inches each). Bend each of the bronze rods into an L, with the short leg being about 8 inches, and insert the short legs in the copper tubes. The bronze rods should be able to rotate freely. Hold the rods parallel to the ground and about 2 inches apart, hands clenched about the copper tubes and knuckles pressed together. Be sure to hold your thumbs well back, so that they do not rest upon the rods or influence them in any manner. Now walk slowly in a straight line, endeavoring to keep the rods level; otherwise, gravity will cause them to swing in either direction. The theory is that the rods will either converge or swing apart naturally when one approaches a point under which there is a buried metallic object or a concentration of moisture. If the bars have swung or crossed at right angles to one another, the object should be directly beneath the handle tips. In experiments with dowsing rods, we have succeeded in tracing the course of water pipes as deep as 6 feet beneath the surface. And at the Wapanucket site, we located Indian refuse pits by this means.

Despite these finds, and the well-authenticated successes of many other dowsers, the validity of the technique remains dubious. Dowsing fails to meet the scientific standard of repeatability, since only some "favored" people are able to do it successfully. Moreover, even the best dowsers appear to have difficulty finding anything when they are blindfolded. This suggests that a good eye for terrain is essential to dowsing success. The actual movements of the dowsing rod, of course, may be controlled unconsciously by slight changes in muscle tension (in the same way that the indicator of a Ouija board is controlled) or, as in the case of the rods that I used, a small tilt of the copper tubes.

Whatever the mechanism, dowsing is fun—like Ouija—and from what I have seen, experimentation in this field is on the increase.

Appendix I : Archaeological Sites
Open to the Public

ALABAMA

Bridgeport
Russell Cave National Monument: 8 miles NW on US 72. Occupied from about 6000 B.C. to A.D. 1650.

Kinlock Knob
Bankhead National Forest: ½ mile W. Petroglyphs.

Moundville
Mound State Monument: On State 69. 40 mounds.

Mount Hope
Bankhead National Forest: 4 miles S. Petroglyphs.

ARIZONA

Camp Verde
Montezuma Castle National Monument: About 5 miles NE off State 79. Five-story cliff dwelling.

Chinle
Canyon de Chelly National Monument: On Navajo Indian Reservation, State 68. Pit houses and cliff dwellings representing four periods of Indian culture from A.D. 348 to 1300.

Clarkdale
Tuzigoot National Monument: 2 miles E off US 89 Alt. Pueblo ruins dating from A.D. 1100 to 1450.

Coolidge
Casa Grande National Monument: 2 miles on State 87, Hohokam tower, ruins.

Flagstaff
Walnut Canyon National Monument: 7½ miles E on US 66, then S for 3 miles on marked road. Over 300 cliff dwellings dating from A.D. 1100 to 1275.
Wupatki National Monument: 45 miles NE off US 89. Over 800 ruins, ancient ball court.

Gila Bend
Painted Rocks State Historical Site: 26 miles NW. Petroglyphs.
Globe
Besh-ba-Gowah: 1 mile S on Pinal Mt. Rd. Pueblo ruins inhabited by
Salado Indians from A.D. 1225–1400.
Grand Canyon National Park
Tusayan Ruin: 22 miles E of Grand Canyon Village. Small pueblo.
Holbrook
Petrified Forest National Park: 19 miles E on US 180. Puerco Ruins,
Indian village. Newspaper Rock, 1 mile S of Puerco River.
Petroglyphs.
Kayenta
Navajo National Monument: 41 miles W off State 464, on Navajo
Indian Reservation. Betatkin and Keet Seel cliff dwellings.
Lupton
Pueblo ruins: Between Lupton and Houck. Basketmaker dwellings,
dating from A.D. 797 or earlier.
Phoenix
Pueblo Grande City Park: Hohokam ruin; continuing periodic exca-
vations.
Roosevelt
Tonto National Monument: 3 miles SE on State 88. Hohokam cliff
dwellings.
Whiteriver
Kinishba Pueblo: 7 miles W on Whiteriver Apache Indian Reservation.
Partially restored ruins dating from A.D. 1050–1350.
ARKANSAS
Arkadelphia
Powell Site: 15 miles NW, S side of Caddo River. Temple mounds.
Eureka Springs
Blue Spring: 7 miles W on US 62, then 1 mile N on gravel road.
Pictographs.
CALIFORNIA
Bishop
Chalfont Valley Petroglyphs: N along Fish Slough Rd. Date unknown.
Fort Ross
Fort Ross State Historic Park. Early 19th-century Russian fur-trading
post and fort.
Indio
Travertine Rock: About 24 miles SW of State 86. Petroglyphs.
Lompoc
Misión de la Purísima Concepción: 2 miles NE. Restored Franciscan
mission.

Santa Barbara
Mission Santa Barbara: Los Olivas and Laguna Sts.
Sequoia and Kings Canyon National Parks
Hospital Rock: 5 miles beyond Ash Mt. Pictographs.
Solvang
Mission Santa Ines.
Tulelake
Lava Beds Monument. Petroglyphs.

COLORADO
Cortez
Mesa Verde National Park: Between Cortez and Mancos on US 160. Pit houses and pueblo ruins and cliff dwellings.
Hovenweep National Monument: 18 miles N of Cortez on US 160, W on graded road from Pleasant View.

FLORIDA
Crystal River
Crystal River State Park: Temple and burial mounds, shell heaps.
Jacksonville
Fort Caroline National Memorial: 10 miles E off State 10. 16th-century French fort.
St. Augustine
Castillo de San Marcos National Monument: 17th-century Spanish fortress.
Fort Matanzas National Monument: 14 miles S off State A1A. 18th-century Spanish fort.

GEORGIA
Blakely
Kolomoki Mounds State Park: 5 miles NW on US 27. Temple and burial mounds.
Cartersville
Etowah Mounds: Temple and burial mounds.
Macon
Ocmulgee National Monument: On US 80 and 129. Temple mounds, earth lodge.
St. Simons Island
Fort Frederica: 18th-century British fort.

ILLINOIS
East St. Louis
Cahokia Mounds State Park: 5½ miles E on US 40 and 66. Temple mounds.
Havana
Dickson Mounds State Memorial: near Havana and Lewiston, off State 78 and 97. Skeletons in burial mound.

Utica

Starved Rock State Park: 1 mile S on State 178. Hopewellian burial mounds.

INDIANA

Anderson

Mounds State Park: 4 miles E on State 32. Mounds.

Evansville

Angel Mounds: 5 miles E on State 266 and 662. Mounds. Excavations during July and August.

Mitchell

Spring Mill State Park: 3 miles E on State 60. Early 19th-century frontier trading post.

IOWA

McGregor

Effigy Mounds National Monument: Off US 18. Mounds in bird and animal shapes.

KENTUCKY

Ashland

Central Park: Burial mounds.

Lexington

Adena Park: Off US 27 and 68. Mound (for permission to visit, apply to University of Kentucky).

Wickliffe

Ancient Burial City (or King Mounds): NW on US 51, 60, and 62. Council houses, burial and temple mounds.

LOUISIANA

Epps

Poverty Point: E on Bayou Macon. Geometric mounds (private property, no admission fee).

Marksville

Marksville Prehistoric Indian Park: 1 mile E.

MAINE

Augusta

Fort Western: Bowman and Cony Sts. 18th-century fort.

Fort Kent

Fort Kent: Off Main St., at end of Meadowbrook Lane. 19th-century blockhouse.

Kittery

Fort McClary Memorial: 2 miles E. 19th-century fort.

Wiscasset

Fort Edgecomb Memorial: S end of Davis Island, 1 mile E. Early 19th-century wooden blockhouse.

MASSACHUSETTS

Pittsfield

Hancock Shaker Village: 5 miles W on US 20. 18th-century com-
munity.

Saugus

The Ironworks: 17th-century blast furnace, forge, and rolling and
slitting mill.

MICHIGAN

Houghton

Isle Royale National Park: Prehistoric camp sites.

MINNESOTA

Pipestone

Pipestone National Monument: 1 mile N on US 75. Ancient quarries
of red stones for ceremonial pipes.

MISSISSIPPI

Natchez

Emerald Mound: 11 miles NE, about 1 mile from Natchez Trace
Parkway, on county road. Temple mound.

MISSOURI

De Soto

Washington State Park: On State 21. Pictographs.

Marshall

Van Meter State Park: 14 miles NW on State 122. Hopewellian
mounds.

MONTANA

Kalispell

Pictographs: W along US 2.

NEBRASKA

Gering

Scotts Bluff National Monument: Extinct bison remains with stone
artifacts.

NEVADA

Moapa

Valley of Fire State Park: SE on State 40. Petroglyphs.

NEW JERSEY

Batsto

Batsto Area of the Wharton Forest: County 52. Revolutionary War
ironworks.

NEW MEXICO

Alamogordo

The Petroglyphs: 35 miles N on US 54, about 5 miles E of Three
Rivers.

Aztec
Aztec Ruins National Monument: N off US 550. Ancient pueblo and kivas.

Bernalillo
Coronado State Monument: 2 miles NW on State 44. Ancient pueblo and kivas.

Espanola
Puye Cliff Dweller and Communal House Ruins: 3½ miles S on State 30, then 9 miles W on State 5.

Folsom
Folsom State Monument: Off US 64. Ancient pueblo and Franciscan mission.

Jemez Springs
Jemez State Monument: About 15 miles N on State 4. Ancient pueblo and Franciscan mission.

Mountainair
Abo State Monument: 10 miles SW on US 60. Ruins of ancient pueblo and mission.
Gran Quivira National Monument: 25 miles S on State 10. Ruins of Franciscan missions.
Quarai State Monument: 9 miles NW off State 10. Ruins of mission church.

Pecos
Pecos State Monument: 2 miles SE of US 85. Ruins of ancient pueblo and mission.

Santa Fe
Bandelier National Monument: 45 miles W off State 4. Ancient pueblos and caves.

Silver City
Gila Cliff Dwelling National Monument: No auto road; write Superintendent, Box 1320. Cliff dwellings.

Thoreau
Chaco Canyon National Monument: 69 miles N on US 66. Pueblo Bonito and ruins of smaller sites.

NEW YORK
Fort Ticonderoga
Fort Ticonderoga: 18th-century fort.

Oswego
Fort Ontario: N of US 104 on E 7th St. 18th-century fort.

Rensselaer
Fort Crailo: 17th-century Dutch fort.

Mt. Gilead

Town Creek Indian Mound State Historic Site: 5 miles E off State 731. Restored temple mound.

New Bern

Tryon Palace Restoration: George St. Reconstructed state capitol.

Roanoke Island

Fort Raleigh National Historic Site. 16th-century British fort.

Winston-Salem

Old Salem: Reception Center, 614 Main St. Long-range restoration of 18th-century Moravian village.

NORTH DAKOTA

Hebron

Crowley Flint Quarry: 17 miles N off US 10. Sources of flint for artifacts.

OHIO

Bainbridge

Slip Mound State Memorial: 3 miles E on US 50. Large central mound of Slip Group.

Chillicothe

Mound City Group National Monument: 3 miles NW on State 104. 24 Hopewellian burial mounds (500 B.C.–A.D. 500).

Story Mound: Delano Ave. Conical Adena mound.

Fort Recovery

Fort Recovery State Memorial: On State 49. 18th-century blockhouse with connecting stockade wall.

Jackson

Leo Petroglyph: 8 miles N. Many petroglyphs.

Kelley's Island

Inscription Rock: In Lake Erie, reached by ferry. Fine examples of pictograph rock.

Lebanon

Fort Ancient: 7 miles SE on State 350. Earthworks, burial mounds, cemeteries, remains of village sites.

Locust Grove

Serpent Mound State Memorial: 4 miles NW on State 73. Large effigy mounds.

Marietta

Mound Cemetery: "Conus" burial mound of chief.

Miamisburg

Miamisburg Mound State Memorial: 1 mile SE on US 25. Largest conical mound in state.

Newark

The Newark Earthworks: Wright Earthworks (James and Waldo Sts.); Moundbuilders State Memorial (SW on State 79); and Octagon State Memorial (W on State 16). Geometric earthworks and effigy mound.

New Philadelphia

Schoenbrunn Village State Memorial: 3 miles E on US 250. Pioneer 18th-century Moravian village.

Rochester

Warren County Serpent Mound: On US 22. Effigy mound.

Sinking Spring

Fort Hill Memorial: About 2 miles N near State 41. Hopewellian earthworks.

Tarlton

Tarlton Cross Mound State Memorial: N near State 159. Effigy mound in form of cross.

OKLAHOMA

Boise City

Black Mesa State Park: 32 miles NW. Cave with ancient pictographs.

PENNSYLVANIA

Chester

Caleb Pusey House: Oldest millhouse in state. Inhabited almost continuously since 17th century. Under restoration; will become state park.

Cornwall

Cornwall Charcoal Furnace: 18th-century iron-casting furnace.

Ligonier

Fort Ligonier: On State 711. 18th-century fortification.

Reading

Hopewell Village National Historic Site: About 14 miles SE on Birdsboro-Warwick Road. 18th-century industrial settlement.

Uniontown

Necessity National Battlefield: 11 miles E on US 40. 18th-century fort and earthworks.

SOUTH CAROLINA

Charleston

Francis Marion National Forest: N on US 17, then NW on State 41. Preliminary excavation of Sewee Indian mound.

Summerville

Old Dorchester Historical State Park: 6 miles NE on State 642. Ruins of Revolutionary fort and settlement.

TENNESSEE

Memphis

Chucalissa Indian Town: 5 miles S on US 61, then 4½ miles W on
Mitchell Road. Temple and burial mounds.

Vonore

Fort Loudoun: 1½ miles N, off US 411. 18th-century French fort.

UTAH

Blanding

National Bridges National Monument: 45 miles W. Ancient cliff
dwellings.

Monticello

Indian Creek Historic State Park: 15 miles N, then 12 miles west, off
US 160. Newspaper Rock, large cliff mural of petroglyphs and
pictographs.

Torrey

Capitol Reef National Monument: 12 miles E on State 24. Petroglyphs
in Fremont River Canyon.

VIRGINIA

Jamestown

Colonial National Historical Park: Remains of early English settlement.

Williamsburg

Colonial Williamsburg: 18th-century state capital.

WASHINGTON

Walla Walla

Whitman Mission National Historic Site: 6 miles W. Portion of early
earthworks and buildings have been excavated.

Yakima

Indian petroglyphs: On US 410.

WEST VIRGINIA

Moundsville

Mammoth Mound: Tomlinson Ave., between 9th and 10th Sts. Large
conical Adena mound.

WISCONSIN

Baraboo

Devil's Lake State Park: 3 miles S on State 123. Effigy mounds.

Black Lion Falls

Gullickson's Glen: 9 miles SW, via County Roads C and X. Artifacts
and petroglyphs.

Fort Atkinson

Mounds.

Lake Mills

Aztalan State Park: 2½ miles E on County B. Mounds.

Prairie du Chien

Wyalusing State Park: 7 miles SE on US 18 and State 35, then 5 miles W on County C. Mounds.

West Bend

Lizard Mound State Park: 20 miles NE on County A. 31 effigy mounds.

WYOMING

Fort Laramie

Fort Laramie National Historic Site: 3 miles SW. Remains of trading center and military post.

CANADA

BRITISH COLUMBIA

Nanaimo (Vancouver Island)

Petroglyph Park: 2 miles S on Hway 1. Ancient rock carvings.

NEW BRUNSWICK

Sackville

Fort Beausejour National Historic Park: 5 miles E on Hway 2. 18th-century French fort.

NOVA SCOTIA

Annapolis Royal

Port Royal National Historic Park: 7 miles on N shore of Annapolis River. 17th-century French settlement.

Cape Breton Island

Fortress of Louisbourg National Historic Park: 18th-century French fortification.

ONTARIO

Amherstburg

Fort Malden National Historic Park: On Hway 18. War of 1812 fortification.

Fort Erie

Old Fort Erie: In Government Park. Fort used in War of 1812.

Kingston

Old Fort Henry: Completely restored 19th-century fort.

Prescott

Fort Wellington National Historic Park: War of 1812 fortification.

QUEBEC

Chambly

Fort Chambly National Historic Park: 17th-century French fort.

St. John

Fort Lennox National Historic Park: 12 miles S on Ile-Aux-Noix. 17th-century French fort, used by British during Revolution and War of 1812.

Appendix II : Archaeological Societies and Related Organizations

With a few exceptions, the archaeological societies listed below are open to all interested persons. A formal education in archaeology or experience in the field is not required for membership. If you are sincerely interested in archaeology or the allied sciences, and wish to learn how and where you may work, you will be welcomed as a member.

The addresses of the current secretaries of some of the societies are not provided, as they are subject to yearly change. If a permanent office exists, the address is given. Universities and museums (Appendix IV) can usually furnish current addresses.

REGIONAL AND NATIONAL ORGANIZATIONS

American Anthropological Association, 1530 P Street, N.W., Washington, D.C. 20005.

Anthropological Association of Canada (Association Anthropologique du Canada), 1575 Forlan Drive, Ottawa.

Archaeological Institute of America, 100 Washington Square East, New York, N.Y. 10003.

Eastern States Archaeological Federation, R.D. 2 Box 166A, Dover, Del. 19901. Member societies: Alabama, Connecticut, Delaware, Florida, Georgia, Maine (2), Maryland (2), Massachusetts, Michigan, Mississippi, New Hampshire, New Jersey, New York, North Carolina, Ohio, Pennsylvania, Rhode Island, South Carolina, Tennessee, Vermont, Virginia, West Virginia, Kentucky, and Ontario and Quebec, Canada.

Society for American Archaeology, 1530 P Street, N.W., Washington, D.C. 20005.

Society for Historical Archaeology, Roderick Sprague, Secretary-Treasurer, Dept. of Sociology and Anthropology, University of Idaho, Moscow, Idaho 83843.

STATE AND PROVINCIAL SOCIETIES
AND ORGANIZATIONS

ALABAMA

Alabama Archaeological Society, Box 6126, University of Alabama Museum, Montgomery. Chapters: Albertville; Auburn; Birmingham; Decatur; East Alabama; Gadsden; Huntsville; Marshall County; Mauvilla; Mobile; Montgomery; Morgan-Limestone; Moundville; Muscle Shoals; Noccalula; Selma; Sheffield; Tuscaloosa.

University of Alabama, Director, Dept. of Archives and History, Montgomery.

ALASKA

University of Alaska, Fairbanks.

ARIZONA

Arizona Archaeological and Historical Society, c/o Arizona State Museum, University of Arizona, Tucson.

Arizona State Museum, Director, Tucson.

ARKANSAS

Arkansas Archaeological Society, Central Office at the University Museum, Arkansas University, Fayetteville.

University of Arkansas Museum and Laboratory of Archaeological Research, Office of the Director, Fayetteville.

CALIFORNIA

Archaeological Research Associates, University of Southern California, Los Angeles.

Archaeological Survey Association of Southern California, Southwest Museum, Los Angeles.

California State Division of Beaches and Parks, P.O. Box 2390, Sacramento.

Central California Archaeological Foundation, Sacramento State College, Sacramento.

Long Beach State College, Dept. of Anthropology, Long Beach.

University of California Archaeological Survey, Los Angeles.

COLORADO

Colorado Archaeological Society, University of Colorado, Boulder. Several local chapters.

State Historical Society of Colorado, State Museum Bldg., E. 14th Ave. and Sherman St., Denver.

CONNECTICUT

Archaeological Society of Connecticut, University of Connecticut, Curator of Anthropological Collection, U-134, Storrs. Chapters: Albert Morgan, Hartford; Bridgeport, Norwalk; New Haven, New Haven.

University of Connecticut, Curator of Anthropological Collection, U-134, Storrs, 06268.

DELAWARE

Archaeological Society of Delaware, Inc., R.D. #2 Box 166A, Dover 19901.

DISTRICT OF COLUMBIA

Anthropological Society of Washington, c/o Smithsonian Institution, Washington.

FLORIDA

Florida Anthropological Society, Dept. of Anthropology, Florida State University, Tallahassee. Chapters: Broward County, Hollywood; Ft. Walton Chapter, Ft. Walton Beach; Indian River, Cocoa; South Florida, Miami; Tampa Bay, Tampa.

GEORGIA

Northwest Georgia Archaeological Society, Shorter College, Rome.

Society for the Preservation of Early Georgia History, Dept. of Archaeology and Anthropology, University of Georgia, Athens.

IDAHO

Idaho Historical Society, 610 Parkway Drive, Boise.

Idaho State College, Office of the Museum Director, Pocatello.

ILLINOIS

Council of Illinois Archaeology, Illinois State Museum, Springfield.

Illinois Archaeological Survey, 137 Davenport Hall, University of Illinois, Urbana.

Illinois State Archaeological Society, Southern Illinois University Museum, Carbondale.

State Conservation Dept., Director, Springfield.

INDIANA

Indiana Historical Society, 140 North Senate Ave., Indianapolis.

IOWA

Iowa Archaeological Society, State University of Iowa, Iowa City.

KANSAS

Kansas Anthropological Society, c/o Kansas State Historical Society, 10th and Jackson Sts., Topeka.

KENTUCKY

University of Kentucky, Dept. of Anthropology, Lexington.

LOUISIANA

Louisiana State University, Dept. of Anthropology, Baton Rouge.

Tulane University, Dept. of Anthropology, New Orleans.

MAINE

Maine Archaeological Society, Robert Abbe Museum of Stone Age Antiquities, Acadia National Park, Bar Harbor, Me. 04609.

MARYLAND

Archaeological Society of Maryland, c/o Maryland Academy of Sciences, 400 Cathedral St., Baltimore 21202.

Archaeological Society of Maryland, Inc., 17 East Branch Lane, Baltimore 21202.

Archaeological Societies and Related Organizations   235

Massachusetts Archaeological Society, Inc., Bronson Museum, 8 North Main St., Attleboro. Chapters: Cape Cod; Cohannet; Haverhill; Manamooskeagin; Massasoit; Norowatuck; Sippican; South Shore; W. Elmer Ekblaw.

MICHIGAN

Aboriginal Research Club, 828 Clay Street, Algonac.

Michigan Archaeological Society, c/o Museum of Anthropology, University of Michigan, Ann Arbor. Chapters: Central Michigan, Lansing; Clinton Valley, Waterford; Genessee County, Fenton; Saginaw Valley, Midland; Southeast, Roseville; Southwest, Benton Harbor; Wright L. Coffinberry, Grand Rapids.

Michigan State University, Dept. of Archaeology and Anthropology, East Lansing.

MINNESOTA

Minnesota Archaeological Society, 2303 Third Ave., South, Minneapolis.

Minnesota Historical Society, University of Minnesota, Minneapolis.

State Archaeologist and Conservation Dept., University of Minnesota, Minneapolis.

MISSISSIPPI

Mississippi Dept. of Archives and History, P.O. Box 571, Jackson.

MISSOURI

Missouri Archaeological Society, 15 Switzler Hall, University of Missouri, Columbia.

MONTANA

Montana Archaeological Society, Montana State University, Missoula.

NEBRASKA

Nebraska State Historical Society, 1500 R. Street, Lincoln.

University of Nebraska State Museum, 101 Merrill Hall, 14th and U. Sts., Lincoln.

NEVADA

Nevada State Museum, Carson City.

NEW HAMPSHIRE

New Hampshire Archaeological Society, c/o Prof. J. Frederick Burtt, 97 Hoyt Ave., Lowell. Chapters: Dartmouth, Claremont; Monadnock, Jeffrey; Seacoast, Exeter.

NEW JERSEY

Archaeological Society of New Jersey, Fairleigh Dickinson University, Madison. Chapters: Shongun, Chatham; Unalachtigo, Hammondton; Unami, Cranbury.

NEW MEXICO

Archaeological Society of New Mexico, c/o Regional Headquarters, National Park Service, Old Pecos Road, Santa Fe. Affiliated societies at: Farmington, Hobbs, Las Vegas, Portales, Silver City, and El Paso (Texas).

New Mexico Science Commission, State Land Office, Santa Fe.

NEW YORK

New York Archaeological Association, State Educational Building, Albany 1. An association of chapters; membership is in the chapters: Auringer-Seelye, Glens Falls; Chenago, Sherburne; Frederick M. Houghton, Buffalo; Long Island, Southold; Metropolitan, New York City; Mid-Hudson, Poughkeepsie; Lewis H. Morgan, Rochester; Orange County, Middletown; Van Epps-Hartley, Claversack.

NORTH CAROLINA

North Carolina Archaeological Society, Box 301, Chapel Hill. Chapters: Catawba, Charlotte; Lower Cape Fear, Wilmington; Neuse River, Smithfield; Tar River, Pikeville; Triangle, Durham; Upper Cape Fear, Dunn.

NORTH DAKOTA

North Dakota State Historical Society, Bismarck.

OHIO

Cleveland Museum of Natural History, Cleveland.

Ohio Academy of Science, Anthropology Section, Ohio Historical Society, 1982 Velma Ave., Columbus 43211.

Ohio Historical Society, Columbus.

OKLAHOMA

Oklahoma Anthropological Society, University of Oklahoma, Norman.

OREGON

Northwestern Anthropological Conference, Portland State College, P.O. Box 751, Portland.

Oregon Archaeological Society, Dept. of Anthropology, University of Oregon, Eugene.

PENNSYLVANIA

Society for Pennsylvania Archaeology. Chapters: Amockwi, Hookstown; Andaste, Towanda; Beaver Valley, Sharpesville; Conestoga, Lancaster; Connonoch, Johnstown; North Central, Williamsport; Lower Susquehanna, Hanover; Susquehannock, Dauphin; Cussewago, Meadville; Forty Fort; Frances Dorrance, Erie, Erie; Forks of the Delaware, Easton; Lenape, Port Jervis; Sheep Rock, Van Buren; Southeastern No. 2, Elkins Park.

RHODE ISLAND

Narragansett Archaeological Society of Rhode Island, 277 Brook St., Providence.

SOUTH CAROLINA

South Carolina Archaeological Society, Columbia.

Appendix III : Archaeological Museums and Special Collections

CALIFORNIA

Antelope Valley Indian Research Museum, Wilsona Routè, Lancaster.

Indian Museum, Lakeport.

Los Angeles County Museum, Exposition Park, Los Angeles.

Robert H. Lowie Museum of Anthropology, University cf California, Berkeley.

Municipal Museum, Riverside.

Museum of Natural History, Santa Barbara.

Oakland Public Museum, 1426 Oak St., Oakland.

San Diego Museum of Man, Balboa Park, San Diego.

Southwest Museum, 10 Highland Park, Los Angeles.

Stanford University Museum, Stanford.

State Indian Museum, 2618 K St., Sacramento.

COLORADO

Colorado State Museum, East 14th Ave. and Sherman St., Denver.

Denver Museum of Natural History, City Park, Denver.

Durango Public Library Museum, Durango.

Gem Village Museum, Inc., Bayfield.

Museum at Mesa Verde National Park.

Trinidad State Junior College Museum, Trinidad.

University of Colorado Museum, Boulder.

Western State College Museum, Gunnison.

CONNECTICUT

Connecticut State Library Museum, 231 Capital Ave., Hartford.

Fort Hill Indian Memorial Association, Gallup Hill, Old Mystic.

Gunn Memorial Library and Museum, Washington.

Mattatuck Historical Society, 119 W. Main St., Waterbury.

Peabody Museum of Natural History, Yale University, 170 Whitney Ave., New Haven.

Somers Mt. Indian Museum, Somers.

University of Connecticut, Storrs (Bull Collection).

DELAWARE

Delaware State Museum, 316 Governors Ave., Dover.

Hagley Museum, Wilmington.

Zwaanendael Museum, Lewes.

DISTRICT OF COLUMBIA

Natural History Building, Smithsonian Institution.

FLORIDA

Florida State Museum, University of Florida, Seagle Bldg., Gainesville.

Fort Pierce Museum, Fort Pierce.

McKee's Sunken Treasure Fortress, US 1, Tavernier.

Museum of Science and Natural History, 3280 S. Miami Ave., Miami.

Museums at these National Monuments: Castillo de San Marcos, St.

240   Archaeological Museums and Special Collections

Augustine; Fort Caroline, Jacksonville; Fort Matanzas, St. Augustine; and these State Parks: Crystal River; Fort Clinch.

Oldest House, St. Augustine.

Southeast Museum of the North American Indian, US 1, Marathon.

South Florida Museum, Bradenton.

Temple Mound Museum, Fort Walton Beach.

University Museum, Florida State University, Tallahassee.

GEORGIA

Emory University Museum, Bishop's Hall, Atlanta.

Museums at these National Monuments: Fort Frederica, St. Simons Island; Ocmulgee, Macon; and State Parks: Etowah Mounds, Cartersville; Kolomoki Mounds, near Blakely.

IDAHO

Idaho State College Museum, Pocatello.

ILLINOIS

Chicago Academy of Science, 2001 N. Clark St., Chicago.

Chicago Natural History Museum, Roosevelt Rd. and Lake Shore Dr., Chicago.

Dickson Mounds State Memorial, US 24, southwest of Peoria.

Illinois State Museum of Natural History and Art, Springfield.

University of Illinois Museum of Natural History, Natural History Bldg., Springfield.

INDIANA

Indiana Historical Society, 140 No. Senate St., Indianapolis.

Indiana State Museum, 311 West Washington St., Indianapolis.

Indiana University Museum of Anthropology, Bloomington.

IOWA

Harlan, on US 59 (Indian artifacts on Indian camping ground south of town).

Museum of Natural History, State University, Iowa City.

Museums at Effigy Mounds National Monument, off US 18, McGregor; and Maquoketa Cave State Park, off US 61, south of Dubuque.

Sanford Museum and Planetarium, 117 East Willow St., Cherokee.

KANSAS

Fort Hayes Kansas State College Museum, Hayes.

Kansas State Historical Society, Memorial Bldg., 10th and Jackson Sts., Topeka.

Museum of Natural History, University of Kansas, Lawrence.

KENTUCKY

Behringer Museum of Natural History, Devow Park, Covington.

Museum of Anthropology and Archaeology, University of Kentucky, Lexington.

Museum at Mammoth Cave National Park, near Cave City.

LOUISIANA

Louisiana State Exhibit Museum, Shreveport.

Louisiana State Museum, New Orleans.

Middle American Research Institute Museum, Tulane University, New Orleans.

Prehistoric Indian Museum, Marksville State Monument, Marksville.

Tulane University, 6823 St. Charles Ave., New Orleans.

MAINE

Robert Abbe Museum of Archaeology, Acadia National Park, Bar Harbor.

Fort Western, Bowman and Cony Sts., Augusta.

Maine Historical Society, Portland.

Wilson Museum, Perkins St., Castine.

MARYLAND

Baltimore Museum of Art, Wyman Park, Baltimore.

Maryland Academy of Sciences, 400 Cathedral St., Baltimore.

MASSACHUSETTS

Aptucxet Trading Post, Bourne.

Berkshire Museum, South St., Pittsfield.

Blue Hills Trailside Museum, 1904 Canton Ave. (State 138), Milton.

Bronson Museum, 8 No. Main St., Attleboro.

Haverhill Historical Society, 240 Water St., Haverhill.

Museum, Saugus Ironworks, Saugus.

Robert S. Peabody Foundation for Archaeology, Phillips Academy, Andover.

Peabody Museum, 161 Essex St., Salem.

Peabody Museum of Archaeology and Ethnology, Harvard University, Cambridge.

Pilgrim Hall, Plymouth.

Sears Museum (Fruitlands Museums), Harvard.

MICHIGAN

Chief Blackbird Home, Harbor Springs.

Detroit Historical Museum, Woodward and Kirby Sts., Detroit.

Grand Rapids Public Museum, 54 Jefferson Ave. S.E., Grand Rapids.

Kelsey Museum of Archaeology, University of Michigan, Ann Arbor.

Marquette Park, French and Indian Museum, St. Ignace.

Michigan Historical Museum, Lansing.

Michigan State Museum, East Lansing.

Museum of Anthropology, Wayne State University, Detroit.

Muskegon County Museum, 1259 Marquette Ave., Muskegon.

MINNESOTA

Minneapolis Public Library, Minneapolis.

Museum of Anthropology, University of Minnesota, 325 Ford Hall, Minneapolis.

Museum, Pipestone National Monument, Pipestone.
Runestone Museum, Alexandria.
The Science Museum, 51 University Ave., St. Paul.

State Historical Museum, State St. at E. Capital, Jackson.
University of Mississippi Museum, University.

Archaeological Research Center, University of Missouri, Van Meter State Park, near Marshall.
Kansas City Museum, 3218 Gladstone Blvd., Kansas City.
Missouri State Museum, Capitol Bldg., Jefferson.
Museum of Anthropology, University of Missouri, 15 Switzler Hall, Columbia.
Museum of Science and Natural History, 2 Oak Knoll Park, St. Louis.

Carter County Museum, County High School, Carter Co.
McGill Museum, Montana State College, Bozeman.
Museum of the Plains Indian, Browning.

Nebraska State Historical Society, 1500 R St., Lincoln.
University of Nebraska State Museum, 101 Merrill Hall, 14th and U Sts., Lincoln.

Nevada State Museum, Carson City.

Dartmouth College Museum, Hanover.

Museum of Natural History, Guyot Hall, Princeton University, Princeton.
Newark Museum, 49 Washington, Newark.
New Jersey State Museum, State House Annex, Trenton.
Paterson Museum, 268 Summer St., Paterson.

Acoma, off US 66, southwest of Albuquerque.
Grant County Museum, Silver City.
Isleta, State 47, south of Albuquerque (pueblo noted for its pottery).
Museum of Anthropology, University of New Mexico, Albuquerque.
Museum of Ceremonial Navajo Art, Santa Fe.
Museum of Indian Arts and Crafts, Gallup.
Museum of New Mexico, Palace Ave., Santa Fe.
Museum, Pecos State Monument, Pecos.
Museums at these National Monuments: Aztec Ruins, Aztec; Bandelier, off US 64, northwest of Santa Fe; Chaco Canyon, off US 66, east of Gallup.
Roswell Museum, Roswell.

Santa Domingo Pueblo, north of Albuquerque (Great Corn Dance, August 14).

School of American Research, Santa Fe.

Zuni, west of Grants (Shalko Dance in December).

NEW YORK

American Museum of Natural History, Central Park West and 79th St., New York.

Blue Mountain Lake Museum, Blue Mountain Lake.

Brooklyn Museum, Eastern Parkway, Brooklyn.

Buffalo Museum of Science, Humboldt Park, Buffalo.

Cooperstown Indian Museum, 1 Pioneer St., Cooperstown.

Mohawk-Caughnawaga Museum, Fonda.

Museum of Primitive Art, 15 West 54th St., New York.

Museum of the American Indian, Broadway at 155th St., New York.

New York State Museum, Washington Ave., Albany.

Rochester Museum of Arts and Sciences, 657 East Ave., Rochester.

NORTH CAROLINA

Brunswick Town State Historical Museum, 255 Pine Grove Dr., Wilmington.

Museum of the Cherokee Indian, Cherokee (west of Asheville).

Museum, Town Creek Indian Mound, State 73, Mount Gilead.

Research Laboratory of Anthropology, Person Hall, University of North Carolina, Chapel Hill.

NORTH DAKOTA

Museum, Fort Lincoln State Park, near Mandan.

OHIO

Cincinnati State Museum, Cincinnati.

Cleveland Museum of National History, Cleveland.

Firelands Historical Museum, Norwalk.

Museum, Fort Ancient State Memorial (State 350, southeast of Lebanon).

Natural History Museum, Mill Creek Park, Youngstown.

Vietzen Archaeology and Pioneer Museum, Elyria.

Visitor Center, Mound City Group National Monument, near Chillicothe.

OKLAHOMA

Black Mesa State Park, Panhandle at New Mexico line.

The Gilcrease Institute of American History and Art, 2401 Newton St., Tulsa.

Indian Council House Museum, Ocmulgee.

Indian Village, south of Anadarko (dances on Saturday night during summer).

Oklahoma Historical Society Museum, Oklahoma City.

Osage House, Pawhuska (west of Bartlesville on US 60).

Southern Plains Indian Arts and Crafts Museum, Anadarko.
Stovall Museum of Science and Industry, University of Oklahoma, Norman.

OREGON

Horner Museum, Oregon State Museum, Corvallis.
Klamath County Museum, Klamath Falls.
Museum of Natural History, University of Oregon, Eugene.
Oregon State Historical Society, 235 S.W. Market St., Portland.

PENNSYLVANIA

Carnegie Museum, Carnegie Institute, Pittsburgh.
Everhart Museum of National History, Science and Art, Nay Aug Park, Scranton.
Museum, Hopewell Village Historic Site, near Reading.
North Museum, Franklin and Marshall College, Lancaster.
Pennsylvania State Museum, Harrisburg.
University Museum, University of Pennsylvania, Philadelphia.

RHODE ISLAND

Haffenreffer Museum of the American Indian, Brown University, Providence.
Mount Hope Museum, Bristol.
Museum of Primitive Cultures, Peacedale.
Roger Williams Park Museum of Natural History, Providence.
Tomaquag Indian Memorial Museum, Burdikville Rd., Ashaway.

SOUTH CAROLINA

Charleston Museum, 125 Rutledge Ave., Charleston.

SOUTH DAKOTA

W. H. Over Museum, University of South Dakota, Vermillion.
Pettigrew Museum, 131 N. Duluth Ave., Sioux Falls.
South Dakota State Historical Museum, Memorial Bldg., Pierre.

TENNESSEE

Chucalissa Indian Museum, Memphis.
The Frank McClung Museum, University of Tennessee, Knoxville.
The Memphis Museum, Memphis.

TEXAS

The A. V. Lane Museum of Archaeology, Southern Methodist University, Dallas.
Museum of Anthropology, University of Texas, Austin.
Texas Western College, Centennial Museum, El Paso.
White Memorial Museum, Brackenridge Park, San Antonio.

UTAH

Moab Museum, Moab.
Museum of Anthropology and Archaeology, University of Utah, Salt Lake City.

VERMONT

Robert Hull Fleming Museum, University of Vermont, Burlington.

Vermont Historical Society Museum, Montpelier.

VIRGINIA

Colonial Williamsburg, Williamsburg.

Valentine Museum, Richmond.

Visitor Centers, Colonial National Historical Park (Jamestown and Yorktown).

WASHINGTON

Eastern Washington State Historical Society and Museum, Spokane.

Washington State Museum, University of Washington, 4037 15th St., N.E., Seattle.

Willis Carey Historical Museum, Chasmere.

Yakima Valley Museum, 2105 Tieton Drive, Yakima.

WEST VIRGINIA

Museum, Mammoth Mound, Moundsville.

WISCONSIN

Douglas County Historical Museum, Superior.

Indian Museum, LaPointe, on Madeline Island (Apostle Islands).

Logan Museum of Anthropology, Beloit College, Beloit.

Milwaukee Public Museum, 818 W. Wisconsin Ave., Milwaukee.

Neville Public Museum, 129 S. Jefferson St., Green Bay.

Oshkosh Public Museum, Oshkosh.

State Historical Society of Wisconsin Museum, Madison.

WYOMING

Wyoming State Museum, State Office Bldg., Cheyenne.

CANADA

Glenbow Foundation, 902 11th Ave., S.W., Calgary, Alberta.

Historical Museum of Medicine Hat, Medicine Hat, Alberta.

Luxton Museum, Banff, Alberta.

Museum of Geology, Paleontology and Archaeology, University of Alberta, Edmonton, Alberta.

Chilliwack Museum, Chilliwack, British Columbia.

Museum of Northern British Columbia, Prince Rupert, British Columbia.

Pacific National Museum, Vancouver, British Columbia.

Provincial Museum of Natural History and Anthropology, Victoria, British Columbia.

Vancouver City Museum, 401 Main St., Vancouver, British Columbia.

Museum, Fort Beausejour National Historic Park, near Sackville, New Brunswick.

New Brunswick Museum, St. John, New Brunswick.
Newfoundland Museum, St. John's, Newfoundland.
Debrissay Museum, Bridgewater, Nova Scotia.
Museum, Fortress of Louisbourg National Historic Park, Cape Breton Island, Nova Scotia.
Assiginack Museum, Manitowaning, Manotoulin Island, Ontario.
Museum, Fort Malden National Historic Park, Amherstburg, Ontario.
Museum, Fort Wellington National Historic Park, Prescott, Ontario.
Museum of Indian Archaeology, University of Western Ontario, London, Ontario.
The National Museum of Canada, Metcalf and McLeod Sts., Ottawa, Ontario.
Royal Ontario Museum, University of Toronto, Toronto, Ontario.
McCord Museum, McGill University, Montreal, Quebec.
Saskatchewan Museum of Natural History, Wascana Park, Regina, Saskatchewan.
University of Saskatchewan Museum, Saskatoon, Saskatchewan.
W. D. MacBride Museum, Whitehorse, Yukon.

Appendix IV : Study Courses

By definition an archaeologist is a student of ancient cultures. He seeks not only to become proficient in the art of excavation, but also to secure the knowledge necessary to grasp the implications of the materials his spade uncovers.

Cultural anthropology is the off-season program of most amateur archaeologists. This study may be pursued in several ways. As a start you can undertake a program of selected reading (see Bibliography) to acquire a background for more advanced study. Many of the local societies offer more formal courses of study in cultural anthropology to their members and you will be welcomed in such study groups. Extension courses in anthropology and archaeology are available at many universities and colleges if you live close enough to attend them. Institutions marked with an asterisk (*) also offer correspondence courses in anthropology, giving credits to those who complete the course in a satisfactory manner (for information, address Correspondence Study, Extension Division).

These suggestions are, of course, substitutes for the more formal, full-time courses available to those who have the time to pursue them.

Below is a partial list of institutions offering educational opportunities in anthropology. The courses are offered by the Department of Anthropology of the respective institution.

ALABAMA

*University of Alabama, University.

ALASKA

University of Alaska, Fairbanks.

ARIZONA

Arizona State College, Flagstaff.

Arizona State University, Tempe.

*University of Arizona, Tucson.

ARKANSAS

*University of Arkansas, Fayetteville.

CALIFORNIA

Long Beach State College, Long Beach.

Sacramento State College, Sacramento.

San Fernando Valley State College, Northridge.

San Francisco State College, San Francisco.
*University of California, Berkeley.
University of California, Davis.
University of California, Los Angeles.
University of California, Riverside.
University of California, Santa Barbara.

COLORADO

Adams State College, Alamosa.
*University of Colorado, Boulder.
University of Denver, Denver.

CONNECTICUT

Yale University, New Haven.

DISTRICT OF COLUMBIA

Catholic University of America, Washington.

FLORIDA

Florida State University, Tallahassee.

ILLINOIS

Knox College, Galesburg.
Southern Illinois University, Carbondale.
University of Chicago, Chicago.

INDIANA

*Indiana University, Bloomington.

IOWA

State University of Iowa, Iowa City.

KANSAS

*University of Kansas, Lawrence.
University of Wichita, Wichita.

KENTUCKY

*University of Kentucky, Lexington.

LOUISIANA

Louisiana State University, Baton Rouge.
Tulane University, Newcomb College, New Orleans.

MAINE

University of Maine, Orono.

MASSACHUSETTS

Boston University, Boston.
Brandeis University, Waltham.
Bridgewater State College, Bridgewater.
Harvard University, Cambridge.
University of Massachusetts, Amherst.

MICHIGAN

Michigan State University, East Lansing.
University of Michigan, Ann Arbor.
Wayne State University, Detroit.

MINNESOTA
 °University of Minnesota, Minneapolis.
MISSOURI
 St. Louis University, St. Louis.
 °University of Missouri, Columbia.
 Washington University, St. Louis.
MONTANA
 Montana State University, Missoula.
NEBRASKA
 University of Nebraska, Lincoln.
NEW HAMPSHIRE
 Dartmouth College, Hanover.
NEW JERSEY
 Princeton University, Princeton.
NEW MEXICO
 University of New Mexico, Albuquerque.
NEW YORK
 Columbia University, New York.
 Hunter College, City University of New York, New York.
 New School for Social Research, New York.
 New York University, New York.
 Skidmore College, Saratoga Springs.
 State University of New York, Harpur College, Binghamton.
 University of Buffalo, Buffalo.
 University of Rochester, Rochester.
NORTH CAROLINA
 Duke University, Duke Station, Durham.
 University of North Carolina, Chapel Hill.
 Wake Forest College, Winston-Salem.
NORTH DAKOTA
 University of North Dakota, Grand Forks.
OHIO
 Miami University, Oxford.
 Ohio State University, Columbus.
 University of Cincinnati, Cincinnati.
OKLAHOMA
 °University of Oklahoma, Norman.
OREGON
 Portland State College, Portland.
 Willamette University, Salem.
PENNSYLVANIA
 Bryn Mawr College, Bryn Mawr.
 Dickinson College, Carlisle.
 Temple University, Philadelphia.

University of Pennsylvania, Philadelphia.
RHODE ISLAND
Brown University, Providence.
SOUTH DAKOTA
University of South Dakota, Vermillion.
TENNESSEE
Scaritt College, Nashville.
University of Tennessee, Knoxville.
Vanderbilt University, Nashville.
TEXAS
*Texas Technological College, Lubbock.
*University of Texas, Austin.
William Marsh Rice University, Houston.
UTAH
*Brigham Young University, Provo.
*University of Utah, Salt Lake City.
WASHINGTON
*University of Washington, Seattle.
Washington State University, Pullman.
WISCONSIN
Beloit College, Beloit.
Lawrence College, Appleton.
University of Wisconsin, Madison.
CANADA
University of Alberta, Calgary, Alberta.
University of Alberta, Edmonton, Alberta.
University of British Columbia, Vancouver, British Columbia.
Victoria College, Victoria, British Columbia.
University of Toronto, Toronto, Ontario.
McGill University, Montreal, Quebec.

MUSEUM AND LABORATORY WORK

One way of picking up a good deal of useful information is to volunteer
to work in the laboratory of a museum or university department of
archaeology. Here the interested amateur assists the professional in the important task of restoring, studying, and interpreting archaeological finds.

FIELD PROGRAMS

Proficiency in excavation is best acquired through practice. Most of
the amateur societies (Appendix II) carry on field work during the out-
door season on a time schedule suited to the amateur. Get in touch with
the society nearest you and become a member of their next expedition.

Several universities offer summer study-dig courses each year. Among them are New York University, the universities of New Mexico, Arizona, Utah, Seattle, Michigan, Indiana, and others. Most take nonmatriculating students.

The Brooklyn Children's Museum, Brooklyn Avenue and Park Place, Brooklyn, N.Y., offers a summer course for qualified high school students in cultural anthropology and archaeology. It includes the excavation of prehistoric and historic sites on Staten Island.

Courses in historical archaeology are now being offered at Arizona State University (Development of Archaeology and Historic Sites), the University of Missouri (Historical American Archaeology), and the University of Pennsylvania (Methods and Problems of Historical Archaeology).

Salvage archaeology of sites threatened by construction of dams and interstate highways offers good opportunities for practical experience locally or farther afield. The organizations to contact are:

National Park Service, Washington, D.C. 20242. Its Inter-Agency Archaeological Salvage Program coordinates the joint efforts of local, state, and federal agencies to study threatened sites.

Smithsonian Institution, River Basin Surveys, 1835 P Street, Lincoln, Nebraska. (Single women are not allowed to participate.)

Amateurs perform particularly useful work on site surveys, such as the Upper Ohio Valley Archaeological Survey directed by Dr. Don Dragoo, curator of the Section of Man, Carnegie Museum, Pittsburgh, Pa.

If you are interested in taking part in a dig, list all of your qualifications in your letter of application. Knowledge of mapping or surveying, photography, or camping, for instance, are all welcome in the field.

Adventurous amateurs who would like to spend part of a summer digging in Britain should order the *Calendar of Excavations* from The Secretary, Council for British Archaeology, 4 St. Andrew's Place, Regents Park, London, N.W.1. This publication is issued monthly from March through September. It costs seven shillings and sixpence (approximately $1.00) and lists all the excavations in Britain where volunteers are needed.

Appendix V : Antiquities Laws

In some areas specific laws have been enacted that relate to archaeological activities. Even where no antiquities laws exist, the common law regulating trespass and protecting property rights is in force. Many property owners are extremely reluctant to permit amateur archaeologists to trespass for the purpose of seeking and excavating Indian sites. This attitude is occasioned by the unethical practice of relic hunters who invade private lands without first asking permission to do so. Growing crops are damaged, hay fields are trampled down, holes are dug and left unfilled by these careless people. Even if no damage is done, many property owners resent unauthorized trespass.

One of the fundamental rules of amateur archaeology is never to invade the rights of a property owner. When you ask for permission, be sure that you explain precisely what you wish to do. Make certain that your permit to trespass includes the right to excavate. Never cut a tree or bush without permission from the owner. Observe all of the restrictions the owner imposes even though they may seem unreasonable to you. If there are cattle or small children in the area, see to it that your activities cause them no injury. In other words, act as you would want others to act on your property. When your work is complete, return the area to its original condition. Never leave open holes, piles of brush, or other rubbish strewn about. Be considerate of others and they will extend the same courtesy to you.

For your own protection you should become familiar with the laws of the state in which you work and the federal laws that apply on all government property. These laws vary from state to state and are subject to change. Areas presently without such regulations may enact them at any time. Also it is well to remember that there are laws in some areas relating to the excavation of human burials. These are not usually a part of the antiquities acts but will be found in the penal code. For example, you may be required to notify the medical examiner in your area if you encounter a human burial. Check on this with a lawyer friend or with the state attorney.

FEDERAL ANTIQUITIES ACTS

Federal land in all states—national parks, monuments, forests, etc.
—are subject to federal legislation (the Antiquities Act of 1906—Public
Law 34-209; 34 Stat; the Historic Sites Act of 1935—Public Law 74-292;
49 Stat. 666; the Historic Preservation Act of 1966—Public Law 89-665;
80 Stat. 915; the Reservoir Salvage Act of 1960—Public Law 86-523; 74
Stat. 220). The government holds that federal lands and national resources, including antiquities, are held in trust for all the people and that
the right and duty to protect them is inherent in the national government.
Under these acts one must obtain specific permission to search for antiquities or to excavate on federal lands. Permission will be granted to reputable
institutions provided that all recoveries are deposited in public repositories
or museums.

The states that have antiquities legislation, the sources of the regulations, and in those states requiring permits, the state authority to which
application should be made are listed below. Unless otherwise noted, the
application should be addressed to the capital of the state.

STATE REGULATIONS

In 1965 twenty-six states had antiquities legislation. By 1972 antiquities laws had been enacted by forty-five states. Only Indiana, New Hampshire, New Jersey, Rhode Island, and Vermont do not have such legislation.

Antiquities legislation, whose constitutionality is sometimes question-
able, can be divided into three categories: that which provides funding for
archaeological research, that which establishes agencies for developing
archaeological resources, and that which exercises control over private
investigation and the disposition of archaeological recoveries.

Legislation designed to control investigation sometimes establishes a
system of permits or licenses, which, under various restrictions, can be
issued to individuals or institutions to enable them to carry out archaeological work. Some permits or licenses are issued upon payment of a fee,
while others are issued to only "qualified persons"; some states require
reports after completion of the work. Some laws establish state ownership
of all or part of the recoveries. Since these laws vary considerably, and
since new laws are being filed daily, it is well for the amateur archaeologist
to keep well informed. To determine precisely the nature of those laws
that pertain in his area of interest, he should apply to the appropriate state
authority. Amateur archaeologists should also familiarize themselves with
other local laws, for sometimes laws under other categories also apply, for
example, common trespass (see Bibliography, General Sources).

ALABAMA. Ala. Code, Title 55, Sec. 272 through 277 (1966). Archaeological excavation prohibited except by state agency. Nonresidents may not excavate. Antiquities may not be taken from the state.

ALASKA. Alaska Comp. Laws Ann., Sec. 38.12.010 through 38.12.050 (Supp. 1970). Laws affect only state-owned lands. Apply: Commissioner of Natural Resources.

ARIZONA. Ariz. Rev. Stat. Ann., Sec. 41.771 through 41.776 (Supp. 1969). Laws affect only state-owned lands. Apply: Director, Arizona State Museum, University of Arizona, Tucson.

ARKANSAS. Ark. Stat. Ann., Sec. 8-801 through 8-808 (1967), Sec. 9-1001 through 9-1017 (1967). Laws affect only state-owned lands but attempt to discourage work on private lands unless conducted in a scientific manner.

CALIFORNIA. Calif. Dept. of Parks and Recreation, Adm. Code, Title 14, Chap. 5, Sec. 1307 through 1309; Calif. Penal Code, Sec. 622½ (West 1939); Calif. Water Code, Sec. 234 (West Supp. 1970); Calif. Pub. Res. Code, Sec. 5097 through 5097.6 (West Supp. 1970). Under the penal code the willful destruction or defacing of archaeological objects on either public or private lands is prohibited. Apply: Director, Division of Beaches and Parks.

COLORADO. Colo. Rev. Stat. Ann., Sec. 131-12-1 through 131-12-6 (1963). Laws affect only antiquities on state-owned land. Apply: State Historical Society.

CONNECTICUT. Conn. Gen. Stat. Ann., Sec. 10-132A (1964), Sec. 10-321 A and B (1967). State archaeologist at University of Connecticut.

DELAWARE. Del. Code. Ann., Title 7, Sec. 5301 through 5306 (1953); Title 7, Sec. 5403 through 5405; Title 29, Sec. 8705 (Supp. 1970). State archaeologist. Laws affect only antiquities on state-owned land. Excavation of private land is discouraged unless it is done in a scientific manner. Apply: Governor of Office of Archaeology.

FLORIDA. Fla. Stat. Ann., Sec. 267 (Supp. 1969). Considerable control is exercised over underwater exploration. The director of the Bureau of Historic Sites and Properties is required by law to be an archaeologist.

GEORGIA. Ga. Code. Ann., Sec. 40-802a through 40-814a (Supp. 1969). Law affects only state-owned lands, but private landowners are asked to permit only qualified persons to explore and excavate. The Georgia Historical Commission is permitted to pay a fee to those who report sites, etc. Apply: Georgia Historical Commission.

HAWAII. Hawaii Rev. Laws, Sec. 734-1 (1968); Sec. 6-1 through 6-15 (1968); Act 216 of 1969; Act 236 of 1969. These various acts are among the most strict of any state antiquities acts. Sec. 267 is concerned with the excavation of human remains. Apply: Department of Land and Natural Resources.

IDAHO. Idaho Code Ann., Sec. 67-4114 through 67-4118 (1957); Sec. 67-4119 through 67-4122 (1963). Laws affect state-owned lands and archaeological sites on private lands that have been so designated and marked by the governor. Apply: Board of Trustees of State Historical Society.

ILLINOIS. Ill. Stat. Ann., Sec. 133c1 through 133c6 (Smith-Hurd Supp. 1970). Laws of 1907, p. 374; Laws of 1925, p. 498. Laws affect only state-owned lands. Apply: State department controlling property.

IOWA. Iowa Code Ann., Title 12, Sec. 303.6; Title 12, Sec. 304.1 through 304.7 (1949); Title 5, Sec. 111.2, 111.35, 111.41, and 111.57 (1949); Title 5, Sec. 111A.1 and 111A.7 (Supp. 1970) Title 12, Sec. 305A.1 through 305.A6 (1969). State archaeologist, Iowa State University. Laws affect only state-owned lands.

KANSAS. Kan. Gen. Stat. Ann., Sec. 74-5401 through 74-5408 (1967). Laws affect only state-owned lands. Apply: Secretary, Kansas Antiquities Commission.

KENTUCKY. Ky. Rev. Stat. Ann., Sec. 164.705 through 164.735 (1967). Laws affect only state-owned lands. Apply: Department of Anthropology, University of Kentucky, Lexington.

LOUISIANA. La. Rev. Stat., Chap. 8, Sec. 521 through 527 (Supp. 1968). Laws relate chiefly to historical sites and research rather than to prehistoric, or archaeological, sites.

MAINE. Me. Rev. Stat. Ann., Title 27, Chap. 13, Sec. 371 through 374 (Supp. 1969). Laws affect only state-owned lands. Apply: Director, Maine State Museum.

MARYLAND. Md. Ann. Code, Art. 66c, Sec. 110B through 110L (Supp. 1968). Laws affect only state-owned lands. Individuals are urged to report the location of sites to the Maryland Geological Survey. Apply: Maryland Geological Survey.

MASSACHUSETTS. Mass. Gen. Laws Ann., Chap. 9, Sec. 26-27; Chap. 40, Sec. 8D, and Chap. 79, Sec. 5A (1963). State Archaeologist Bronson Museum, 8 North Main Street, Attleboro, Massachusetts 02703. Additional laws are under consideration.

MICHIGAN. Mich. Comp. Laws, Sec. 299.51 through 299.55 (1948); Sec. 399.4 (1913). Laws affect only state-owned lands. Apply: Director, Department of Natural Resources.

MINNESOTA. Minn. Stat. Ann., Sec. 138.31 through 138.41 (1963) 138.51 through 138.64 (1965). State archaeologist, University of Minnesota. Laws affect only state-owned lands. Apply: Director, State Historical Society.

MISSISSIPPI. Miss. Code, Sec. 6192-101 through 6192-123. Law affects state-owned lands and such sites on private lands that have been designated, with the permission of the owner, as state archaeological landmarks. Apply: Board of Trustees, Department of Archives and History.

MISSOURI. Mo. Stat. Ann., Sec. 560.473 (Supp. 1970). Law affects only state park land, not other state-owned lands.

MONTANA. Mon. Rev. Codes Ann., Sec. 75-1202 through 75-1206 (1967). The wording of the law is not clear; it does not specifically differentiate between state-owned and private lands. Apply: Commissioner of Public Lands.

NEBRASKA. Neb. Rev. Stat., Sec. 39-1363 (1959). The laws of this state are not clear, but archaeological work on private lands does not seem to be affected. Apply: Conservation and Survey Division, University of Nebraska.

NEVADA. Nev. Rev. Stat., Sec. 381-200 through 381-260 (1953). Law affects only state-owned lands. Apply: Board of Directors, Nevada State Museum.

NEW MEXICO. N. M. Stat. Ann., Sec. 4-27-4 through 4-27-16 (1969). State archaeologist, Museum of New Mexico. Laws affect only state-owned lands. Apply: Cultural Properties Review Commission and State Archaeologist.

NEW YORK. N.Y. Education Law, Sec. 233 (McKinney 1970); Conservation Law, Sec. 831-4 (Supp. 1971). State archaeologist. Laws affect only state-owned lands and Indian cemeteries designated by the State Historic Trust. Apply: Head of State Departments with approval of Commissioner of Education.

NORTH CAROLINA. N.C. Gen. Stat., Sec. 70-1 through 70-4 (1935); Sec. 121-1 through 121-13.1 (1955). Laws affect only state-owned lands. Apply: Director, State Museum or Director, Department of Archives and History.

NORTH DAKOTA. N.D. Code, Sec. 55-12-07 (Supp. 1965); N.D. Cent. Code, Sec. 55-03-1 through 55-03-07 (1965); Sec. 55-10-01 through 55-10-10 (1967). Owners of private land may issue written permits, for others or may excavate on their own land without a state permit. Apply: Superintendent, State Historical Society.

OHIO. Ohio Rev. Code Ann., Sec. 149.30 through 149.301 (1969). Provides for the acquisition of archaeological sites by the State Historical Society. No actual antiquities laws exist.

OKLAHOMA. Okla. Stat. Ann., Title 70, Chap. 50, Sec. 3309 (1965); Title 74, Chap. 9A, Sec. 241 (Supp. 1970). A license is required to explore or to excavate on all land, federal, state, or private, and one half of all material recovered must be deposited with the Museum of Science and History at the University of Oklahoma. License fee: $50; renewal $25. Apply: Chairman, Department of Anthropology, University of Oklahoma, Norman.

OREGON. Ore. Rev. Stat. Sec. 273-705 (1967), Sec. 273-711 (1967), Sec. 352-090 (1967), Sec. 273-715 (1967). Laws affect only state-owned lands. Apply: State Land Board and President, University of Oregon, Eugene.

PENNSYLVANIA. Pa. Stat. Ann., Title 71, Sec. 716 (1963), Title 18, Sec. 4863 (1963). The manufacture, sale, or offering for sale of fraudulent archaeological specimens is prohibited.

SOUTH CAROLINA. SC Code, Sec. 9-331 (1969), Sec. 54-321 through 54-328 (1969). First act is enabling legislation for South Carolina Institute of Archaeology and Anthropology. Second act applies to underwater archaeology. Apply: Institute of Archaeology and Anthropology, University of South Carolina.

SOUTH DAKOTA. S.D. Code, Sec. 1-20-1 through 1-20-16 (1970). Law affects only state-owned lands. Apply: Secretary, State Historical Society.

TENNESSEE. Tenn. Code Ann., Chap. 468, Sec. 1 through 19 (Supp. 1970). State archaeologist. The provisions of the law apply in specific counties, depending on population. Sec. 16 authorizes the state archaeologist to issue permits to citizens of the state to surface hunt or to excavate in search of artifacts. Artifacts may not be removed from the state for more than 364 days in any one year. Apply: State Archaeologist, Division of Archaeology, Department of Conservation.

TEXAS. Tex. Rev. Civ. Stat., Art. 6145-9 (Supp. 1969). Law affects state-owned lands and sites designated as historic landmarks. Damaging or excavating on private land without the consent of the owner is forbidden. Apply: Antiquities Commission.

UTAH. Utah Code Ann., Sec. 63-11-2 (1960). Law affects only state-owned lands. Apply: State Park and Recreation Commission.

VIRGINIA. Va. Code Ann., Sec. 10-135 through 10-145.1 (1966); Sec. 10-146 through 10-150 (1966). An enabling act only.

WASHINGTON. Wash. Rev. Code, Sec. 27.44.00 through 27.44.020 (1964); Wash. Rev. Code, Sec. 27.48.010 (1964). Relates only to burials, petroglyphs, and paintings.

WEST VIRGINIA. W.Va. Code Ann., Sec. 5-12-1 through 5-12-5 (Supp. 1970). Forbids excavation of archaeological sites on state land or on private land when investigation rights have been previously acquired by the state. Apply: Antiquities Commission.

WISCONSIN. Wis. Stat. Ann., Sec. 27-012 (Supp. 1969). State archaeologist. Laws affect only state-owned lands. Apply: Director, State Historical Society (with approval of state archaeologist).

WYOMING. Wyo. Stat. Ann., Sec. 36-11 through 36-13 (1959); Sec. 36-44.6d (Supp. 1969). Laws affect only state-owned lands. Archaeological materials may not be removed from the state without the approval of the State Board of Land Commissioners. Apply: State Board of Land Commissioners.

MEXICO

The law relating to the preservation, ownership, excavation, and export of objects of antiquity is complex and comprehensive. In general, no person may search for, collect, or excavate in search of antiquities of any sort without permission from the federal government and the province in which the work is to be done. Permission to search for or to excavate antiquities will not be granted to any but professional persons who represent a qualified and reputable institution. Antiquities may not be taken out of the country except by special permit. These laws are strictly enforced and any attempt to evade their provisions will be prosecuted with vigor.

CANADA

All provinces and territories have laws regulating the excavation and investigation of archaeological sites. The antiquities laws differ slightly for each province, so that anyone wishing to carry on archaeological activity should contact the proper authority for permission:

Department of Anthropology, University of Alberta, Calgary, Alberta.

Curator of Anthropology, The Provincial Museum, Victoria, British Columbia.

Department of Sociology and Anthropology, University of Manitoba, Winnipeg, Manitoba.

Director, New Brunswick Museum, 277 Douglas Ave., St. John, New Brunswick.

Minister of Provincial Affairs, St. John's, Newfoundland.

Director, Nova Scotia Museum, Halifax, Nova Scotia.

Royal Ontario Museum of Archaeology, 100 Queens Park, Toronto, Ontario.

Deputy Minister, Ministry of Cultural Affairs, Quebec, Quebec.

Curator of Archaeology and Ethnology, Saskatchewan Museum of Natural History, Wascana Park, Regina, Saskatchewan.

Commissioner, Yukon Territory, Whitehorse, Yukon Territory.

Glossary

A.D. Used as a prefix to a date, it denotes so many years "In the year of our Lord" (*Anno Domini*) after the beginning of the Christian calendar.

ALTITHERMAL. The term used by Ernst Antevs (1948) to describe the second of his Neothermal periods. Dating from about 7,000 to 4,000 years ago, this was a warm period. Often the term "Long Drought" is used for this period in the western United States. It has also been called the Climatic Optimum and the Thermal Maximum.

ANATHERMAL. Antevs' name for the first of the Neothermal periods. Dating from 9,000 to 7,000 years ago, this period started off cool and became somewhat warmer with the passage of time.

ARCHAIC. A cultural stage in the eastern United States before the introduction of agriculture and pottery. Some archaeologists divide this stage into two or three subperiods characterized by technical advances in stonework. Various writers have used the term with slightly different connotations. It has been used to designate early ceramic stages in Mexico.

ARTICULATED. A term used by physical anthropologists to indicate that bones are in the position in which they were during the life of a mammal.

ARTIFACT. Anything made by man. In archaeology it is applied to tools, implements, and other objects that are demonstrably of human manufacture.

ASPECT. A group of foci or components (which see) that display a great many of the specific elements of a culture (traits).

ATLATL. A Mexican term meaning spear thrower. These artifacts are found in many American culture categories north of Mexico. The atlatl is simply a stick with a hook at one end that fits into a depression in the butt of a spear. It is used to lengthen the arm and thus to add leverage and speed to the throw. Atlatl weights are objects of stone fastened to the throwing stick for added weight. These may be perforated so that the stick passes through the artifact, or they may be grooved for lashing to the stick.

BASAL GRINDING. Often projectile points, particularly those from a Paleo-Indian culture, are ground along the base and lower edges so that

260

the lashings will not be cut. Sometimes the same result is obtained by the removal of small chips. This is called basal thinning.

B.C. Used as a suffix to a date it denotes so many years "Before Christ," or before the Christian calendar.

BLADE. This term is used by archaeologists in several ways. (1) It can refer to a fragment of stone removed from a parent core. The blade, in this instance, will be used in the manufacture of an artifact in what is known as the "blade and core industry." (2) That portion of an artifact, usually a projectile point or a knife, beyond the base or tang. (3) In certain cultures small artifacts are called microblades.

BLANK. A fragment of stone that has been worked roughly into shape but which must be further chipped to form the intended artifact.

BLOWOUT. A geological term used to designate an area from which the top-soil, and perhaps some of the lower soils, have been removed by wind action.

B.P. Used as a prefix to a date and meaning "Before the Present." In carbon dating, 1950 is commonly used as a point in the present from which to proceed. Thus, 4250 B.P. would mean 4250 years prior to 1950, or B.C. 2300.

BRECCIA. A composite rock in which angular stone fragments are cemented together by a natural adhesive.

BURIN. A chisel-like artifact made from a flake. This tool may have been used in the working of ivory or bone.

CALCIUM CARBONATE. A natural calcium-carbon-oxygen combination, as in limestone. This is often the adhesive in composite rocks.

CALICHE. A crust of calcium carbonate often present in semiarid or arid areas, either on top of or within the soil.

CARBON 14 DATING. A small but definite amount of the radioactive isotype C^{14} is found in all living things and is constantly replenished by the intake of carbon dioxide from the atmosphere. On death it disintegrates at a known rate. Since the remaining C^{14} in any specimen can be measured, any organic material, such as textiles, burnt bone, charcoal, etc., can be measured. A carbon date is given as B.P. (which see).

CERAMICS. A term used by archaeologists for pottery objects made from clay.

CHANNEL FLAKE. The long flake removed longitudinally from the base of a fluted (Paleo-Indian) projectile point.

CHRONOLOGY. The order or sequence in which events took place. An absolute chronology refers to a sequence of events that can be determined from a specific date.

COMPLEX. A grouping of related traits that together form a unit of culture. For example, the agricultural complex would consist of all of the traits—tools and nonmaterial concepts—that cluster about the planting, raising, cooking, and storing of the products of the farmer.

COMPONENT. A site, or any one of several cultures present at a given site. Usually a component has chronological and geographical connotations. The terms *focus* and *phase* are used by some archaeologists instead of *component*.

CONCHOIDAL. The shell-like shape of the fractured surface of such stones as chert or flint.

CORE. A piece of stone from which flakes or blades have been chipped away. Artifacts made from cores are called "core tools."

CROSS-BEDDING. Layers of soil which lie at an angle to the plane of the principal beds.

CULTURE. The way in which the members of a human group live, think, act, create, and manufacture tools and products.

CULTURE PATTERN. Sum total of elements or traits within a culture.

DENDROCHRONOLOGY. Dating by means of tree rings. Variations in the width of the annual growth rings reveal variations in climate and rainfall.

DEPOSIT. A natural deposit of soil (or rock) that has been laid down by any of the forces of nature, such as wind, water, ice.

DIAGNOSTIC. Especially meaningful or significant.

DIFFUSION. The movement of culture traits or ideas from one place to another.

EOLIAN. A term applied to layers of sand or silt deposited by wind action.

EROSION. A slow wearing away of the soil or rock by the action of water. Often spoken of as "weathering."

FLAKE TOOL. Stone tool produced by chipping large flakes from a core.

FLUTED. The groove or channel, particularly of a Paleo-Indian projectile point.

FOCUS. A group of components that possess similar traits. The components will probably not be identical but should have a sufficient number of significant traits in common to indicate a relationship.

GRAVER. A small, extremely sharp, pointed stone tool manufactured from a flake by chipping it on two edges at one end. Common on Paleo-Indian sites.

GROUND STONE. Artifacts made by the process of pecking and grinding. Sometimes called polished tools.

HEMATITE. An oxide of iron, deep red in color. Used by the Indian as a paint when ground and mixed with grease or oil. In some few instances artifacts have been made of hematite.

HORIZON. If used in connection with a specific site it usually means a certain level. In cultural anthropology the term may be used for a particular "level of development." Soil horizon refers to a zone or layer of soil.

INDUSTRY. A word used by archaeologists to group together all of the artifacts made of a certain material (the flint industry, for example).

INHUMATION. Burial in the earth.

IN SITU. The term used in archaeology to indicate that an artifact or object is in the place in which it was originally deposited.

LACUSTRINE. Used in reference to water-deposited material.

LAMINA. Flat stratum of clay, or fine sand, usually applied to a thin layer or bed. Also used to denote a layer of sedimentary rock (shale).

LANCEOLATE. Lance-shaped; said of narrow, tapering projectile points.

LITHIC. Stone. Lithic materials or artifacts are those made of stone.

LOESS. A deposit of very fine wind-blown material.

MANO. A word of Spanish origin (*mano de piedra*) meaning "hand stone." An artifact used in the hand for grinding seeds or stone materials for pigment on the metate (which see).

MEDITHERMAL. Last of divisions of the Neothermal period, dating from about 4,000 years ago to present.

METATE. A word of Mexican origin applied to slabs of stone on which grain was placed to be ground by the mano. Usually troughlike.

MICROLITHS. Small stone artifacts made from prismatic flakes. Too small for hand use, they may have been set in bone or wooden shafts to make a composite cutting tool.

MIDDEN. A deposit of refuse material. Often called a kitchen midden.

MORAINE. A bank or layer of mud, gravel, and stones deposited by a glacier.

NEOTHERMAL. A period of time beginning about 9,000 years ago to the present.

OBLIQUE FLAKING. A flaking technique in which the flake scars appear from left to right diagonally across the face of an artifact.

PATINA. The altered surface and coloring of an object or an artifact made by natural weathering or exposure to soil acids.

PERIODS. A time division of the history of a large region.

PETROGLYPH. A carving or inscription on stone.

PHASE. Archaeological remains of what is presumed to be a single tribe or people at a given period in their history.

PICTOGRAPH. Scratched or picked drawing on stone; conveys information by means of pictures of events or objects described.

PLANOCONVEX. Said of an artifact with one flat and one convex side.

PLAYA. A geological term used to denote a shallow basin-like area in which surface water collects. Found mainly in arid regions.

PLUVIAL. A designation used to denote periods of moisture in a normally arid area.

POLISHED TOOLS. Artifacts made by the technique of pecking and grinding.

POTSHERD. Pottery fragment.

PREHISTORY. Generally speaking, the study of cultures as they existed before the beginnings of written records.

PROJECTILE POINT. The point of any weapon such as a spear, dart, arrow, or lance.

RETOUCH. The technique of removing small flakes by pressure in the sharpening or resharpening of a stone artifact.

SCRAPER. A stone artifact used in the scraping of hides or soft materials. The term is often modified by a prefix which indicates the shape of the artifact—snub-nosed scraper, thumbnail scraper, end or side scraper, etc.

SERRATED. Possessing a notched or saw-tooth edge.

SILT. A geological term denoting a soil composed of extremely fine grains.

SITE. Any locality occupied or utilized by man that has been known to archaeology by reconnaissance or excavation.

STAGE. An established plateau in historical development. A cultural level reached by a large group of people (the agricultural stage, for example).

STRATIFICATION. A term used to denote the presence of a number of horizons or strata, where the earlier materials are overlaid by the later.

TEMPER. Sand, grit, plant fibers, and other material mixed with the clay of a vessel to prevent it from cracking during drying process.

TERRACE. A geological term denoting the previous location of the shore of a body of water or a valley floor on which a stream once flowed.

TILL. Unstratified soil consisting of sand, gravel, clay, and unsorted stones, deposited directly by a glacier.

TRADITION. Way of making an artifact that has continued for a long time in a given area.

TRAIT. A specific element of culture.

TRANSVERSE FLAKING. A technique similar to oblique flaking, but in which the flake scars lie at right angles to the central line of an artifact.

TYPE SITE. A site that establishes the typical content of a particular culture (Sandia cave, for example).

TYPOLOGY. A system of arranging artifacts according to classes or types.

VARVES. Layers formed in the beds of lakes from the soil carried by contributing streams. Usually applied to paired layers of alternating fine and relatively coarse materials marking the deposits of a specific year.

Bibliography

This bibliography is by no means a complete listing of all the materials available on the subject of archaeology. It merely represents an attempt to select those that will be particularly helpful to the beginner who wants to acquire a broad, general knowledge of the field. For those wishing to start their own collections of reference materials, the inexpensive paper editions indicated are especially recommended. More specialized technical works are included for the advanced amateur interested in particular sites, methods, or techniques.

While the emphasis is on North American archaeology, materials dealing with Old World areas have been included in some instances to provide background information or to suggest how specialized techniques (as in underwater archaeology) may be adapted to different locales.

Films, slides, and filmstrips are useful for demonstration or discussion purposes at club meetings. They are available from the sources indicated on a rental or purchase basis.

GENERAL SOURCES

Abstracts of New World Archaeology. Society for American Archaeology; Washington, D.C. Vol. 1, 1960; Vol 2, 1962. Very helpful.

Anthropological Bibliography of the Eastern Seaboard. Eastern States Archaeological Foundation; Trenton, N.J. Vol. 1, 1800-1946; Vol. 2, 1946-1959. Good for those interested in areas east of the Mississippi.

Thomas, William L., Jr., and Pikelis, Anna M. (eds). *International Directory of Anthropological Institutions.* Wenner-Gren Foundation for Anthropological Research, Inc.; New York, 1953. World-wide listing of universities, museums, societies, and other institutions concerned with the field of archaeology. Information about courses, collections, sources of advice.

GENERAL ANTHROPOLOGY AND PREHISTORY

Bass, William M. *Human Osteology—A Laboratory and Field Manual of the Human Skeleton.* Missouri Archaeology Society; Columbia, Mo.,

1971. Profusely illustrated with drawings of the various bones of the body at various ages. Should be in the field kit of every archaeologist.

Bibby, Geoffrey. *The Testimony of the Spade.* Alfred A. Knopf; New York, 1956. A history of archaeological discoveries—largely by amateurs—throughout the Old World.

Braidwood, Robert J. *Prehistoric Men* (5th ed.). Chicago Natural History Museum, Popular Series (Anthropology), No. 37; Chicago, 1961 (paper). An excellent short account of Old World prehistory for the general reader.

Brennan, Louis A. *American Dawn.* Macmillan; New York, 1970. The most recent information on migrations from the Old World, new data on sea levels, carbon 14 dating, etc.; must reading for every amateur archaeologist.

———. *No Stone Unturned.* Random House; New York, 1959.

Ceram, C. W. *The First Americans.* Harcourt, Brace; New York, 1971. North American archaeology written in a most entertaining manner.

———. *Gods, Graves, and Scholars.* Alfred A. Knopf; New York, 1951. A history of archaeology in which romantic excursions go hand in hand with scientific endeavor. Mostly Old World, but one section on Middle America.

Cornwall, Ian W. *The World of Ancient Man.* John Day; New York, 1964. Exclusively Old World prehistory.

Gardou, C. H. *Before Columbus.* Crown; New York, 1971. Links between the Old World and ancient North America.

Kroeber, A. L. *Anthropology* (rev. ed.). Harcourt, Brace; New York, 1948. A rather scientific text chiefly used in archaeological courses.

———. *Anthropology Today: Selections.* Sol Tax (ed.). University of Chicago Press; Chicago, 1962. (Also Phoenix paper edition.) The paper edition is a very comprehensive scientific inventory brought up to date from the original edition.

Linton, Ralph. *The Tree of Culture.* Alfred A. Knopf; New York, 1955. Cultural anthropology, interestingly written.

McGimsey, Charles R., III. *Public Archaeology.* Seminar Press; New York and London, 1972. A compendium of all state antiquities laws.

Marriott, Alice, and Rachlin, Carol K. *The Story of the American Indian.* G. P. Putnam's Sons; New York, 1969.

Muller, Herbert J. *The Uses of the Past.* New American Library, New York, 1954. (Also Mentor paper edition.) A rather philosophical discussion of culture; nonarchaeological.

Oakley, Kenneth P. *Man the Tool-Maker.* British Museum (Natural History); London, 1956 (paper). (Also Phoenix paper edition, 1957.) A concise, useful account of prehistoric techniques. Excellent for making comparisons between Old and New World techniques. For the advanced amateur.

Chapter 1: Before You Start to Dig

Braidwood, Robert J. *Archaeologists and What They Do.* Franklin Watts New York, 1960. A very good account of the archaeologist at work.

Kenyon, Kathleen M. *Beginning in Archaeology* (rev. ed.). Frederick A. Praeger; New York, 1957 (paper). Classic introduction to archaeology by an outstanding authority on the Middle East. Contains sections on American archaeology by Saul S. and Gladys D. Weinberg.

Petrie, William M. F. *Methods and Aims in Archaeology.* Macmillan; London, 1904. The classic by an English authority is worth reading for its presentation of the philosophy and responsibilities of archaeologists.

Wheeler, Mortimer. *Archaeology from the Earth.* Penguin Books; London, 1956 (paper). Philosophy and methods described by a distinguished authority who has directed excavations in Britain, France, and India.

Wissler, Clark. *The Archaeologist at Work.* American Museum of Natural History, Science Guide No. 116; New York, 1946. Reprinted from *Natural History,* Vol. 51, No. 3, 1943.

Woolley, Leonard. *Digging Up the Past.* Penguin Books; London, 1950 (paper). What archaeology is about, as revealed by excavations at Ur, Knossos, Egypt, and other Old World sites.

Chapter 2: Who Lived Where

GENERAL READING

Bandelier, Adolph F. A. *The Delight Makers.* Dodd, Mead; New York, 1947. A fictionalized account of prehistoric times in Frijoles Canyon, N.M., where the author conducted surveys between 1880 and 1886.

Birket-Smith, Kaj. *The Eskimos* (rev. ed.). Humanities Press; New York, 1959. Excellent.

Embree, Edward R. *Indians of the Americas.* Houghton Mifflin; Boston, 1939. Slightly out of date, but still a good description of the various kinds of culture in the Americas.

Gladwin, Harold S. *Men Out of Asia.* McGraw-Hill; New York, 1947. (Also paper edition.) Slightly fanciful, but widely read by amateurs. Intriguing, although contains much data that is disputed.

Goddard, Pliny E. *Indians of the Northwest Coast.* American Museum of Natural History; New York, 1934. Good, solid facts. Should be read by everyone interested in this area.

————. *Indians of the Southwest.* American Museum of Natural History; New York, 1931. "Must" reading for anyone interested in the area.

Griffin, James B. (ed.). *Archaeology of the Eastern United States.* University of Chicago Press; Chicago, 1952. A good, solid book. By all means should be read by those interested in the area covered.

Hibben, Frank C. *Digging Up America.* Hill and Wang; New York, 1960. New World prehistorical archaeology by an authority on the Southwest. Some of the author's theories have been questioned, but he writes an interesting story.

―――. *The Lost Americans.* Thomas Y. Crowell; New York, 1961 (Apollo paper edition). An excellent popular discussion of ancient man in America.

Jenness, Diamond. *Indians of Canada.* National Museum of Canada, Canadian Dept. of Mines Bulletin No. 65; Ottawa, 1934. A bit out of date, but still solid material on the area.

Jennings, Jesse D., and Norbeck, Edward (eds.). *Prehistoric Man in the New World.* University of Chicago Press; Chicago, 1963. A very scholarly presentation that might prove rather dry for the amateur.

Johnson, Frederick (ed.). *Man in Northeastern North America.* Papers of the Robert S. Peabody Foundation for Archaeology, Vol. 3; Andover, Mass., 1946. A "must" for those working in the area.

Kidder, Alfred V. *Introduction to the Study of Southwestern Archaeology.* Yale University Press; New Haven, 1962. Excellent for those interested in this area.

MacGowan, Kenneth, and Hester, Joseph A. *Early Man in the New World.* Peter Smith; Gloucester, Mass. (Also Anchor paper edition.) A brief, introductory text for the layman.

McNickle, D'Arcy. *They Came Here First.* J. B. Lippincott; Philadelphia, 1949. Popular archaeology. Quite good. Deals with New World prehistory.

Marriott, Alice L. *The First Comers.* David McKay; New York, 1960. Another popular introduction to New World archaeology. Good for young readers.

Martin, Paul, *et al. Indians Before Columbus.* University of Chicago Press; Chicago, 1949. Now somewhat out of date, but still good anthropology.

Mason, Ronald J. "The Paleo-Indian in the Eastern United States," *Current Anthropology,* Vol. 3, No. 3; Chicago, 1962. The best paper yet published on the subject, of which the author has a deep understanding. Recommended reading for all who are interested in the area.

Pohl, Frederick J. *Atlantic Crossings Before Columbus.* W. W. Norton; New York, 1961. Most amateurs will be deeply interested in this story.

―――. *The Lost Discovery.* W. W. Norton; New York, 1962. A good exposition of the methods of the science, although most archaeologists do not agree with the theories, which are subject to question.

Shetrone, Henry C. *The Moundbuilders.* Kennikat Press; Port Washington, N.Y. Excellent.

Wedel, Waldo R. *Prehistoric Man on the Great Plains*. University of Oklahoma Press; Norman, 1961. Highly recommended reading for the area.

Wissler, Clark. *The American Indian* (3d ed.). Peter Smith; Gloucester, Mass. A widely used text, now somewhat outdated.

―――. *Indians of the Plains*. American Museum of Natural History; New York, 1934. Excellent. Should be read by those interested in the area.

Wormington, H. M. *Ancient Man in North America* (4th ed.). Denver Museum of Natural History, Popular Series No. 4; Denver, 1957. An absolute "must" for all amateurs. Somewhat outdated.

―――. *Prehistoric Indians of the Southwest*. Denver Museum of Natural History, Popular Series No. 7; Denver, 1956. Good for the area.

SPECIALIZED READING

Amsden, Charles A. *Prehistoric Southwesterners from Basketmaker to Pueblo*. Southwest Museum; Los Angeles, 1949.

Antevs, Ernst. "The Spread of Aboriginal Man to North America," *Geographic Review*, 25, No. 2; 1935.

Cross, Dorothy. *Archaeology of New Jersey* (2 vols.). Archaeological Society of New Jersey; Trenton, 1956.

Dragoo, Don W. "Archaic Hunters of the Upper Ohio Valley," *Carnegie Museum Annals*, 35, No. 10; Pittsburgh, 1959.

―――. "Mounds for the Dead," *Carnegie Museum Annals*, 37; Pittsburgh, 1963.

Ferguson, Alice L. L., and Henry G. *The Piscataway Indians of Southern Maryland*. The Alice Ferguson Foundation; Acookeek, 1960.

Fowler, Melvin L. "Summary Report of Modoc Rockshelter," *Illinois State Museum Reports of Investigations*, No. 8; Springfield, 1959.

Giddings, James L. *The Archaeology of Cape Denbigh*. Brown University Press; Providence, 1964.

Greenman, Emerson F. *Cultural Relationships of Archaeological Sites in the Upper Great Lakes*. Michigan Academy of Science, Arts and Letters; Ann Arbor, 1938.

―――. *The Younge Site*, University of Michigan; Ann Arbor, 1937.

Guthe, Alfred K. *The Late Prehistoric Occupation of Southwestern New York*. New York State Archaeological Association; Albany, 1958.

Harp, Elmer, Jr. *The Cultural Affinities of the Newfoundland Dorset Eskimo*. National Museum of Canada, Bulletin No. 200; Ottawa, 1964.

―――. "New World Affinities of the Cape Dorset Culture," *Papers of the University of Alaska*, Vol. 1, No. 2; 1953.

Harrington, Mark R. *Gypsum Cave, Nevada*. Southwest Museum Papers, No. 8; Los Angeles, 1933.

―――. "The New Tule Springs Expedition," *The Master Key*, No. 29, Southwest Museum; Los Angeles, 1952.

Johnson, Frederick (ed.). *The Boylston Street Fish Weir* (2 vols.). Papers of the Robert S. Peabody Foundation for Archaeology. Vol. 2, 1942; Vol. 4, 1949. Andover, Mass.

Mayer-Oakes, William J. "The Prehistory of the Upper Ohio Valley," *Car negie Museum Annals;* Pittsburgh, 1955.

Moorehead, Warren K. *The Archaeology of Maine.* Andover Press; Andover, Mass., 1922.

———. *Archaeology of the Arkansas River Valley.* Dept. of Archaeology, Phillips Academy; Andover, Mass., 1931.

———. *Exploration of the Etowah Site in Georgia.* Yale University Press; New Haven, 1932.

Prufer, Olaf H., and Baby, Raymond S. *Paleo-Indians of Ohio.* State Historical Society; Columbus, 1963.

Rainey, Froelich G. *Archaeology of Central Alaska.* Papers of the American Museum of Natural History; New York, 1932.

———. *Eskimo History.* American Museum of Natural History, Anthropological Papers. Vol. XXXVII, Pt. 4. New York, 1941.

Ritchie, William A. *An Introduction to Hudson Valley Prehistory.* New York State Science Service; Albany, 1958.

———. *Traces of Early Man in the Northeast.* New York State Science Service; Albany, 1957.

Strong, William D. *An Introduction to Nebraskan Archaeology.* Smithsonian Misc. Collections. Vol. XLIII, No. 10. Washington, D.C., 1935.

Webb, William S. "Indian Knoll," University of Kentucky *Reports in Anthropology and Archaeology,* Vol. 4, No. 3; Lexington, 1946.

———, and Baby, Raymond S. *The Adena People, No. 2.* The Ohio State University Press; Columbus, 1957.

———, and Snow, Clarence E. "The Adena People," University of Kentucky *Reports in Anthropology and Archaeology,* Vol. 6; Lexington, 1945.

Wheat, Joe Ben. *Mogollon Culture Prior to* A.D. *1000.* American Anthropological Association, Memoir No. 82; Washington, D.C., 1955.

Winters, Harold D. "An Archaeological Survey of the Wabash Valley in Illinois," *Illinois State Museum Report* No. 10; Springfield, 1963.

Witthoft, John. "A Paleo-Indian Site in Eastern Pennsylvania," *Proceedings of the American Philosophical Society,* Vol. 96, No. 4; Philadelphia, 1952.

Chapter 3: How to Know Where to Dig

GENERAL READING

Cotter, John L., and Hudson, J. Paul. *New Discoveries at Jamestown.*

U.S. Government Printing Office; Washington, D.C., 1957 (paper). Colonial life reconstructed through historical archaeology.

Holmquist, June D., and Wheeler, Ardis H. *Diving Into the Past*. Minnesota Historical Society; Minneapolis, 1964 (paper). Underwater archaeology.

Horner, Dave. *Shipwrecks, Skin Divers, and Sunken Gold*. Dodd, Mead; New York, 1965. How and where to skin dive successfully for sunken treasure.

Hume, Ivor Noel. *Here Lies Virginia*. Alfred A. Knopf; New York, 1963. The chief archaeologist of Colonial Williamsburg describes the work of historic site archaeology at three Virginia sites: 16th-century Roanoke Island, 17th-century Jamestown, and 18th-century Williamsburg.

McGregor, John C. *Southwestern Archaeology*. John Wiley; New York, 1941. For those interested in the area.

Robbins, Roland W., and Jones, Evans. *Hidden America*. Alfred A. Knopf; New York, 1959. Colonial site archaeology at its best. Very interesting.

Silverberg, Robert. *Sunken History: The Story of Underwater Archaeology*. Chilton; Philadelphia, 1963. Describes what can be accomplished by this technique. Old World areas.

Wagner, Kip. "Drowned Galleons Yield Spanish Gold," *National Geographic;* January, 1965. Underwater archaeology off the Florida coast.

SPECIALIZED READING

Avery, T. Eugene. *Interpretation of Aerial Photographs*. Burgess Publishing Co.; Minneapolis, 1962.

Bullen, Ripley, P. *Excavation in Northeastern Massachusetts*. Papers of the Robert S. Peabody Foundation for Archaeology, Vol. 1, No. 3; Andover, Mass., 1949.

———, and Sleight, Frederick W. *Archaeological Investigations of the Castle Windy Midden, Florida*. William L. Bryant Foundation, American Studies No. 1, Central Florida Museum; Orlando, 1959.

Byers, Douglas S. *Two Sites on Martha's Vineyard*. Papers of the Robert S. Peabody Foundation for Archaeology, Vol. 1, No. 3; Andover, Mass., 1940.

Cressman, Luther S. *Archaeological Researches in the Northern Great Basin*. Carnegie Institute of Washington, Publication No. 538; 1942.

Cross, Dorothy. *Archaeology of New Jersey*. (2 vols.). Archaeological Society of New Jersey; Trenton, 1956.

Chapter 4: What You Will Find

GENERAL READING

Griffin, James B. (ed.). *Archaeology of the Eastern United States*. University of Chicago Press; Chicago, 1952. A good, solid book. By all means should be read by those interested in the area covered.

Hill, A. *Beginner's Book of Basic Anatomy.* Reinhold; New York, 1962.

Kidder, Alfred V. *Introduction to the Study of Southwestern Archaeology.* Yale University Press; New Haven, 1962. Excellent for those interested in this area.

King, Blanche B. *Under Your Feet.* Dodd, Mead; New York, 1939.

McGregor, John C. *Southwestern Archaeology* (2d ed.). University of Illinois Press; Urbana, 1965. For those interested in the area.

Miles, Charles. *Indian and Eskimo Artifacts of North America.* Henry Regnery; Chicago, 1962.

Wedel, Waldo R. *Prehistoric Man on the Great Plains.* University of Oklahoma Press; Norman, 1961. Highly recommended reading for the area.

Wormington, H. M. *Ancient Man in North America* (4th ed.). Denver Museum of Natural History, Popular Series No. 4; Denver, 1957. An absolute "must" for all amateurs. Somewhat outdated.

———. *Prehistoric Indians of the Southwest.* Denver Museum of Natural History, Popular Series No. 7; Denver, 1956. Good for the area.

SPECIALIZED READING

Bolton, Reginald P. *Indian Remains in Northern Vermont.* Museum of the American Indian, Heye Foundation; New York, 1930.

Bushnell, David L. *Mounds and Other Ancient Earthworks of the United States.* Smithsonian Institution Publication 300 A; Washington, D.C., 1929.

Cushing, Frank H. *A Study of Pueblo Pottery.* Bureau of American Ethnology, Annual Report 4. Government Printing Office; Washington, D.C., 1882.

Dewdney, Selwyn, and Kidd, Kenneth E. *Indian Rock Paintings of the Great Lakes.* University of Toronto Press; Toronto, 1962.

Holmes, William H. *Pottery of the Ancient Pueblos.* Bureau of American Ethnology, Report 4. Government Printing Office; Washington, D.C., 1882.

Kellar, James H. *The Atl-Atl in North America.* Indiana Historical Society, Vol. III, No. 3; Indianapolis, 1955.

Mallery, Garrick. *Pictographs of the North American Indians.* Bureau of American Ethnology, Annual Report 4. Government Printing Office; Washington, D.C., 1882.

Prufer, Olaf H. "Fluted Points and Ohio History," *Explorer,* Vol. 4, No. 3. Cleveland Museum of Natural History; Cleveland, 1962. Excellent.

Rainey, Froelich G. *Archaeology of Central Alaska.* Papers of the American Museum of Natural History; New York, 1932.

Ritchie, William A. *A Lamoka Lake Site.* Lewis H. Morgan Chapter, New

York State Archaeological Association; Rochester, New York, 1932.
————. *An Archaeological Survey of the Trent Waterway in Ontario, Canada*. Lewis H. Morgan Chapter, New York State Archaeological Assn.; Rochester, 1949.
————. *An Early Site in Cayuga County*. Lewis H. Morgan Chapter, New York State Archaeological Assn.; Rochester, 1945.
————. *An Introduction to Hudson Valley Prehistory*. New York State Science Service; Albany, 1958.
————. *A Prehistoric Fortified Village Site at Canandaigua, Ontario County, New York*. Research Records of the Rochester Museum of Arts and Sciences; Rochester, 1946.
————. *Archaeological Evidence for Ceremonialism in the Owasco Culture*. Lewis H. Morgan Chapter, New York State Archaeological Assn.; Rochester, 1947.
————. *A Stratified Prehistoric Site at Brewerton, New York*. Lewis H. Morgan Chapter, New York State Archaeological Assn.; Rochester, 1946.
————. *A Unique Prehistoric Workshop Site*. Research Records of the Rochester Museum of Arts and Sciences; Rochester, 1938.
————. *Certain Recently Explored New York Mounds and Their Relationship to the Hopewell Culture*. Research Records of the Rochester Museum of Arts and Sciences; Rochester, 1938.
————. *Dutch Hollow, An Early Historic Period Site in Livingston County, New York*. New York State Archaeological Assn.; Albany, 1954.
————. *New Evidence Relating to the Archaic Occupation of New York*. Lewis H. Morgan Chapter, New York State Archaeological Assn.; Rochester, 1936.
————. *Recent Discoveries Suggesting an Early Woodland Burial Cult in the Northeast*. New York State Science Service; Albany, 1955.
————. *The Chance Horizon*. New York State Science Service; Albany, 1952.
————. *The Stony Brook Site and its Relation to Archaic and Transitional Cultures on Long Island*. New York State Science Service; Albany, 1959.
————. *Traces of Early Man in the Northeast*. New York State Science Service; Albany, 1957.
————. *Two Prehistoric Villages at Brewerton, New York*. Research Records of the Rochester Museum of Arts and Sciences; Rochester, 1940.
————, and Dragoo, Don. *The Eastern Dispersal of the Adena*. New York State Science Service; Albany, 1960.
————, and Miller, Schuyler P., *An Early Owasco Sequence in Eastern New York*, New York State Science Service; Albany, 1953.
Smith, Carlyle S. *The Archaeology of Coastal New York*. American Mu-

seum of Natural History, Anthropological Papers, Vol. 43, No. 2; New
York, 1950.

Witthoft, John. "A Paleo-Indian Site in Eastern Pennsylvania," *Proceedings
of the American Philosophical Society*, Vol. 96, No. 4; Philadelphia,
1952.

Chapter 5: How to Plan an Excavation

Breed, Charles B. *Surveying* (2d ed.). John Wiley; New York, 1957.

Detweiler, A. H. *Manual of Archaeological Surveying.* Stechert-Hafner
Service Agency; New York, 1948.

Heizer, Robert F., *Manual of Archaeological Field Methods* (2d ed.). The
National Press; Palo Alto, Calif., 1950. Includes a detailed discussion
of archaeological methods.

Robbins, Maurice. *An Archaic Village in Middleboro, Massachusetts.*
Massachusetts Archaeological Society, Inc.; Attleboro, 1960.

Chapter 6: What You Need to Know About Soils

GENERAL READING

Croneis, Carey, and Krumbein, William C. *Down to Earth: An Introduction to Geology.* University of Chicago Press; Chicago, 1961 (Phoenix
paper edition). The origin of the earth presented as the background
to the pageant of life. Lively and interesting.

SPECIALIZED READING

Benninghoff, William S. *Review of C. J. Heusser's Late Pleistocene Environment of the North Pacific Coast, North America.* American Association for the Advancement of Science; Washington, D.C., 1960.

Haury, Emil W. *The Stratigraphy of Ventana Cave, Arizona.* University
of New Mexico Press; Albuquerque, 1950.

Hibben, Frank C., *Evidences of Early Occupation of Sandia Cave, New
Mexico and Other Sites in the Sandia-Manzano Area.* Smithsonian
Misc. Collections 99, No. 3; Washington, D.C., 1941.

Johnson, Frederick (ed.). *The Boylston Street Fish Weir* (2 vols.). Papers
of the Robert S. Peabody Foundation for Archaeology. Vol. 2, 1942;
Vol. 4, 1949. Andover, Mass.

Pyddola, Edward. *Stratification for the Archaeologist.* Lawrence Verry,
Inc.; Mystic, Conn., 1961.

Chapter 7: How to Excavate a Site

Heizer, Robert F. *Manual of Archaeological Field Methods* (2d ed.). The National Press; Palo Alto, Calif. 1950. Includes a detailed bibliography of archaeological methods.

Wissler, Clark. *The Archaeologist at Work.* American Museum of Natural History, Science Guide No. 116; New York, 1946. Reprinted from *Natural History,* Vol. 51, No. 3, 1943.

Chapter 8: How to Record Data

Dobbs, Horace. *How to Use Your Camera Under Water.* A. S. Barnes; New York. For the underwater archaeologist.

Schenck, Hilbert, and Kendall, Henry W. *Underwater Photography.* Cornell Maritime Press; Cambridge, Md., 1954.

Soday, Frank J. *Tennessee Archaeological Field Manual.* Misc. Papers of the Tennessee Archaeological Society; Knoxville, 1957.

Sussman, Aaron. *Amateur Photographer's Handbook* (7th ed.). Thomas Y. Crowell; New York, 1965. Everything you need to know about cameras and films, picture-taking, developing, and printing.

Chapter 9: How to Preserve and Restore Your Finds

Leechman, Douglas. *Technical Methods in the Preservation of Anthropological Specimens.* National Museum of Canada, Canadian Dept. ot Mines Bulletin No. 67; Ottawa, 1928.

Chapter 10: How to Date Archaeological Finds

GENERAL READING

Bothwell, Don, and Higgs, Eric (eds.). *Science in Archaeology.* Basic Books; New York, 1963.

Douglass, Andrew E. "The Secret of the Southwest Solved by Talkative Tree Rings," *National Geographic;* December, 1929. A popular account of tree-ring dating.

Kroeber, A. L. *Anthropology Today: Selections.* Sol Tax (ed.). University of Chicago Press; Chicago, 1962. (Also Phoenix paper edition.) The paper edition is a very comprehensive scientific inventory brought up to date from the original edition.

Libby, Willard F. *Radiocarbon Dating* (2d ed.). University of Chicago Press; Chicago, 1955.

Poole, Lynn and Gray. *Carbon 14 and Other Scientific Methods that Date the Past.* McGraw-Hill; New York, 1961.

SPECIALIZED READING

Flint, Richard F. *Glacial and Pleistocene Geology*. John Wiley and Sons; New York, 1957.

————, and Deevey, Edward S., Jr. "Radiocarbon Dating of Late-Pleistocene Events," *American Journal of Science*, Vol. 249; New York, 1951.

Johnson, Richard B. *Proton Magnetometry and Its Application to Archaeology*. Indian Historical Society; Indianapolis, 1955.

Lee, Thomas E. "The Antiquity of the Sheguiandah Site," *The Canadian Field Naturalist*, Vol. 71, No. 3; 1957.

————. "The Prehistory of Manitoulin Island, Ontario," *New World Antiquity*, Vol. 9, 8/9; London, 1962.

Chapter 11: How to Write a Site Report

Greenman, Emerson. *The Younge Site*. University of Michigan; Ann Arbor, 1937.

Robbins, Maurice. *An Archaic Village in Middleboro, Massachusetts*, Massachusetts Archaeological Society, Inc.; Attleboro, 1960.

Witthoft, John. "A Paleo-Indian Site in Eastern Pennsylvania," *Proceedings of the American Philosophical Society*, Vol. 96, No. 4; Philadelphia, 1952.

Chapter 12: Historical Archaeology

Carter, William H. *North American Indian Trade Silver*, Vols. I, II. North American Indian Publications; 788 Dundas St., London, Ontario, Canada.

Davis, M. B. "Phytogeography and Palynology on Northeastern United States," *The Quaternary of the United States*, H. E. Wright, Jr., and D. G. Frey, eds. Princeton University Press; Princeton, N.J., 1965.

Dimbley, G. *Plants and Archaeology*. John Baker; London, 1970.

Hume, Ivor Noël. *Historical Archaeology*. Alfred A. Knopf; New York, 1969.

Struever, S. "Flotation Techniques for the Recovery of Small-Scale Archaeological Remains," *American Antiquity*, Vol. 33, No. 3; 1968.

Usher, Peter J. "Fur Trade Posts of the Northwest Territories," report NSRG 71-4. Available without charge from the Chief, Northern Science Research Group, Department of Indian Affairs and Northern Development, 400 Laurier Ave. West, Ottawa 4, Ontario, Canada.

Yarnell, R. A. "Aboriginal Relationships Between Culture and Plant Life in the Upper Great Lakes Region," Anthropological Papers, No. 23, Museum of Anthropology, University of Michigan, Ann Arbor.

MAGAZINES

American Anthropologist. American Anthropological Association, 1530 P Street, N.W., Washington, D.C. Bi-monthly. Articles of anthropological and archaeological interest

American Antiquity. Society for American Archaeology, 1530 P Street, N.W., Washington, D.C. Quarterly. Covers the field of New World archaeology. Illustrated. Has useful section on current research.

Archaeology. Archaeological Institute of America, 100 Washington Square East, New York, N.Y. 10003. Quarterly. Illustrated popularly written scholarly articles on archaeology in all parts of the world.

Arizona Highways. Arizona Dept. of Highways, Phoenix, Ariz. 85009. Monthly. Beautifully illustrated. Articles on archaeological sites in state.

National Geographic. National Geographic Society, Washington, D.C. Monthly. Frequent articles of archaeological interest. Popularly written and well illustrated.

Natural History. American Museum of Natural History, Central Park West at 79th Street, New York, N.Y. 10024. Ten issues per year. Occasional articles of archaeological interest.

Popular Archaeology. DeBoer Publication Corp., 260 North Rock Road, P.O. Box 18387, Wichita, Kans. 67218. Intended to be "a timely link between amateur and professional."

Scientific American. 415 Madison Avenue, New York, N.Y. 10017. Monthly. Well-written articles for the advanced amateur, usually on scientific aspects of archaeology.

Southwestern Lore. Colorado Archaeological Society, University of Colorado, Boulder. Archaeology of the area.

FILMS, SLIDES, AND FILMSTRIPS

Aboriginal Peoples of Minnesota (Minnesota Study Series). Filmstrip. University of Minnesota, Audio-Visual Education Service, Wesbrook Hall, Minneapolis, Minn. The history of Minnesota's Indians from prehistoric to modern times. Produced in collaboration with Dr. Lloyd A. Wilford, professor of anthropology, University of Minnesota.

Bull Brook Site. 48 2 × 2 slides, color. University of Wisconsin, Bureau of Audio-Visual Instruction, 1312 W. Johnson Street, Madison, Wis. Excavation of a Paleo-Indian site north of Ipswich, Mass. Prepared by Douglas S. Byers, director of the Robert S. Peabody Foundation for Archaeology, Phillips Academy, Andover, Mass.

Culture Sequences in Southern and Eastern Florida. 12 2 × 2 slides, color. University of Wisconsin, Bureau of Audio-Visual Instruction, 1312

W. Johnson Street, Madison, Wis. Pottery sequences in Florida Glades and Indian River areas, with associated artifacts. Prepared by Dr. Irving Rouse, Dept. of Anthropology, Yale University.

Dangerous River. 16mm film, sound, 17 minutes, color or black and white. Bailey Films, Inc., 6509 De Longpre Ave., Hollywood, Calif. Smithsonian Institution archaeologists explore area of Bighorn River, Wyoming. Indian relics and fossils of the region.

Dating Their Past. 16mm film, sound, 29 minutes, black and white. Nebraska Council for Educational Television, Lincoln, Neb. Determining the age of prehistoric relics uncovered in the Great Plains area. Prepared for National College Educational Television.

The Early Hunters (Great Plains Trilogy Series II). 16mm film, sound, 29 minutes, black and white. University of Nebraska, Bureau of Audio-Visual Instruction, Lincoln, Neb. The hunting life of people who came to America from Asia. How they coped with the world of the Ice Age.

Emerald and Anna Mounds. 25 2 × 2 slides, color. University of Wisconsin, Bureau of Audio-Visual Instruction, 1312 W. Johnson St., Madison, Wis. Excavation of Emerald and Anna Mounds in Mississippi. By John L. Cotter.

The Foragers (Great Plains Trilogy Series I). 16mm film, sound, 29 minutes, black and white. University of Nebraska, Bureau of Audio-Visual Instruction, Lincoln, Neb. The changing fortunes of the plainsmen from 2000 B.C. to A.D. 500 as revealed by archaeological excavations.

From Nomad to Villager (Great Plains Trilogy Series II). 16mm film, sound, 29 minutes, black and white. University of Nebraska, Bureau of Audio-Visual Instruction, Lincoln, Neb. How the prehistoric Indians changed their way of life: the development of new tools, pottery, religious ceremonies, as revealed by burials.

Indian Life in Early Canada. Filmstrip, 48 frames, black and white. Stanbow Productions, Inc., 12 Cleveland St., Valhalla, N.Y. The customs and activities of Indians in Canada before the coming of the white man. Produced by the National Film Board of Canada.

Learning About the Past. 16mm film, sound, 10 minutes, color or black and white. Indiana University, Audio-Visual Center, Bloomington, Ind. Archaeologists excavate Indian mound: field work, sorting, and collecting artifacts.

Man, Animal, Climate and Earth (Great Plains Trilogy Series II). 16mm film, sound, 29 minutes, black and white. University of Nebraska, Bureau of Audio-Visual Instruction, Lincoln, Neb. The mysteries of early man revealed from discoveries of early human camping sites in southwestern Nebraska.

Plainsmen of the Past (Great Plains Trilogy Series II). 16mm film, sound, 29 minutes, black and white. University of Nebraska, Bureau of Audio-

Visual Instruction, Lincoln, Neb. The prehistory of the Great Plains as revealed through the work of archaeologists.

Point of Pines. 16mm film, sound, 22 minutes, color. New York University, Film Library, 26 Washington Place, New York, N.Y. The excavation of prehistoric Indian sites by the Archaeological Field School of Arizona.

Prehistoric Farmers (Great Plains Trilogy Series II). 16mm film, sound, 29 minutes, black and white. University of Nebraska, Bureau of Audio-Visual Instruction, Lincoln, Neb. Social organization of prehistoric inhabitants as suggested by cultural archaeology. The crops, houses, and tools brought by new groups pushing into the Plains area.

Index

knives, 66-67
Krueger Enterprises, Inc., 198, 201-202

land bridge at Bering Strait, 4-5, 6
laterization, effect of, on soils, 99
Leo petroglyph, Jackson County, Ohio, 21
level-stripping method of excavation, 118-119
Llano complex projectile points, 57
local history of Indian site, 29

magnetic properties of soils, 218
magnetism, use of, in archaeological field, 218-220
maize, cultivation of, 10, 11, 13, 17
Major John Bradford house, Kingston, Mass., *frontis*
maps, U.S. Geological Survey, 30, 32-33, 34, 84, 151-152
Massachusetts Archaeological Society, 41, 114, 160
mesa towns, 130
metal, artifacts made of, 53
metal detector, 218
Mexican antiquities laws, 259
Middle West, prehistoric culture of, 21-22
migration valve, 5, 27 (*table*)
mine detector, 218
Mogollon culture of prehistoric America, 9, 12-13, 17
mound building, 12, 21-22, 23
mounds at excavation sites, 130-132
mountain lion petroglyph from Arizona's Petrified Forest, 18
multistoried communal houses, 13, 17, 18-19
museums and special collections, 239-247

national archaeological societies, 233
Newfoundland, Eskimos in, 15
Norsemen in America before Columbus, 4, 15

Northeast, prehistoric culture of, 26-27
Northern area, prehistoric culture of, 15
Northwest Coast, prehistoric culture of, 15-16
notchers, 68

oceanographers' contributions to archaeology, 202-203
organic material:
    effect of, on soils, 98, 100, 218
    isolation of, by flotation, 146-148
Oriental traits found in South America, 4

Paleo-Indians, culture of, 7, 8, 9-10, 15, 16, 21, 22, 26, 34, 43, 55, 109, 190, 191
    artifacts of, 9, 43, 48, 49, 56-60, 67
parent material, effect of, on soils, 98, 100
Pebble Tool culture, 7-8
pecking technique in making artifacts, 50-56
pedalfer soils, 104
pedocal soils, 104
percussion technique of chipping, 48, 49
perforators or drills, 68
petroglyph of mountain lion, 18
petrology, 190-191
photography, archaeological, 152, 168-172
    aerial, 37
    use of, in excavating, 122, 145
pit houses, 17-18
pits at excavation sites, 122, 124-125, 156, 207
plains area, prehistoric culture of, 19-20
Plano tradition projectile points, 57, 60
Pleistocene, culture changes in, 5-6, 7
Pleistocene animals, 5, 9, 10, 19, 22
plotting sites for digging, 34-37
podzolization, effect of, on soils, 99
Polaroid Land cameras, 171
polishing and rubbing stones, 73

site history in site report, 206
site location, and preliminary survey records, 152-154
site location, determining choice of, 28-45
  area survey, 28-37, 44-45
  field check, 37-44
site report, writing of, 204-212
skeleton:
  bones of, 137-145
  determining age of, 136
  determining sex of, 136, 145
sketch map, preparation of, 84-85
slope of the land, effect of, on soils, 99-100
Snaketown, Arizona, 17
soapstone, artifacts made of, 51
soils:
  classification of, 102-104
  definitions of, 98
  erosion effects on, 100, 104-107
  factors in formation of, 98-100
  soil profile, 100-102
Southeast area, prehistoric culture of, 22-23
Southwest area, prehistoric culture of, 16-19
Spaniards, coming of, to New World, 12
spear points of Paleo hunters, 9
spear thrower weights, 72
spectrographic analysis of materials, 202
spelunking, 2
state antiquities regulations, 254-259
state archaeological societies, 234-238
state lands, permission for invasion of, 39, 254-259
steatite, artifacts made of, 51
Steward Observatory at University of Arizona, 191
stone artifacts, 47-56, 208-209
stone sinkers, 71
stratification:
  and chronology, 189-190

stratification (cont.)
  influence of, on excavation method, 117
stratigraphic column—animals and cultural variations, 55
stratigraphy record, 162-164, 207
study courses in archaeology, 248-252
subsistence requirements of Indians, 29-32
survey maps, 32-34, 44-45, 149-152
survey records, 149-154
survey symbols, 44
Sweet's Knoll Site, excavation of, 84-85, 211

teeth, human, 145
Temple Mound culture, 12, 22, 23
test pitting, in exploratory excavations, 112-114
test trenching, in exploratory excavations, 112
textiles:
  artifacts of, 54, 210
  cotton cloth weaving of the Anasazi, 18
  in Paleo culture, 16
thermoremnant magnetism, 218
throwing sticks, 58, 72
time as factor in soil formation, 98, 100
topographical maps, 32-34, 84
totem poles, 16
trade goods of Indians, 54
traits of culture, 46
trash pit, 219
tree-ring technique of dating, 191-193
trespassing, 39, 84
tundra, 15

underground dwellings, 17-18
underwater archaeology, 202-203
unit-level method of excavation, 119-120
U.S. Geological Survey, see maps, U.S. Geological Survey

vertebrae, human, 139

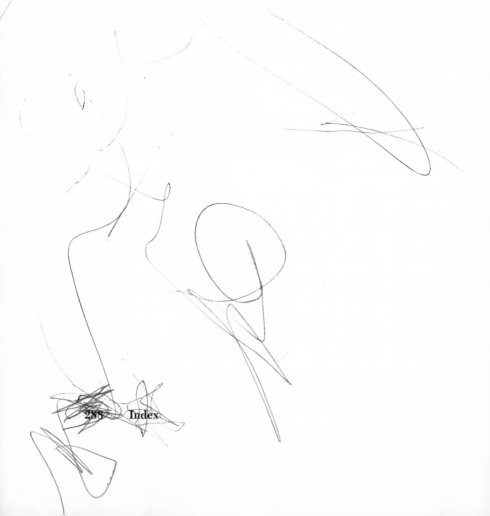

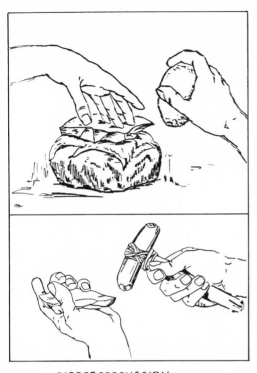

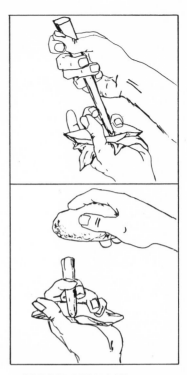

DIRECT PERCUSSION

**INDIRECT PERCUSSION
AND PRESSURE FLAKING**

In direct percussion the material to be flaked may be held in one hand or against an anvil of stone or wood. The hammer may be a hafted fragment of stone, bone, or wood, or simply a stone. The anvil technique is most successful for removing large, thin or deep, wide flakes. The hand technique is used for smaller, thicker flakes.

In indirect percussion (bottom) the material is held in the hand or rested against an anvil. A fragment of green bone or antler tine is held at the point on the edge where the flake is to be detached. Pressure flaking (top) is usual in the final finishing process. The material is held firmly in one hand as pressure is applied with a pointed flaking tool held in the other.

find. On close examination, many of them will prove to be delicate tools. In this period, too, the stoneworkers were extremely selective, demanding the best material, such as flint or chert. The Paleo-Indians apparently traveled long distances to obtain the material they wanted rather than use inferior local stones. At the Wapanucket #8 site in

Massachusetts, for example, the material used by the Paleo-Indians came from nearly 200 miles northwest of the site, in the Hudson River valley of New York State.

Artifacts can be recognized as such if: (1) there are indications of a regular pattern of chipping that has modified the shape of the object; (2) the shape is similar to other recognizable artifacts; (3) a substantial number of similarly shaped objects are found at the site; or (4) there are indications of use—a battered edge or a polished and ground surface, for example. In case of doubt, save the object until you can get the benefit of expert opinion. It is better to save, check, and discard than to use snap judgment and possibly discard artifacts that may be diagnostic of the site or the period.

PECKED, GROUND, AND POLISHED ARTIFACTS

Another large group of artifacts typical of Late Archaic or Woodland sites is made by a technique known as *pecking* and *grinding*. Such tools as axes, pestles for grinding nuts or grain, and gouges and chisels for woodworking were made by this technique. A pebble or a fragment of material conforming roughly to the size and shape of the finished tool was selected. This was battered or pecked into shape by repeated blows from a hammerstone. You will see evidence of this battering or crushing action in the small pits that cover the surface of the artifact. This was followed by grinding or rubbing on an abrasive surface. Sandstone was often used as a polishing agent. Usually only a portion of the battered surface, such as the cutting edge, will be ground. The rest of the artifact will keep its battered or pecked surface. Occasionally the entire surface of an artifact will be ground so that there will no longer be any evidence of the pecking process. Often the cutting edge will appear to be highly polished, usually by use rather than by design.

It is easy to be misled by the natural grindings and polishing often seen in pebbles that have been subjected to water, wind, and sand action on an exposed beach. Man-made artifacts, however, reveal polish or grinding scars oriented in one direction and not at all angles, as is the case in natural polishing. If you suspect that a fragment has been ground or polished by man, clean off the dirt and hold the artifact to the light so it will show clearly the character of the work. You will soon learn to detect the difference between the work of man and that of nature.

Steatite (soapstone) is a very soft material, but it was used occasionally for such artifacts as vessels and pipes.

In some areas during the Late Archaic, soapstone (steatite) was used for the manufacture of vessels for cooking and storing foods and for pipes. In the Arctic Coast and Northern areas lamps or stoves for heating and cooking were also made from this material. Soapstone is very soft and can be scratched with the fingernail. If rubbed or scraped fragments of steatite appear at a site, save and record them carefully. They are an excellent index of the period of the culture, and you may even recover enough fragments to reconstruct a vessel. Soapstone is too soft for most purposes, but occasionally an ornament or utilitarian artifact will be made of it. Small fragments of hematite (iron oxide) or graphite may be found bearing scratches or grooves on their surfaces. These are paint stones. They are scraped or ground to obtain a powder called pigment, which served as a base for paint. Keep these fragments, as they are in a sense an artifact.

Recover and preserve all fired clay fragments. These are diagnostic, or especially significant, and will supply considerable information concerning the period and derivation of the culture. The fragments from a vessel may be widely scattered about a site, but it is interesting and informative to bring them together. From them it is often possible also to reconstruct the shattered vessel. On some sites in the Southwest, however, there is such an abundance of potsherds (the archaeological term for pottery fragments) that archaeologists save only rim sherds, decorated sherds, or those which indicate unusual shape or function.

Many artifacts are made of bone, antler, or shell and these will be recovered at sites where conditions have allowed them to be preserved. It is surprising how these fragile materials will sometimes resist the destructive forces of nature and remain in recognizable condition in the earth. Often artifacts of this material are preserved

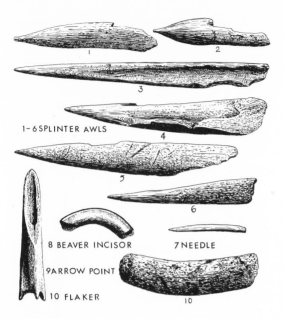

1-6 SPLINTER AWLS

8 BEAVER INCISOR   7 NEEDLE

9 ARROW POINT

10 FLAKER

Antler tines were used for a variety of purposes. Teeth were set in antler tine or wooden handles and used as awls. Sometimes teeth were drilled and used as beads or ornaments.

in shell heaps where the natural lime acts as a preservative. Charring by fire is another means of preservation of such artifacts as projectile points, needles, awls, punches, fishhooks, scrapers, and beads of bone. Rounded, polished, or ground surfaces or drilled holes will serve to identify artifacts of these materials. Scattered about the refuse pits and hearths of a village you will find the broken and burned fragments of bone from the food cooked and eaten by the occupants. Some long bones were split to obtain the marrow, which was considered a delicacy by the Indians. If they are in large enough fragments or show a characteristic shape, they can be identified and will furnish considerable information concerning the food habits of the culture.

Shell was often used for making beads, ornaments, spoons, and even such tools as scrapers and hoes. Small shells—periwinkle, for example—became beads by the simple process of grinding the two ends. When recovered from inland sites far removed from their source, shells may often furnish important clues concerning migration or trade routes. Shell beads that I took from an inland site near Brookfield, Massachusetts, have been identified as those of a salt-

In post-Paleo times at least three cultural centers arose in the area—the Mogollon, Hohokam, and Anasazi. The Mogollon people lived in the mountainous country of southern New Mexico, chiefly along the Mimbres River valley. A primitive type of maize, dated about 300 B.C., came from Tularosa Cave I, in Mogollon territory; from Tularosa Cave II in the same area came the earliest known pottery, dated about one hundred years later.

The Mogollon culture reached its peak during the Mimbres period, between A.D. 1050 and 1200. This period was characterized by beautiful black-on-white pottery decorated with naturalistic figures. Burials were often accompanied by handsome pottery bowls of this type, which were ceremonially "killed" by having a hole knocked in the bottoms. The spirit believed to be in the pottery was thus released to accompany the spirit of the deceased to a better world.

The Hohokam were lowland desert-dwellers who inhabited central and southern Arizona, to the west of the Mogollon. They were skilled shell and stone carvers and made a distinctive buff-colored pottery with red painted decoration. Their homes were single-room lodges of adobe (brush and mud). The greatest Hohokam town, called Snaketown by its excavators, lay near the site of present-day Phoenix. Here were found vestiges of the overflow ditches and irrigation canals that explain the ability of the Hohokam to grow maize and cotton. Ball courts uncovered at Snaketown and other large Hohokam villages bear marked similarities to those built and used for ceremonial games by the early Mexicans and Maya to the south. Because the Hohokam cremated their dead, little is known of their physical appearance.

During the late 1200's intruders from the north began to drift into Hohokam territory, settling near the Salt River. These "Salado" people, so-called after the Spanish word for salt, brought with them such Anasazi traits as multistoried communal houses and burial of the dead. Casa Grande, in Arizona, is the only surviving example of the "great houses" built by the Salado people. Although differing from each other in almost every respect, the Hohokam and Salado peoples lived peacefully side by side.

The Anasazi (Basket Maker and Pueblo) lived in the "four corners" region where the states of Utah, Colorado, Arizona, and New Mexico meet. Before the year A.D. 400 the early Basket Makers had an essentially Archaic culture. They lived in underground dwell-

Above, this striking petroglyph of a mountain lion was found in Arizona's Petrified Forest. (U.S. Dept. of the Interior, National Park Service)

Left, the famous Cliff Palace was one of the first major ruins discovered at Mesa Verde, in Colorado. It dates from the Great Pueblo period (about A.D. 1200 to 1300). (U.S. Dept. of the Interior, National Park Service)

ings, or pit houses, used a primitive spear and thrower as their chief weapon, and were skillful weavers of baskets. In addition to basketry, they wove sandals and other articles of clothing, utilizing plant fibers and strips of rabbit fur.

Significant changes took place as farming became more important in the Anasazi economy. Underground dwellings were roofed over with poles and adobe to provide better protection from the weather. From the pit houses gradually developed more permanent, multiple-room dwellings of coursed masonry (stone set in adobe mortar), which were built on the open mesa, or tableland. Often rising as high as four stories, these houses were joined together to form compact villages. Cotton cloth was woven, the bow and arrow came into use, and fired clay pottery of fine design and decoration replaced the earlier basketry.

After about 1200 the Anasazi moved from the mesas to caves. There they built pueblos, or cliff dwellings, perhaps as a defense against intruders who had moved into the area. Important pueblo centers rose at Chaco Canyon in northwestern New Mexico, at Mesa Verde in southwestern Colorado, and in the Kayenta region of northeastern Arizona. Pueblo Bonito ("beautiful village"), one of the most famous of the Chaco Canyon apartment houses, contained in its heyday 800 rooms and 32 kivas, or ceremonial chambers. It housed over 1,200 inhabitants, and was until the 1880's the largest apartment building anywhere in the world.

Other arts also reached their highest development in the Great Pueblo period (Pueblo III or Golden Age), which lasted from about 1000 to 1400. The striking black-on-white and polychrome ware of Chaco, Kayenta, and Mesa Verde replaced the earlier crude gray utilitarian ware. Pottery of many varieties and outstanding craftsmanship—jugs, water jars, bowls, ladles—was made by all of these people.

Then, in 1276, drought struck the region. For almost a quarter of a century little rain fell, crops failed, and springs dried up. The economic decline was followed, or accompanied by, an actual invasion of the territory by desert nomads, probably Apache and Navajo. The Anasazi moved away toward the south. These events led to an intermixing of the various peoples of the Southwest, but some of the old Anasazi traits, although greatly affected by European cultures, still survive in the area among the modern Hopi, Zuñi, and others.

Plains

From southern Alberta and Saskatchewan to northern Texas stretches the great grassy steppe country that has supported vast herds of grazing animals for thousands of years. Before the retreat of the last great ice sheet, mastodon, mammoth, the large, straight-horned bison, and other Pleistocene animals roamed the southern portion of the range. But they became extinct at the end of the Ice Age. Their final disappearance depleted the food resources so severely that man, too, vanished from the area.

When climatic conditions improved, grass grew in abundance once more on the western Plains. First to return were the herds, this time the modern bison (buffalo) and lesser grazing animals. Man returned, following his prey along the rivers. But in the interim his artifacts had undergone considerable change. No longer did he hunt with hand-thrown weapons tipped with fluted points. Now he possessed the bow, and arrows tipped with stone points resembling those of the eastern Archaic culture.

Later, Woodland people entered the area from the east, bringing with them cordmarked (decorated with the imprint of twisted cords) pottery and agriculture. Archaeologists of the River Basin survey

One of the most remarkable of the Adena or Hopewell effigy mounds is the 1,350-foot-long Serpent Mound, in Adams County, Ohio. Resembling a huge, partially coiled snake, it holds a 30-foot "egg" between its jaws. (Development Department, State of Ohio)

have discovered evidences of hundreds of farming towns lining the rivers of the Great Plains, principally along the Nebraska and Republican rivers and other tributaries of the Missouri. These Plains farmers cultivated corn, squash, and tobacco, and lived in round or square earthen lodges. Some of their villages lasted almost into historic times.

During the 1500's, however, the Plains bison began to increase in numbers and to spread over a wide area. Abandoning the hard, dull work of farming, the plains Indians took up bison hunting. These were the only ancient Americans ever to abandon farming after having learned it.

Historical archaeology in this area is important because it indicates a period of rapid change. The horse, a common animal in the Americas during the Ice Age, became extinct when it ended. The introduction of the horse about 1700 from Spanish settlements in the Southwest greatly increased the hunting efficiency of the Plains Indians as well as their ability to defend or enlarge their territory. When other Woodland people were forced out of their homeland by the westward pressure of colonial settlements along the Atlantic coast, they were compelled to forsake their traditional way of life and adopt that of the Plains bison hunters.